HOME-KITCHEN FOOD STORAGE

Pantry-shelf Storage, Room Temperature

food item	storage time	keep in mind
baking powder, baking soda	18 months	keep dry, tightly covered
bouillon cubes & powders	1 year	
breads & rolls	3 days	in original wrapping
cake mixes	1 year	keep dry
cakes, baked	2-3 days	refrigerate if with cream or custard filling
canned foods, all kinds	1 year or more	use oldest first
coffee, vacuum can	1 year, un-opened	store in refrigerator or freezer 1 week after opening
coffee, instant	6 months, unopened	store in refrigerator or freezer 1 week after opening
coffee lightener, nondairy	6 months	keep dry
cookies, packaged	4 months, unopened	1 week after opening
crackers	3 months	keep dry, tightly closed
crumbs, cracker/bread	6 months	keep dry, tightly closed
flour, all-purpose/cake	6 months	keep dry, tightly closed
frostings, mixes & canned	6 months	
fruit, dried	6-8 months	
gelatin, unflavored/fruit	6 months	keep dry
herbs & spices, whole	1 year	keep tightly closed
herbs & spices, ground	6 months	keep tightly closed
honey	1 year	do not refrigerate
hot-roll/quick-bread mixes	1 year	keep dry
jam, jelly	1 year	refrigerate after opening
molasses	1 year	
nonfat dry milk	6 months	keep dry; refrigerate after reconstituting
oil, salad & cooking	3 months	keep tightly closed
pancake, waffle mixes	6 months	keep dry, tightly closed
pasta	6 months, unopened	keep dry
peanut butter	6 months	2 months after opening
piecrust mixes	6 months	
pies & pastries	3 days	refrigerate cream, custard
pudding mixes	1 year	
rice, brown & wild	1 year	
rice, white	2 years	
rice, flavored mixes	6 months	
salad dressings	6 months	refrigerate after opening
sauce/soup/gravy mixes	3 months	
sauces/ketchup, barbecue	2 months	keep tightly closed
shortening, hydrogenated	8 months	keep tightly closed
soft drinks	3 months	
sugar, granulated	2 years	keep dry
sugar, brown & confectioners	4 years	
syrups	1 year	close tightly after use
tea, loose or bags	6 months	
tea, instant	1 year	
vegetables: onions, potatoes, rutabagas, sweet potatoes, winter squash	1 week	keep dry; provide for air circulation, will keep 2-3 months at 55°

Refrigerator Storage, Fruits & Vegetables
(in crisper or closed plastic bags)

food item	storage time	keep in mind
apples	1 month	or store at room temperature
apricots, avocados, pears, melons, bananas, grapes, nectarines, peaches, plums	5 days	ripen before refrigerating
berries & cherries	3 days	
citrus fruits	2 weeks	or store at room temperature
pineapples	2 days	
asparagus	3 days	
beets, carrots, parsnips, radishes, turnips	5 days	remove tops before storing
cabbage, cauliflower, celery, cucumbers, green beans, eggplant, peppers	1 week	
tomatoes	1 week	ripen tomatoes before refrigerating
corn on the cob	1 day	refrigerate in husks
lettuce, spinach, all green leafy vegetables	5 days	remove damaged leaves before refrigerating
lima beans, peas	5 days	leave in pods

Refrigerator Storage, Dairy Products
(tightly covered or wrapped)

food item	storage time	keep in mind
butter	2 weeks	
buttermilk	2 weeks	
cheese, spreads	2 weeks	if mold forms on hard cheese, remove before serving — it will do no harm
cheese, cottage & ricotta	5 days	
cheese, cream & neufchatel	2 weeks	
cheese, sliced	2 weeks	
cheese, in whole cuts	2 months	
cream, sweet/sour	1 week	ultrapasteurized, 1 month in original carton
eggs, whole in shell	1 month	
whites, separated	4 days	tightly covered
yolks, separated	4 days	cover with water
margarine	1 month	
milk, whole & skim	1 week	
milk, reconstituted nonfat, opened condensed & evaporated	1 week	

Refrigerator Storage, Meat, Fish & Poultry (uncooked)

food item	storage time	keep in mind
beef, pork, lamb & veal: steaks, chops, roasts	5 days	leave in store plastic wrap or rewrap loosely
ground & stew meats	2 days	
fresh sausage	2 days	
variety meats	2 days	
bacon, frankfurters	1 week	after opening
ham, canned	6 months	unopened
ham, slices	3 days	
ham, whole	1 week	
luncheon meats, cold cuts	5 days	after opening
sausage, dry & semidry	3 weeks	
fish, shellfish (all kinds)	1 day	keep closely wrapped
poultry, fresh or thawed	2 days	

Refrigerator Storage, Leftovers & Packaged Foods (after opening)

food item	storage time	keep in mind
broth, gravy, soup	2 days	tightly covered
cakes, pies: cream or custard fillings	2-3 days	
casserole dishes, stews	3 days	
coffee	1 week	after opening
coffee lighteners, frozen	3 weeks	after thawing
flour: rye, whole wheat, wheat germ	1 year	tightly covered container — not original package
fruits	3 days	
juices, beverages	6 days	
meat, fish, poultry	2 days	remove stuffing from poultry
nutmeats	6 months	tightly covered
pickles, olives	1 month	original container
refrigerated doughs: rolls, biscuits, cookies, breads	check final-use date on package; do not open until ready to use	
salad dressings	3 months	original container
salads: potato, chicken, fish, coleslaw	2 days	tightly covered
wine, white table	3 days	after opening

Continued on back Endsheet

food item	storage time	keep in mind
breads, rolls (baked)	3 months	overwrap commercial wrappings
breads, unbaked loaves	3 months	overwrap commercial wrappings
cakes: butter, pound-type	6 months	unfrosted, overwrap
cake, angel food	2 months	overwrap
cake, frosted layer	4 months	
coffee lighteners	1 year	
doughnuts, danish pastry	3 months	overwrap
fish (fat types): trout, mackerel, salmon	3 months	overwrap if package damaged
fish, (lean types): cod, flounder, sole	6 months	if thawed, do not refreeze
shellfish, breaded, cooked	3 months	
lobster, scallops	3 months	
king / queen crab	10 months	
shrimp, uncooked, unbreaded	1 year	
fruit	1 year	
ice cream, sherbet	1 month	overwrap leftovers
main-dish pies, fish or meat	3 months	
main-dish pies, poultry	6 months	
meats, beef roasts, steaks	1 year	overwrap
ground beef	4 months	overwrap
lamb, veal roasts, & steaks	9 months	overwrap
pork chops	4 months	overwrap
pork roasts	8 months	overwrap
pancake / waffle batter	3 months	
pies, unbaked	8 months	
pies, ready to thaw & eat	4 months	
poultry: chicken, turkey parts	6 months	
whole chicken, turkey	1 year	
duck, goose	6 months	
turkey rolls, roasts	6 months	
vegetables, all	8 months	

USEFUL SUBSTITUTIONS

if the recipe calls for	use instead
2 tablespoons all-purpose or whole wheat flour (for thickening)	1 tablespoon cornstarch or arrow-root or potato starch or quick-cooking tapioca
1 cup beef or chicken broth	1 bouillon cube or 1 envelope or 1 rounded teaspoon bouillon powder + 1 cup boiling water
2 egg yolks	1 whole egg
1 cup grated coconut	1⅓ cups flaked coconut
1 pound fresh mushrooms	12 ounces canned mushrooms, drained, or 3 ounces dried mush-rooms, rehydrated
1 teaspoon lemon juice	½ teaspoon distilled white vinegar
1 teaspoon grated lemon peel	½ teaspoon lemon extract
1 cup homogenized milk	1 cup skim milk + 2 tablespoons butter or margarine; or ½ cup evaporated milk + ½ cup water, or ¼ cup powdered whole milk + 1 cup water
1 square (1 ounce) unsweetened chocolate	3 tablespoons cocoa + 1 table-spoon butter or margarine
½ cup butter or margarine	7 tablespoons vegetable shortening
1 cup sifted cake flour	⅞ cup sifted all-purpose flour
1 teaspoon baking powder	½ teaspoon cream of tartar + ¼ teaspoon baking soda
1 cup sour cream (for use in cooking)	1 tablespoon lemon juice + evaporated milk (undiluted) to make 1 cup, or ⅓ cup butter + ¾ cup yogurt or buttermilk

1 cup buttermilk or sour milk	1 tablespoon lemon juice or white vinegar + milk to make 1 cup (let stand 5 minutes)
1 cup honey or corn syrup	1¼ cups sugar + ¼ cup liquid
1 tablespoon snipped fresh herb	1 teaspoon dried herb, same kind
1 medium onion, chopped	1 tablespoon instant minced onion, rehydrated
1 cup light cream or half-and-half	3 tablespoons butter + ⅞ cup milk
1 cup heavy (whipping) cream	⅓ cup butter + ¾ cup milk
2 cups tomato sauce	¾ cup tomato paste + 1 cup water
1 cup tomato juice	½ cup tomato sauce + ½ cup water
1 small clove garlic	⅛ teaspoon garlic powder or ¼ tea-spoon commercial garlic juice
1 tablespoon gelatin	1 envelope
1 cake compressed yeast	1 envelope active dry yeast
1 cup yogurt (in cooking)	1 cup buttermilk

FOOD-MEASURE EQUIVALENTS

start out with	to end up with
apples, 3 medium (1 pound)	3 cups sliced
bananas, 3 medium (1 pound)	1½ cups mashed
bread, 1-pound loaf	14 to 20 slices
bread, 1 slice (including crust)	½ cup crumbs
butter or margarine, ¼ pound	½ cup (1 stick or cube)
cheese, ¼ pound	1 cup shredded
cheese, cottage, 8-ounce container	1 cup
cheese, cream, 3-ounce package	6 tablespoons
chocolate, unsweetened, 1 square	1 ounce
chocolate, semisweet pieces, 6 ounces	1 cup
coconut, flaked, 3½-ounce can	1⅓ cups
coconut, shredded, 4-ounce can	1⅓ cups
cream, heavy or whipping, 1 cup	2 cups whipped
cream, sour, 8-ounce container	1 cup
egg whites, large, 8 to 10	1 cup
egg yolks, large, 12 to 14	1 cup
flour, all-purpose, 1 pound	about 3½ cups
flour, cake, 1 pound	about 4 cups
lemon, 1 medium	3 tablespoons juice, 1 tablespoon grated peel
lime, 1 medium	2 tablespoons juice, 1 teaspoon grated peel
milk, evaporated, 5⅓ or 6-ounce can	⅔ cup
12- or 14½-ounce can	1⅔ cups
sweetened condensed, 14-ounce can	1¼ cups
nuts, 1 pound almonds in shell	1 to 1¼ cups nutmeats
almonds, 1 pound shelled	3 cups
brazil nuts, in shell, 1 pound	1½ cups nutmeats
brazil nuts, shelled, 1 pound	3¼ cups
filberts, in shell, 1 pound	1½ cups nutmeats
filberts, shelled, 1 pound	3½ cups
peanuts, in shell, 1 pound	2 to 2½ cups nutmeats
peanuts, shelled, 1 pound	3 cups
pecans, in shell, 1 pound	2¼ cups nutmeats
pecans, shelled, 1 pound	4 cups
walnuts, in shell, 1 pound	2 cups nutmeats
walnuts, shelled, 1 pound	4 cups
onion, 1 large	¾ to 1 cup chopped
orange, 1 medium	¼ to ⅓ cup juice, 2 tablespoons grated peel
potatoes, 1 pound sweet, white	2¼ cups diced
raisins, 1 pound	3 cups
rice, long grain regular, 1 cup	3 cups cooked
salad oil, 16 ounces	2 cups
sugar, 1 pound granulated	2¼ to 2½ cups
brown, 1 pound	2¼ cups (packed)
confectioners, 1 pound	4 to 4½ cups
syrup, corn, 16 ounces	2 cups
maple, 12 ounces	1½ cups

Famous Brands

MEAT COOKBOOK

Brand Name Publishing Corp.

Acknowledgments

The editors wish to thank the following companies for permission to use their recipes, photographs, and product names in this volume:

American National Cowbelles, Inc.

Seven Seas® Brand is a registered trademark of Anderson, Clayton & Co.

Armour Food Company/A ConAgra Company

Beatrice/Hunt-Wesson Foods

Caloric Corporation

Campbell Soup Company

Corning Glass Works

Butter Buds® and Sweet 'N Low® are registered trademarks of the Cumberland Packing Corporation

Florida Department of Citrus

Hamilton Beach Scovill Inc.

Hernke Foods, Inc.

Geo. A. Hormel & Co.

Idaho Potato Commission

Kikkoman International Inc.

Lea & Perrins, Inc.

Lipton® Recipe Soup Mix and Lipton® Cup-a-Soup™ Instant Soup are trademarks of Thomas J. Lipton, Inc., Englewood Cliffs, NJ 07632

Wish-Bone® Dressing is a registered trademark of Thomas J. Lipton, Inc., Englewood Cliffs, NJ 07632

McIlhenny Company (Tabasco)

Miller Beer Co., makers of Lowenbrau beer

New Zealand Lamb Company

Ocean Spray Cranberries, Inc.

Oster

Consumer Products Division, Reynolds Metal Company

Ste. Pierre Smirnoff Fls., Division of Heublein, Inc., Hartford, CT

Solo Food Products, Division of Sokol & Company

Sunbeam is a registered trademark of Sunbeam Corporation

Sun-Maid Growers of California

Uncle Ben's, Inc.

Published by Brand Name Publishing Corp., 1950 Craig Road, St. Louis, Missouri 63146 and Brand Name Books, Inc., 122 East 25th Street, New York, New York 10010.

Printed in Italy by Mondadori, Verona

Invitation

The Famous Brands Cookbook Library invites you, the modern cook, to a new experience in your own kitchen. Have you ever wished you had a larger repertoire of company's-coming menus? Ever searched for a different and exciting way to prepare favorite products? Ever felt that if you could just have a certain technique explained simply, you could master an entire new world of cooking?

The solutions to these dilemmas and others are the cornerstone of the twelve volumes that comprise *The Famous Brands Cookbook Library.* Whether you are just getting to know your kitchen—or have a long-standing relationship with it—the recipes and hints provided here offer the very best and latest information available from the test kitchens of many of America's finest food companies. Once you have had a chance to discover the treasures inside this volume, you'll want to collect each of the other volumes in this series—and an invaluable home cooking library will be yours.

Famous Brands Desserts
Famous Brands Every Oven Microwave Cookbook
Famous Brands Great Vegetable Dishes
Famous Brands Meat Cookbook
Famous Brands Chicken & Poultry
Famous Brands Breads, Quick Breads, & Coffee Cakes
Famous Brands Soups & Salads
Famous Brands Pasta Dishes
Famous Brands Fish & Seafood Cookbook
Famous Brands Cooking with Eggs & Cheese
Famous Brands Main Dishes
Famous Brands Chocolate Classics

Front cover: *Roast Beef (page 40).*

Back cover: *Ham with Honey Beer Basting Sauce (page 77).*
Courtesy Miller Brewing Co.

The Many Merits of Meat

When the question before the house is "What's for dinner?" it is safe to assume that no one really cares which vegetable is on the menu, whether or not there's to be a salad, or even if anyone had the kindness to whip up something special for dessert. The matter of concern here is the heart of the meal, the foundation upon which all the rest is built. In a word, the meat. A repertory of recipes for a wide variety of meat dishes, a knowledge of how to cook and serve all kinds of meat, can be the making of a home cook's culinary reputation.

Here, in the *Famous Brands Meat Cookbook,* is all the information you need to build such a reputation for yourself. You'll find dozens of inventive ways to deal with the many available cuts of beef, lamb, pork, and veal. Downright goodness is the key to all of them—imaginative seasonings, new approaches to old favorites, dishes that are truly quick/easy for delicious busy-day meals, production-number inspirations for memorable parties, and, most important to every home cook, dozens of recipes for family-meal meats that can make the week-in, week-out task of menu-making a real pleasure.

Beef is the best-liked meat in this country; consequently there are more recipes here for beef than for any other kind of meat. But pork and lamb and veal are generously treated, each with its share of recipes. You'll want to try them all.

There are main dishes in this volume, of course, but the bounty of goodness by no means stops there. Appetizer recipes featuring meat are here, too, as well as soups and stews, a wide spectrum of casserole dishes, new ventures in burgers and sandwiches, great adventures in barbecuing, and some new-territories explorations of unusual meat specialties, many of which are quick-to-make wonders.

Turn the pages and begin a great learning experience with meat dishes.

CONTENTS

Sensational Starters

Any meal will be off to a great start with tasty appetizers—
pâtés, puffs, rolls, antipasti, dips, and spreads—made with
your favorite meats.

Dressed-up Cold Cuts

Caviar Spread

Makes about 1½ cups
- 1 package (8 ounces) cream cheese, softened
- ⅓ cup mayonnaise
- 2 tablespoons lemon juice
- 1 tablespoon milk
- 1 jar (2 ounces) red caviar (about ¼ cup)
  Turkey, beef, or liverwurst

In a large bowl, beat cream cheese until smooth. Add mayonnaise, lemon juice, and milk. Mix well. Stir in caviar. Cover and chill. Serve with turkey, beef, or liverwurst.

Cranberry-Sour Cream Sauce

Makes 1 cup
- ⅓ cup sour cream
- 1½ teaspoons horseradish
- ¾ cup Ocean Spray Whole Berry Cranberry Sauce
  Beef or ham

In a bowl, combine all ingredients. Cover and chill. Serve with beef or ham.

Apricot Spread

Makes 1 cup
- ½ cup apricot preserves
- ½ cup chili sauce
- ¼ cup mayonnaise
- 1 teaspoon spicy brown mustard

In a bowl, combine all ingredients. Cover and chill. Serve with ham, bologna, turkey, or salami.

Gazpacho Sauce

Makes about 1½ cups
- ½ cup Ocean Spray Jellied Cranberry Sauce
- ½ cup chili sauce
- ¼ cup finely chopped green pepper
- ¼ cup finely chopped onion
- ¼ cup finely chopped cucumber
  Beef, ham, or liverwurst

In a saucepan, heat jellied cranberry sauce and chili sauce over low heat until thoroughly combined and smooth. Cool. Stir in vegetables. Cover and chill. Serve with beef, ham, or liverwurst.

Ham 'n' Cheese Balls

Makes 40 appetizers
- ½ cup butter
- 1½ cups shredded cheddar cheese
- ¼ cup finely chopped baked ham
- ¼ teaspoon Worcestershire sauce
  Dash cayenne
- 1 cup all-purpose flour

In a mixing bowl combine butter, cheese, ham, and seasonings. Blend in flour and mix well. Shape dough into balls the size of large marbles and place on baking sheet. Bake in a preheated 350°F. oven for 15 to 18 minutes. Serve piping hot or spread uncooked balls out in a single layer in a shallow pan. Place in a freezer and freeze until hard. Remove from freezer and pack in freezer bags.
To serve, remove the number desired for serving and bake as above.

Sesame Beef Sticks

Makes about 25 appetizers
- ½ cup Wish-Bone Italian Dressing
- 3 tablespoons sugar
- 1 tablespoon soy sauce
- 1 pound boneless sirloin or round steak, cut into thin 3-inch strips
  Sesame seed

In large shallow baking dish, blend all ingredients except beef and sesame seed; add beef. Cover and marinate in refrigerator, turning occasionally, at least 2 hours.
Remove beef and thread on small skewers, reserving marinade. Roll beef in sesame seed; broil, turning once and spooning on reserved marinade, until done.

Dressed-Up Cold Cuts. Ocean Spray Cranberries

Ribbon Bologna Wedges

Makes 32 wedges

   1 jar (5 ounces) cheese spread with olives and
      pimiento
  12 thin slices large bologna sausage
   ¼ cup finely chopped walnuts or pecans
      Finely snipped parsley

Spread cheese evenly on bologna slices. Sprinkle each slice with nuts. Pile 6 slices on top of each other. Sprinkle parsley on top. Cover with plastic wrap and chill. To serve, cut each pile into 16 wedges and insert a colored toothpick in each.

Veal Roll-Ups

Makes 8 servings

   1 veal round steak or veal cutlets (about 2 to 2½
      pounds), cut ¼ inch thick
   8 thin slices boiled ham
   4 slices process Swiss cheese
   1 egg, lightly beaten
   2 tablespoons milk
      Fine, dry bread crumbs
   1 can (10½ ounces) condensed cream of
      mushroom soup
   2 tablespoons dry white wine
   ½ cup milk
      Paprika

Cut veal into 8 pieces. Pound each to ⅛-inch thickness. Top each piece with a ham slice. Cut each cheese slice in 4 strips; place 2 strips each on ham slice. Roll meat around cheese. Secure with wooden toothpicks. Mix egg and 2 tablespoons milk. Dip rolls in egg mixture, then in crumbs. Place, seam side down, in a shallow baking dish. Combine soup, wine, and ½ cup milk in a saucepan. Heat. Pour around rolls. Cover baking dish with aluminum foil; bake in a preheated 350°F. oven for 1 hour, or until meat is tender. Sprinkle with paprika. Bake 10 minutes until lightly browned.

Ham 'n' Cheese Roll-Ups

Makes about 25 hors d'oeuvres

   1 package (8 ounces) cream cheese, softened
   1 tablespoon Lea & Perrins Worcestershire Sauce
   1 teaspoon chopped chives or parsley
   ½ teaspoon powdered mustard
   5 thin slices boiled ham
      Rye bread rounds

In a small bowl blend cream cheese, Lea & Perrins, chives, and mustard. Spread over ham. Roll up, jelly roll fashion. Cover and chill at least 2 hours. Cut each roll into ¾-inch slices. Place each slice on bread round.

Pâtés

Basically, even if this sounds like heresy, a pâté is a meat loaf. The greatest of meat loaves, the superlative in meat loaves, but meat loaf all the same.

Pâtés range all the way from simple unbaked ones to those in pastry jackets (pâté en croute) or in aspic (en gelée) made with stock and wine. Most pâtés are made of ingredients very finely ground or puréed, although there are country pâtés (pâté de campagne) of rougher texture. Pâtés may be plain (if that is the right word to describe anything so smooth, so almost insupportably delicious) or have inclusions such as pistachio or pine nuts (pignolias) or, most elegantly, truffles. Many are brandy flavored and well seasoned—but gently, so that the brandy and/or seasoning is a subtle touch, not an overpowering one. Some have thin slices of meat—tongue, ham, chicken, or such exotica as stuffed breasts of quail—in the pâté, surrounded by the forcemeat. Even the homely hard-cooked egg sometimes appears in the center of a pâté.

These delights need little embellishment. Serve in slices or in cubes, with good crusty bread and sour pickles—tiny French cornichons are ideal.

Pâtés may be made of livers of all sorts, of forcemeat—finely chopped or puréed filling—of chicken, pork, veal, ham (often with bacon), duck, flavorful fish such as salmon, and even canned tuna, or a combination of several ingredients.

Hurry-Up Harlequin Canapés

Makes 48 canapés

   1 package (12 ounces) corn muffin mix
   ¼ cup grated Parmesan cheese
   2 cans (3 ounces each) potted meat
   3 cans (4 ounces each) Vienna sausages
  28 cocktail onions
   ½ cup sliced sweet pickles
   ½ cup sliced stuffed olives

Prepare corn muffin mix according to package directions and spread evenly in a well-buttered 15½x10½x1-inch jelly roll pan or bake-broil serving tray. Sprinkle top with Parmesan cheese. Spoon potted meat in 3 narrow rows crosswise and at each end of pan. Cut Vienna sausages in half lengthwise; arrange V-shaped rows between rows of potted meat, alternating with the cocktail onions. Arrange rows of sliced pickles and olives in the remaining spaces. Bake in a preheated 400°F. oven for 20 to 25 minutes, or until browned. Cut into small rectangles.

Cheese-Sausage Rolls

Makes 50 to 60 servings
- 16 sausage links
- 16 slices thin-sliced white bread
- 1 cup shredded cheddar cheese
- ¼ cup butter

Cook sausage links until done. Drain on paper towels. Cut crusts from bread. Combine cheese and butter. Spread on both sides of bread. Roll a sausage in each slice and fasten with wooden toothpicks. Bake on an oiled baking sheet in a preheated 400°F. oven for 10 to 12 minutes. Slice each roll into 3 or 4 slices and serve piping hot.

Instant Liver Pâté

- 1 roll (8 ounces) braunschweiger (liver sausage)
- ½ cup butter or margarine, softened
- 1 teaspoon dry mustard
- 1 teaspoon brandy
- 1 container (4 ounces) whipped cream cheese
- 1 tablespoon mayonnaise
- Pimiento, finely chopped
- Parsley, finely chopped
- Sieved hard-cooked egg yolk
- Bacon-flavored crackers

Fold an 18x18-inch sheet of Heavy Duty Reynolds Wrap aluminum foil in half lengthwise. Repeat folding in half to form a 1¼-inch band. Fold ends of band together into a seam to form a ring. Form foil ring into heart shape and tape outside of heart to platter. Beat together braunschweiger, butter, mustard, and brandy until smooth. Pack mixture into mold. Cover with Reynolds Plastic Wrap and refrigerate several hours. Remove plastic wrap and foil strip. Combine cream cheese and mayonnaise; frost heart. In center, make a small heart of chopped pimiento. Outline with parsley, then egg yolk. Spread on bacon-flavored crackers.

Zippy Beef-Olive Spread

Makes 1½ cups
- 1 teaspoon instant minced onion
- 1 tablespoon dry sherry
- 1 package (8 ounces) cream cheese, at room temperature
- 2 tablespoons mayonnaise
- 1 package (3 ounces) smoked sliced beef, finely snipped
- ¼ cup chopped stuffed olives
- Whole wheat bread or unsalted crackers

Soften onion in sherry. Blend cream cheese with mayonnaise; add the sherry-onion mixture. Stir in beef and olives. Serve with triangles of whole wheat bread or unsalted crackers.

Dipsy Dip

Makes 1½ cups
- ¾ cup finely chopped bologna
- ½ cup chopped pitted ripe olives
- 2 tablespoons chopped pimiento
- 2 tablespoons sweet pickle relish
- ¼ teaspoon garlic salt
- Assorted crackers

Combine bologna, olives, pimiento, pickle relish, and garlic salt. Stir in enough mayonnaise to make mixture of dip consistency. Cover and chill. Serve with assorted crackers.

Paprika Meatballs

Makes 16 meatballs★
- 1 pound lean ground beef
- ⅓ cup liquid Butter Buds
- 3 tablespoons minced onion
- 2 tablespoons fine bread crumbs
- ¼ teaspoon garlic powder
- ⅛ teaspoon dry mustard
- ⅛ teaspoon pepper
- 1 medium-size ripe tomato, chopped
- ½ teaspoon basil
- ¼ teaspoon thyme
- 2 cups low-fat milk, divided
- 1 packet Butter Buds
- 3 tablespoons all-purpose flour
- 2 teaspoons paprika

In large bowl, combine beef, Butter Buds, onion, bread crumbs, garlic powder, mustard, and pepper and mix thoroughly. Shape mixture into 16 cocktail-size meatballs. Brown in large non-stick skillet over medium heat about 10 to 15 minutes, or until meatballs are browned on all sides. Remove from skillet and drain off excess fat. Combine tomato, basil, and thyme in same skillet. Cook until tomato is very soft, about 5 to 10 minutes. In saucepan, heat 1½ cups milk until warm. Add Butter Buds and stir until dissolved. Add flour and paprika to remaining milk and stir to a smooth paste. Add to heated milk mixture and blend thoroughly. Slowly add cooked tomato to milk mixture, stirring constantly. Transfer mixture to large skillet and add meatballs. Heat thoroughly just until hot. Do not boil.

★By using Butter Buds instead of butter in this recipe, you have saved 180 calories and 30 mg cholesterol per serving.

Swedish Meatballs

Makes 6 to 8 servings

    2 cups fresh bread cubes
    ½ cup milk
    ¼ cup butter or margarine
    1 onion, finely minced
    3 eggs, beaten
    1 teaspoon salt
    ¼ teaspoon pepper
    2 teaspoons paprika
    2 teaspoons ground nutmeg
    1 teaspoon dry mustard
 1½ pounds ground beef
    1 teaspoon mixed herbs
    1 clove garlic, minced
    2 cups beef bouillon
    2 teaspoons bitters
    1 beef bouillon cube
    2 teaspoons tomato paste
    ¼ cup all-purpose flour
    2 cups sour cream

Combine bread cubes and milk and let stand. Preheat Multi-Cooker Frypan to 300°F. Melt 1 tablespoon of the butter in frypan. Cook onion until tender but not browned. Squeeze as much of the milk out of the bread as possible and place bread in a mixing bowl. Add the cooked onion, eggs, salt, pepper, paprika, nutmeg, and mustard. Blend well. Add beef and mixed herbs. Blend lightly but thoroughly with your hands until well mixed. Turn frypan to 320°F. Shape mixture into balls 1 inch in diameter. Heat remaining 3 tablespoons butter in frypan. Brown meatballs well on all sides in hot butter. Remove meatballs from pan. Cook garlic in pan drippings 1 minute. Combine beef bouillon, bitters, bouillon cube, tomato paste, and flour. Stir well. Cook, stirring until mixture thickens and comes to a boil. Stir in sour cream and heat, but do not boil. Return meatballs to pan and let simmer at very low temperature until well heated.

Q. *How can I avoid having my meatballs fall apart while they are cooking?*
A. Try plunging them—momentarily—into rapidly boiling water before you begin to cook them. They'll keep their shape, and the hot water seals in their flavor.

Ham Balls in Zesty Orange Sauce. Corning Glass Works

Ham Balls in Zesty Orange Sauce

Makes 6 to 8 servings

    1 pound ground ham
    ½ pound ground fresh pork
    ½ cup cracker crumbs
    ½ cup chopped onion
    ½ teaspoon dry mustard
    ½ cup milk
    2 eggs
    ⅓ cup firmly packed dark brown sugar
 1½ tablespoons cornstarch
    ¼ teaspoon ground cloves
 1½ cups orange juice

You will need: Pyrex 10-inch pie plate; Corning Ware 2½-quart covered shallow casserole

Combine ham, pork, crumbs, onion, mustard, milk, and eggs in a large bowl; mix well. Form into 1½-inch balls and place in pie plate. Bake in 350°F. oven 30 minutes. Meanwhile, combine brown sugar, cornstarch, and cloves in casserole; stir in orange juice. Cook over medium heat, stirring constantly until thickened. Reduce heat; keep sauce warm until ham balls are cooked. Drain ham balls on paper towels, then add to sauce in casserole. Cover; simmer 15 to 20 minutes, until both ham balls and sauce are hot.

Empañadas (page 17). Lea & Perrins

Walnut-Beef Miniatures

Makes 100 meatballs

 1 pound ground beef chuck
 ½ cup soda cracker crumbs
 ½ cup finely chopped walnuts
 ¼ cup canned applesauce
 ½ teaspoon salt
 ⅛ teaspoon pepper
 ⅛ teaspoon ground nutmeg
 2 tablespoons butter
 2 tablespoons all-purpose flour
 1½ cups beef bouillon

Combine chuck, cracker crumbs, walnuts, and applesauce in a mixing bowl. Add salt, pepper, and nutmeg, and blend thoroughly. Shape meat lightly into 1-inch cocktail-size balls. Brown meatballs on all sides in melted butter in a large skillet. Remove meatballs as they are browned and set aside. Blend flour into drippings in skillet. Add bouillon and cook, stirring constantly, until mixture thickens slightly and comes to a boil. Taste, and add additional salt and pepper if desired. Add meatballs to sauce and simmer 10 to 15 minutes. Cool meatballs as quickly as possible. Ladle into freezer containers, leaving at least 1 inch headroom. Seal, label, and freeze.

To serve, remove from containers and heat in the top of a double boiler over hot water or in a large skillet over very low heat, stirring occasionally. Turn meatballs into a chafing dish and serve piping hot with toothpicks inserted into meatballs.

Oslo Meatballs

Makes 6 to 8 servings

 1 pound boneless beef chuck, cut in 1-inch pieces
 ½ pound boneless pork shoulder, cut in 1-inch pieces
 2 slices bread, torn in pieces
 1 egg
 1 teaspoon salt
 ¼ teaspoon pepper
 ¼ teaspoon ground nutmeg
   Quick White Sauce (see index)
 ½ envelope onion soup mix
 ½ cup sour cream

Assemble Food Grinder with fine disc and large bowl. Grind beef, pork, and bread. Add egg, salt, pepper, and nutmeg; mix well. Shape into walnut-size balls. Brown meatballs in hot skillet. When brown, remove meatballs with slotted spoon. Prepare white sauce in large saucepan. Stir in onion soup mix. Add meatballs to sauce and simmer covered 10 minutes. Just before serving, add sour cream and mix well.

Roquefort Meatballs

Makes 60 meatballs

 1½ pounds ground beef chuck
 1 package (3 ounces) Roquefort cheese, crumbled
 ¾ teaspoon salt
 ⅛ teaspoon pepper
 ¼ cup butter
 ½ cup dry red wine

Combine beef, cheese, salt, and pepper and blend well. Shape into tiny balls using 1 heaping teaspoon of meat for each ball. Melt butter in a skillet. Brown meatballs in hot butter, turning as needed to brown on all sides. Add wine; cover and cook slowly about 5 minutes, or until done. Serve from a chafing dish with toothpicks.

Unexpected Guests?

When afternoon guests linger for cocktails and you can't run out to the store, spicy meatballs save the day. Add ¼ teaspoon ginger to 1 pound ground beef along with your usual spices. Shape into tiny meatballs, brown quickly, and serve for cocktails with your favorite dip. Make them up in advance, cook, store in the freezer, and you'll never be caught unprepared.

Far East Appetizer Meatballs

Makes 8 servings

 1 can (12 ounces) Spam
 ⅔ cup dry bread crumbs
 ½ cup chopped well-drained bean sprouts
 ¼ cup chopped green onions
 ¼ teaspoon powdered ginger
   Pepper to taste
   Far East Dipping Sauce (recipe follows)

Grind Spam or process in food processor using chopping blade until finely chopped. Combine Spam with bread crumbs, bean sprouts, onion, ginger, and pepper. Using about 1 teaspoon for each meatball, shape mixture into 24 balls. Place on rack in shallow baking pan; bake in 425°F. oven 15 minutes. Cool to room temperature. Spear meatballs on cocktail toothpicks and dip into hot Far East Dipping Sauce.

Far East Dipping Sauce

 1 cup tomato juice
 ⅓ cup finely chopped green onions
 ¼ cup finely chopped green pepper
 ¼ teaspoon ground ginger

In small saucepan, combine all ingredients. Bring to a boil; simmer uncovered 5 minutes. Serve hot.

Porcupine Meatballs

Makes 6 servings
- 1 cup raw converted rice
- 1 pound ground round steak
- ¼ cup minced onions
- 1 teaspoon salt
- ½ teaspoon black pepper
- 2 cans (10¾ ounces each) Campbell's Condensed Tomato Soup

Mix rice, ground round, onions, salt, and pepper. Shape mixture into 24 1-inch balls. Drop balls into boiling water to cover. Simmer over low heat for 1 hour, or until rice is tender and meatballs are easily pierced. By this time almost all the water will have been absorbed and some of the rice will be cooking in the liquid remaining. Add soup and stir very gently to blend. Reheat until bubbly.

Liver Dumplings

Makes 6 to 8 servings
- ½ pound lean fresh pork
- ½ pound kidney suet
- 1 pound calves' liver
- 1 onion, chopped
- 1 teaspoon butter
- 12 slices white bread, crusts removed
- 1 cup heavy cream
- 2 eggs, well beaten
- 1½ teaspoons salt
- ½ teaspoon pepper
- ¼ teaspoon ground nutmeg
- 1 clove garlic, mashed
- 1 cup all-purpose flour (about)
- 3 cans (10½ ounces each) Campbell's Condensed Beef Broth
- 3 soup cans water
- ½ cup dry bread crumbs
- ¼ cup butter

Grind pork, suet, and liver coarsely. Sauté onion in 1 teaspoon butter until soft but not brown. Add to meat along with bread, cream, eggs, salt, pepper, nutmeg, garlic, and enough flour to make a stiff dough. Blend well, mashing mixture thoroughly. Combine soup and water in a large kettle. Bring to a boil; lower heat to simmering. Shape liver mixture into 24 balls, using lightly moistened hands. Drop into simmering soup and simmer 20 minutes. Remove from stock with a slotted spoon and place on a platter. Combine crumbs and ¼ cup butter and stir over low heat until crumbs are brown. Sprinkle crumbs over dumplings. Dumplings can also be served in the broth in which they were cooked for a hearty main dish soup.

Stuffed Grape Leaves

Makes 8 servings
- 1 medium-size onion, finely chopped
- 2 eggs
- 1 cup uncooked rice
- 1 pound ground hamburger
  Salt, pepper, paprika, dry mint leaves
- 1 jar California grapevine leaves
  Few pats butter
- 3 fresh juicy lemons

Blend the onion, 1 egg, rice, hamburger, and spices. Float the grapevine leaves in a large bowl of water to dilute the brine content. Snip the stem from each leaf as it is used. Place the leaf underside up, and position a small dab of the hamburger mixture in one corner. Then roll the leaf over the hamburger, tucking in the sides and end as you roll. (If the leaves are loosely wrapped, the rice will unravel the leaves as it cooks and expands.) Place the tightly rolled grapevine leaf at one side of a medium-size saucepan. Place the succeeding leaves closely against the first leaf. The entire batch will result in about 3 layers of leaves. Place a heavy dish or two face down on the leaves and cover the leaves gently with cold water to the level of the dishes. Drop a few pats of butter over the top of the water. Heat until water boils, then reduce heat and simmer until rice is well cooked. In a bowl place 1 raw egg and the juice from the lemons. Beat the egg and lemon juice with a fork for about 100 strokes. Slowly pour the water from the saucepan into the bowl of egg-lemon juice. Then slowly pour the egg-lemon base over all the grapevine leaves in the saucepan, which has been removed from the heat. Since the egg-lemon sauce will settle quickly, the leaves should be placed in the bowl one at a time, which will result in the bottom leaves being inverted to the top and vice versa. Let the leaves stand about 5 minutes. Serve hot or cold.

Shaping Ground-Meat Mixtures

Use your hands if you wish to form ground-meat mixtures into patties or loaves or balls. But be sure to rinse your hands in cold water before plunging in—it will keep the mixture from sticking to your fingers. Although hands are the best kitchen tools ever invented, there are alternatives. Melon ballers shape small, neat, cocktail-size meatballs, and ice-cream scoops provide big, hearty meatballs. Flatten the ice-cream-scoop balls, and presto! meat patties, ready to cook.

Ham Buffet Mold (page 16). Campbell Soup Company

Last-Minute Antipasto

Makes 8 servings
- 1 head Boston lettuce
- ¼ pound hard salami, thinly sliced
- 4 ounces provolone cheese
  Cherry tomatoes
- 1 jar (6 ounces) marinated artichoke hearts
- 1 jar (3¾ ounces) marinated mushrooms
- 1 can (2 ounces) flat anchovy fillets
  Ripe olives
  Hot pickled peppers
  Oil and vinegar

Line serving platter with lettuce leaves. Roll salami slices. Cut cheese into triangle-shaped wedges. Arrange ingredients on lettuce. Cover with Reynolds Plastic Wrap and refrigerate. To serve, drizzle with oil and vinegar.

Tenderloin of Beef

Makes 16 servings
- 1 whole beef tenderloin, about 4 to 6 pounds
- 1 clove garlic, halved
  Party rye bread slices

Rub tenderloin all over with cut side of garlic. Place on a rack in a shallow roasting pan, tucking narrow end under to make roast uniformly thick. Insert meat thermometer into center of thickest part. Roast in a preheated 450°F. oven for 45 to 60 minutes, or to rare (140°F. on the roast meat thermometer). Place meat on a carving board. At serving time, cut into very thin slices and serve with party rye bread.

Last-Minute Antipasto, Instant Liver Pâté (page 9). The Reynolds Wrap Kitchen

Glazed Corned Beef

Makes 20 servings

  1 whole corned beef brisket, about 4 pounds
  1 large onion, sliced
  2 whole garlic cloves
  2 bay leaves
    Whole cloves
  1 tablespoon Grey Poupon mustard
  2 tablespoons firmly packed light brown sugar
    Party rye bread slices

Place beef in a large Dutch oven. Cover with 4 cups boiling water. Add onion, garlic, and bay leaves. Bring water to a boil; reduce heat and cover. Simmer about 3½ hours, or until meat is fork-tender. Remove meat from water and place in a shallow baking pan, fat side up. Score fat and stud with cloves. Brush with mustard and sprinkle brown sugar over top. Bake in a preheated 350°F. oven for 15 to 20 minutes, or until well glazed on the top. Place meat on a cutting board. At serving time, cut in very thin slices and serve with party rye bread.

Beef Tartare

Makes 4 servings

  4 slices white bread, buttered
  1 pound beef sirloin, raw
  2 tablespoons chopped onion
  2 tablespoons chopped pickled beetroot
  2 tablespoons capers
  2 tablespoons chopped parsley
  4 egg yolks
  1 teaspoon salt
    Pinch pepper

Scrape beef, or put once through meat grinder. Divide among the slices of bread and spread evenly. Garnish with onion, beetroot, capers, and parsley. Serve with yolks of egg, each ensconced in its shell, in the middle of each piece. Sprinkle with salt and pepper.

Ham Pie with Cheese Biscuit Topping

Makes 6 servings

  2 cans (10½ ounces each) Campbell's Condensed Cream of Celery Soup
  ⅔ cup light cream
  4 cups diced cooked ham
  3 cups biscuit mix
  1½ cups grated cheddar cheese
  1 cup milk

Combine soup, cream, and ham. Divide mixture equally among 6 individual casseroles of 1-cup capacity each. Combine biscuit mix and cheese. Toss to blend. Stir in milk and mix until dough cleans the bowl. Knead dough a few times on a lightly floured board until smooth. Roll out dough to ½-inch thickness and cut into rounds large enough to cover the tops of the casseroles. Bake in a preheated 350°F. oven for 30 minutes, or until filling is bubbly and crust is brown.

Ham Buffet Mold

Makes 8 to 10 servings

  1 can (10¾ ounces) Campbell's Condensed Tomato Soup
  ¾ cup water
  2 envelopes unflavored gelatin
  ½ cup cold water
  1 package (3 ounces) cream cheese
  2 tablespoons lemon juice
  1 tablespoon grated onion
  ½ cup mayonnaise
  2 teaspoons prepared mustard
  2 cups finely chopped boiled or smoked ham
    Salad greens
    Hard cooked eggs, sliced
    Stuffed olives

Combine soup and ¾ cup water and bring to a boil. Soak gelatin in ½ cup cold water for 5 minutes. Stir softened gelatin into hot soup. Add cream cheese and beat until smooth. Cool until slightly thickened. Stir in remaining ingredients. Pour mixture into a lightly oiled 6-cup mold. Chill for 4 hours, or until the mold is firm. To unmold, dip mold into lukewarm water for a few seconds, tap to loosen, and invert on a platter. Garnish with a variety of salad greens, hard-cooked egg slices, and stuffed olives.

Empanadas

Makes about 4 dozen

  1 package (8 ounces) cream cheese, softened
  ½ cup butter or margarine, softened
  1½ cups all-purpose flour
  1 tablespoon olive or salad oil
  2 tablespoons minced onion
  ½ pound ground lean beef
  1 can (8¼ ounces) tomatoes, drained and crushed
  2 tablespoons chopped raisins
  2 tablespoons chopped pitted green olives
  1 tablespoon Lea & Perrins Worcestershire Sauce
  ½ teaspoon salt
  ½ teaspoon oregano leaves, crumbled
  1 hard-cooked egg, chopped
  1 egg yolk
  1 tablespoon water
  ¼ cup sesame seed

In the large bowl of an electric mixer, blend cream cheese and butter. Gradually add flour; blend until dough is smooth. Divide dough into 3 balls; cover and chill until firm, about 30 minutes. In a medium skillet, heat oil. Add onion; sauté for 3 minutes. Add meat; cook and stir until browned, about 5 minutes. Stir in tomatoes, raisins, olives, Lea & Perrins, salt, and oregano. Simmer uncovered for 5 minutes, stirring occasionally. Stir in chopped egg; cool. On a lightly floured board, roll each ball of dough separately to ⅛-inch thickness. With a 3-inch biscuit cutter, cut out circles. Spoon about 1 teaspoon of the meat mixture onto one side of each circle. Moisten edges with water; fold pastry over filling to form a a semicircle; press edges to seal; crimp with fork tines. Repeat. Prick tops of turnovers to allow steam to escape. Mix egg yolk with water; brush over tops of turnover. Sprinkle with sesame seed. Place on cookie sheets. Bake in a preheated hot oven (400°F.) until golden, about 12 minutes. Serve hot.

Ham Pancakes

Makes 6 servings (2 crêpes each serving)
- ½ **cup all-purpose flour**
- 1 **teaspoon** *each* **sugar and salt**
- 2 **tablespoons melted butter**
- ¾ **cup milk**
- 3 **egg yolks**
- 3 **egg whites, stiffly beaten**
- 2 **cups ground cooked or smoked ham**
- 3 **hard-cooked eggs, chopped**
- 1 **cup grated Swiss cheese**
- 2 **cans (10¾ ounces each) Campbell's Condensed Cheddar Cheese Soup**
- ½ **cup light cream**

Sift flour, sugar, and salt into a bowl. Add melted butter, milk, and egg yolks and beat until smooth. Fold in egg whites. Lightly grease a 6-inch skillet. Heat skillet and pour in about 2 tablespoons of the batter. Spread evenly over bottom of skillet. Cook until golden brown on each side. Repeat, using all batter. In a bowl, combine ham, hard-cooked eggs, ¾ cup of the grated cheese, and ½ cup of the cheddar cheese soup. Spoon filling on pancakes and roll up. Place filled pancakes in a greased shallow baking pan. Combine remaining soup with cream; beat until smooth. Spoon over pancakes. Sprinkle top with remaining grated cheese. Bake in preheated 400°F. oven 20 minutes, until brown.

Pork Satay

Makes 6 to 8 servings
- ½ **pound lean boneless pork**
- 2 **tablespoons soy sauce**
- 2 **tablespoons thick steak sauce**
- 10 **dried apricots**
- ¼ **cup creamy or chunky peanut butter**
- ½ **teaspoon salt**
- 5 **drops hot pepper sauce**

Cut the pork into ¾-inch cubes and combine with soy sauce and steak sauce. Cover and refrigerate for several hours, stirring occasionally. Meanwhile, simmer apricots in ¾ cup water for 5 minutes. Place apricots and their cooking liquid in a blender container or food processor. Add peanut butter, salt, and hot pepper sauce. Cover and process until smooth. Reheat when ready to serve. Thread the marinated pork cubes on skewers. (If you use wooden skewers, soak them in water 2 hours before using.) Brush with any remaining soy sauce mixture. Cook over hot coals or under broiler for 6 to 8 minutes, turning often. Serve with the warm apricot-peanut butter sauce for dipping.

Spareribs Chinese

Makes 4 to 6 servings
- 4 **pounds pork spareribs**
- ½ **cup Kikkoman Soy Sauce**
- ⅓ **cup honey**
- ¼ **cup dry sherry**
- 1 **clove garlic, crushed**
- ¼ **teaspoon ground ginger**

Cut ribs into serving pieces; place in shallow, foil-lined pan, meaty side down. Combine remaining ingredients; brush ribs thoroughly with sauce. Cover and bake at 350°F. 1 hour. Turn ribs over, pour remaining sauce over ribs, and brush with sauce. Bake uncovered 30 minutes longer; brush occasionally.

Appetizer Kebabs

Miniature kebabs, smaller than the dinner-size ones, make excellent appetizers, They can be small versions of the main-dish kind, or you can go in different directions. Tiny meatballs alternating with small mushrooms are excellent. So are chunks of chicken liver and water chestnuts, threaded on a small skewer with bits of bacon separating them. A slice of bacon, threaded accordian-style around three plump oysters, makes a triple-barreled angel on horseback. Or substitute little bay scallops for the oysters. These and many other combinations can be cooked in advance and kept warm in a chafing dish, or grilled to order on a small hibachi.

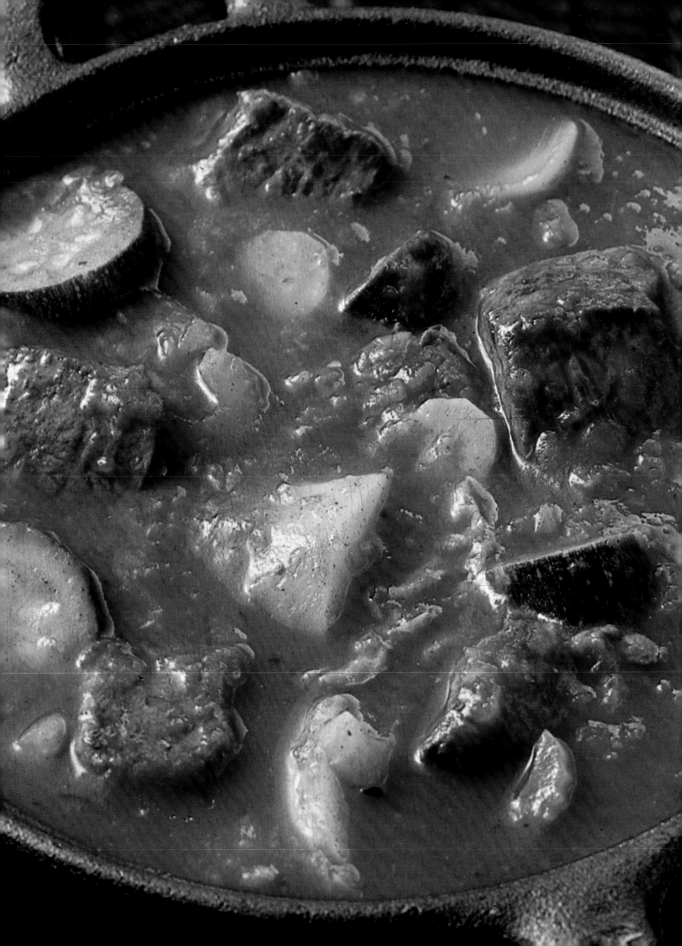

A Kettle of Soups and Stews

A perfect first course? Try a homemade, richly flavored soup. A wintery evening's repast? Select a hearty, meaty stew.

Hearty Beef-Vegetable Soup

Makes 6 to 8 servings

    2 pounds stewing beef, cut into 1-inch pieces
    6 cups hot water
    ½ cup chopped onion
    1 can (6 ounces) Hunt's Tomato Paste
    2 teaspoons salt
    1 teaspoon ground allspice
    ¼ teaspoon thyme
    ¼ teaspoon coarsely ground pepper
    2 beef bouillon cubes
    1 bay leaf
    3 carrots, sliced ¼-inch thick
    3 ribs celery, sliced ¼-inch thick
    3 zucchini, sliced ½-inch thick
    2 potatoes, quartered
    ¼ head cabbage, cut in 1-inch pieces

Combine first 10 ingredients in a Dutch oven or large kettle. Bring to boil; simmer covered about 2 hours, or until meat is tender. Remove bay leaf. Add carrots and remaining ingredients. Simmer covered 30 minutes longer, or until vegetables are tender.

South of the Border Stew

Makes 6 servings

    1 can (40 ounces) Dinty Moore Beef Stew
    1 can (12 ounces) whole-kernel corn with red
        peppers, drained
    1 teaspoon taco sauce
    Corn chips

In medium saucepan, combine stew, corn, and taco sauce; heat to serving temperature. Sprinkle with corn chips and serve.
Note: You may want to substitute 1 tablespoon chili powder for taco sauce.

Scandinavian Soup

Makes 6 servings★

    4 ounces lean beef round, cut into ½-inch cubes
    1 teaspoon vegetable oil
    ⅓ cup diced celery
    1 tablespoon finely chopped onion
    1 small clove garlic, crushed
    1 teaspoon salt
    ½ teaspoon thyme
    ¼ teaspoon dry mustard
    5 cups water
    1 bay leaf
    1 packet Butter Buds
    ½ cup diagonally sliced carrots, ¼ inch thick
    ⅛ teaspoon white pepper
    1 cup frozen cut green beans
    ¾ cup uncooked small macaroni shells

In large skillet, brown beef in oil 3 to 4 minutes. Add celery, onion, garlic, salt, thyme, and mustard. Cook until celery is tender, about 7 to 8 minutes. Add water, bay leaf, and Butter Buds. Reduce heat and add carrots, pepper, green beans, and macaroni. Simmer 10 minutes, or until vegetables and macaroni are tender. Remove bay leaf before serving.
★By using Butter Buds instead of butter in this recipe, you have saved 125 calories and 47 mg cholesterol per serving.

Hearty Beef-Vegetable Soup. Beatrice/Hunt-Wesson Foods

Hearty Party Soup

Makes 10 servings

- 1 large soup bone, split
- 2 pounds soup meat
- 1 tablespoon salt
- ½ medium-size cabbage, sliced
- 2 onions, chopped
- 6 carrots, pared and cut in 3-inch pieces
- 2 stalks celery, cut up
- ¼ green pepper, seeded and cut up
- 1 can (1 pound 13 ounces) tomatoes
- 1 cup cut green beans
- 1 cup peas
- 1 can (12 ounces) whole kernel corn
- 1 potato, peeled and cubed
- 2 tablespoons snipped parsley
- ½ cup catsup
- 1 teaspoon sugar
- 1 teaspoon salt
- ¼ teaspoon pepper

Place soup bone, soup meat, and salt in a large kettle with 4 quarts of water. Bring to a boil and simmer 20 minutes. Skim off any foam that rises to the top of soup. Add cabbage, onions, carrots, celery, pepper, and tomatoes. Simmer covered about 30 minutes. Add remaining ingredients. Simmer covered about 2 hours. Taste for seasoning. Remove meat and bone from soup. Cut up pieces of meat and return to soup. Cool soup by setting kettle in ice water. Skim all fat from top of soup. Reheat slowly just before serving. Serve piping hot.

Stew 'n' Dumplings

Makes 6 servings

- 1 can (40 ounces) Dinty Moore Beef Stew
- 2 cups biscuit mix
- ⅔ cup milk
- 2 tablespoons finely chopped parsley

In large skillet or pot, heat stew to bubbling. In bowl, stir biscuit mix, milk, and parsley to make a soft dough. Drop dough by spoonfuls onto hot stew. Cook uncovered over low heat 10 minutes. Cover and cook 10 minutes more.

Variations

Add 1 can (16 ounces) mixed vegetables, drained
Add 1 can (4½ ounces) mushroom slices, drained
Add 1 can (8 ounces) tomato sauce

Basic Beef Stock

A homemade beef stock specially prepared for a specific recipe or on hand for last-minute menus provides the core for many of your favorite beef dishes.

Makes 2 quarts

- 4 pounds shank soup bones
- 2 pounds marrowbone, cut in 3-inch pieces
- 1 calf's foot or veal knuckle
- 3 leeks
- 1 onion, studded with 3 whole cloves
- 2 cloves garlic
- 1 stalk celery with leaves
- 1 carrot
- 1 teaspoon thyme
- 1 bay leaf
- 12 peppercorns
- 4 sprigs parsley
- Salt to taste

Place 4 quarts cold water in an 8-quart pot. Add all ingredients except salt. Bring to a boil. Remove scum as it accumulates on surface. Allow stock to boil about 20 minutes. Lower heat, cover, and simmer 2 hours. Skim off any additional scum, add salt, and simmer 1½ hours longer. Cool. Place in refrigerator until cold enough to skim off fat. Strain and store in freezer for future use.

If storing in refrigerator, leave fat on top of stock during storage. Skim before using. The stock will keep about 4 days. Reboil for longer refrigerator storage.

Note: To make Brown Stock, brown bones in oven before adding to pot. Since the best stock flavor is obtained if all ingredients are the same temperature when cooking begins, be certain to cool browned bones before adding them to stock pot.

Mulligan Soup

Makes 2 servings

- 1 can (7½ ounces) Dinty Moore Brunswick Stew
- 1 can (8 ounces) stewed tomatoes
- ⅓ cup water

In small saucepan, combine all ingredients; bring to a boil. Simmer 2 minutes, stirring occasionally, and serve.

Mexican Meatball Soup

Makes 6 servings
    1 pound lean ground beef
    ½ cup Sun-Maid® Seedless Raisins
    ¼ cup long-grained rice
    1 teaspoon salt
    ¼ teaspoon freshly ground pepper
 1½ teaspoons dried mint leaves, crumbled
    ½ teaspoon oregano
    ¼ teaspoon cumin
    3 cans (10½ ounces) beef broth
    1 can (16 ounces) stewed tomatoes
    1 small head cabbage (1½ pounds)
    2 medium carrots, cut in ¼-inch slices
    2 medium zucchini (8 ounces), cut in ¼-inch
       slices
    ¼ cup dry sherry

Combine ground beef, raisins, rice, ¼ cup water, salt, pepper, mint, oregano, and cumin. Mix well. Form 18 1¾-inch meatballs. Bring beef broth and 1 quart of water to a boil in a large pot. Add meatballs; reduce heat to low and cook for 20 minutes. With a slotted spoon, remove meatballs and set aside. Add tomatoes to the broth. Cut cabbage into 6 wedges. Add cabbage and carrots to boiling broth. Reduce heat and simmer partially covered for 8 minutes. Add meatballs and zucchini. Simmer 2 minutes longer. Lace with sherry and serve.

Choucroute

Makes 8 to 10 servings
    ½ pound Italian sausages
    1 can (5 ounces) Hormel Chicken Vienna
       Sausages
    2 cups chopped onions
    1 large clove garlic, minced
    3 pounds sauerkraut, rinsed and drained
 1½ cups beer
    1 cup water
    1 apple, peeled, cored, and chopped
    4 peppercorns
    3 whole cloves
    1 bay leaf
    1 can (12 ounces) Spam
    ½ pound kielbasa

In large skillet (at least 10 inches in diameter), brown sausages on all sides over low heat. Remove from skillet; drain off all but 2 tablespoons drippings. Sauté onions and garlic over medium heat until onions are lightly browned, stirring often. Add sauerkraut, beer, water, and apple; bring to a boil. Tie peppercorns, cloves, and bay leaf together in a piece of cheesecloth; add to skillet. Cut Spam into 6 slices; stir into sauerkraut mixture with kielbasa and sausages. Lower heat; cover and simmer 2 hours. Discard cheesecloth bag before serving.

Stew Stroganoff Style

Makes 6 to 8 servings
    3 tablespoons oil
 2½ pounds boneless beef for stew, cut into 2-inch
       pieces
 2½ cups (½ pound) sliced mushrooms
    3 tablespoons all-purpose flour
 2½ cups boiling water
    ¼ cup minced onion
    ¼ teaspoon minced garlic
    1 beef bouillon cube
    2 tablespoons Lea & Perrins Worcestershire Sauce,
       divided
    1 teaspoon salt
    1 cup sour cream
    2 tablespoons tomato paste
    2 tablespoons chopped parsley
       Cooked noodles (optional)

In a large heavy saucepot or Dutch oven heat oil. Add meat, a few pieces at a time; brown well on all sides. Remove meat; set aside. Add mushrooms to saucepot; sauté for 5 minutes. Stir in flour; cook and stir for 2 minutes. Gradually stir in water. Add onion, garlic, bouillon cube, 1 teaspoon of the Lea & Perrins, salt, and reserved meat. Bring to boiling point. Reduce heat and simmer covered until meat is tender, about 1½ hours. Combine sour cream, tomato paste, and remaining 1 tablespoon Lea & Perrins; stir into meat. Heat, but do not boil. Stir in parsley. Serve over cooked broad noodles, if desired.

About Overseasoning

Too much of any seasoning—salt, pepper, herbs, spices—can be a disaster, ruining a dish with bitter, strident flavor. Add seasoning a little at a time, tasting as you go. Too much of other seasonings generally can't be rectified, but there are several things you can do to compensate for oversalting. In gravy, soup, or stew, add more liquid. Or add a few pinches of brown sugar, which will offset the saltiness without substituting a too-sweet taste. Or add a few thin slices of potato to the dish, cook until potatoes are translucent, then remove and discard.

Flemish Carbonnades (page 27). Campbell Soup Company

Beef Goulash (page 23). McIhlenny & Co.

Beef Goulash

Makes 6 to 8 servings

- 2 cups Brown Sauce Base (recipe follows)
- ¼ cup butter or margarine
- 4 cups sliced onions
- 2 cloves garlic, minced
- 3 pounds boned round or chuck, cut in 1-inch cubes
- 1 can (8 ounces) whole tomatoes, drained, cut in pieces
- 4 teaspoons paprika
- ½ teaspoon salt
- ½ teaspoon dried leaf marjoram
- 1 bay leaf

Make Brown Sauce Base. In large saucepot or Dutch oven, melt butter; add onions and garlic and cook until lightly browned. Add beef; brown on all sides. Stir in tomatoes, Brown Sauce Base, paprika, salt, marjoram, and bay leaf. Cover and simmer 1½ to 2 hours, stirring occasionally, until meat is tender.

Note: Serve over noodles, spaetzle, mashed potatoes, or rice. If desired, Tabasco hot pepper sauce may be added when serving.

Brown Sauce Base

Makes about 1 cup

- 2 tablespoons butter
- 2 tablespoons flour
- 1 cup canned beef broth or 1 beef bouillon cube dissolved in 1 cup water
- ¼ teaspoon Tabasco pepper sauce

Melt butter in saucepan and cook until golden brown. Blend in flour and cook over low heat, stirring constantly, until dark brown. Stir in broth and add Tabasco. Cook, stirring constantly, until sauce thickens and comes to a boil. If desired, serve with additional Tabasco sauce.

Sukiyaki Skillet

Makes 8 servings

- 1 pound boneless beef for stew
- 2 tablespoons oil
- 2 medium onions, sliced
- 1 cup Uncle Ben's® Converted® Brand Rice
- 3 cups water
- 2½ teaspoons salt
- 1 small can mushrooms (stems and pieces)
- 1 large green pepper, cut in large cubes
- 5 to 6 large stalks celery, cut in 1-inch pieces
- 1 can (1 pound) bean sprouts
- 1 package (10 ounces) frozen chopped spinach, almost thawed
- 3 tablespoons soy sauce
- 1 tablespoon sugar

Cut stew meat into thin slices. Brown meat and onions in oil in a large skillet. Cover and cook slowly about 10 minutes. Add rice, water, salt, and mushrooms with their liquid. Cover and cook slowly until rice is tender, about 25 minutes. Add pepper, celery, bean sprouts, spinach, soy sauce, and sugar. Cover and cook until spinach is tender, 5 to 8 minutes. Do not overcook; vegetables should be crisp. Toss lightly to mix ingredients. Serve with extra soy sauce if desired.

Braised Beef 'n' Vegetables (page 25). Armour Food Company

Veal Stew (page 27). Hamilton Beach Scovill, Inc.

Steakhouse Stew

Makes 6 servings

2 **pounds boneless beef for stew, cut into 1½-inch pieces**
¼ **cup all-purpose flour**
3 **tablespoons oil**
1 **cup coarsely chopped onions**
1 **can (8 ounces) tomato sauce**
¾ **cup water**
3 **tablespoons Lea & Perrins Worcestershire Sauce**
2 **tablespoons vinegar**
2 **tablespoons tomato paste**
2 **tablespoons sugar**
½ **teaspoon salt**
1 **can (4 ounces) sliced mushrooms**
   Cooked noodles (optional)

Dredge beef with flour; shake off excess. In a large heavy saucepot, heat oil. Add beef, a few pieces at a time; brown well on all sides. Remove beef; set aside. Add onions to fat remaining in saucepot; sauté until tender, about 5 minutes. Stir in reserved meat along with remaining ingredients except mushrooms. Bring to boiling point, stirring occasionally. Reduce heat and simmer covered until meat is tender, about 1½ hours, stirring occasionally. Stir in mushrooms; heat only until hot. Serve over cooked noodles, if desired.

Kentucky Burgoo

Makes 8 to 10 servings

2 **tablespoons bacon fat**
1 **pound lean shin bones of beef, with meat**
1 **pound shoulder of veal, cubed**
1 **chicken (1¼ pounds)**
2 **teaspoons salt**
2 **cups chopped onions**
1 **tablespoon bacon fat**
1 **clove garlic, minced**
1 **cup diced raw potatoes**
5 **stalks celery, diced**
1 **can (1 pound) tomatoes**
3 **carrots, pared and diced**
1 **green pepper, seeded and chopped**
1 **cup butter beans or lima beans**
¼ **teaspoon crushed red pepper or dash cayenne**
2 **whole cloves**
1 **bay leaf**
1 **tablespoon dark brown sugar**
   Dash pepper
1 **cup sliced okra**
3 **ears or 1 can (12 ounces) corn**
¼ **cup butter**
½ **cup all-purpose flour**
½ **cup snipped parsley**

Heat 2 tablespoons bacon fat in a Dutch oven. Add beef bones and veal and brown well. Add chicken, 2 quarts of water, and salt. Cover and cook over low heat until veal and chicken are tender. Remove from broth. When cool enough to handle, remove all skin and bones. Cut meat into bite-size pieces and return to broth. In a skillet, cook onions in 1 tablespoon bacon fat until pale golden. Add to broth with garlic, potatoes, celery, tomatoes, carrots, green pepper, butter beans, red pepper, cloves, bay leaf, brown sugar, and pepper. Cook slowly, about 1½ hours. Add okra and corn; cook 15 minutes. Blend butter and flour. Stir into burgoo until thickened. Correct seasoning. Sprinkle with parsley.

Casserole Toppers

Some go on early in the game, some are added the last few minutes of cooking—either way, toppings for casseroles are many and various, all add the finishing touch, the final fillip that makes a good dish better. Bread crumbs are good, are better for having been sautéed lightly in butter. Crushed chips—corn or potato—are very tasty. Crushed crackers ditto—plain, buttery, cheese- or otherwise flavored. Just a sprinkling of paprika shows you cared, and helps the top of the dish to brown. Crunchy dry cereal is fine. So are broken-up pretzels. Cheese, grated or cut in neat squares or triangles, makes a deliciously chewy topping. Biscuits—homemade or from a dairy-case package—bake up high and handsome, and can take the place of a filler ingredient in the dish itself. Mashed potatoes, plain or cheese-flavored or -sprinkled, make a fine topping and serve the same purpose. Or sprinkle the top of the dish with toasted slivered almonds. Whatever, do something—don't let a casserole come naked to the table.

Stew 'n' Corn Bread Casserole

Makes 6 to 8 servings

1 **cup green pepper, cut in ½-inch chunks**
2 **tablespoons butter or margarine**
1 **can (24 ounces) Armour Star Beef Stew**
1 **can (15 ounces) kidney beans, drained**
1 **can (8¼ ounces) tomatoes, chopped and drained**
2 **tablespoons chili powder**
1 **package (15 ounces) corn bread mix, mixed according to package directions**

Heat oven to 425°F. Cook green pepper in butter or margarine 5 minutes; drain. Combine green pepper, stew, kidney beans, tomatoes, and chili powder; pour into lightly greased 13x9-inch baking dish. Spread corn bread mix on top. Bake at 425°F. for 20 minutes.

Braised Beef 'n' Vegetables

Makes 4 servings

 1 1½ pound Naturally Tender Beef bottom round steak, cut in 3x¼-inch strips
 2 tablespoons vegetable oil
 2 teaspoons salt
 ½ teaspoon thyme
 ¼ teaspoon pepper
 1 teaspoon Armour Star Beef Flavor Instant Bouillon or 1 Armour Star Beef Flavor Bouillon cube dissolved in 1 cup boiling water
 2 packages (10 ounces each) frozen Italian green beans, thawed
 2 cups sliced mushrooms
 ¾ cup buttermilk
 1 teaspoon cornstarch
   Red onion rings
   Parsley sprigs

In large fry pan, cook beef on medium-high heat in oil 10 minutes; drain. Combine salt, thyme, and pepper; sprinkle on beef. Add bouillon to beef; simmer covered 1 hour and 30 minutes. Stir in green beans and mushrooms; simmer covered 15 minutes. Combine buttermilk and cornstarch; gradually add to beef mixture. Cook over low heat, stirring until thickened. Garnish with onion and parsley.

Ranchero Supper Stew

Makes about 6 servings

 2 tablespoons oil
 1½ pounds beef cubes
 1 envelope Lipton Onion or Beefy Onion Recipe Soup Mix
 2 cans (16 ounces each) whole tomatoes, undrained
 1 cup water
 2 teaspoons chili powder
 2 carrots, thinly sliced
 1 green pepper, chopped
 ½ cup celery, thinly sliced
 2 potatoes, diced

In large skillet, heat oil and brown beef; add Lipton Onion Recipe Soup Mix blended with tomatoes, water, and chili powder. Simmer, stirring occasionally, 30 minutes. Add carrots, green pepper, celery, and potatoes; simmer covered 45 minutes, or until vegetables are tender and gravy is slightly thickened.

Raisin-Anise Beef Stew

Makes 6 servings

 2 medium-size onions, sliced
 2 tablespoons vegetable oil
 2 pounds beef for stewing, cut in 1½-inch chunks
 1 cup Sun-Maid® Seedless Raisins
 1 can (10½ ounces) condensed beef broth
 ¼ cup cider vinegar
 2 teaspoons anise seed
 1½ teaspoons salt
 1 pound butternut squash

In a Dutch oven, lightly brown the onions in the oil. Add the meat, raisins, beef broth, vinegar, anise seed, and salt and bring to a boil. Reduce heat, cover, and simmer for 1 to 1½ hours, or until the meat is nearly tender. Check the stew during cooking; if the mixture is too dry, add a little hot water. Meanwhile, peel squash, cut in half, and scoop out the seeds. Cut in chunks and add to the stew during the last 30 minutes of cooking time. Continue cooking unil the meat and squash are very tender.

Raisin-Anise Beef Sandwiches

Omit squash. Spoon meat mixture into warm sesame seed rolls. Add a dollop of sour cream or plain yogurt. Makes 8 to 10 sandwiches.

Far East Beef Stew

Makes 4 servings

 1 can (24 ounces) Armour Star Beef Stew
 1 can (8½ ounces) water chestnuts, drained and sliced
 ½ cup green onions and tops, cut in 1-inch pieces
 ¼ cup soy sauce
 ⅛ teaspoon ground ginger
   Hot cooked rice
   Chow mein noodles

In fry pan, combine stew, water chestnuts, green onions, soy sauce, and ginger; simmer 10 minutes. Serve over rice. Garnish with noodles.

Frozen Meats

Most cuts of meat can be cooked directly from the frozen state, requiring about 1½ times as long to cook as the same cut unfrozen. Because roast cooking times are less certain than with unfrozen meat, be sure to use a meat thermometer, inserting it as soon as the meat is sufficiently thawed by the oven heat to accept it.

Fruited Pork Stew

Makes 4 servings

- 1 pound boneless pork for stewing, cut into 1-inch cubes
- 2 small onions, quartered
- 1 tablespoon vegetable oil
- 1 cup chicken broth
- 1 teaspoon salt
- ¼ teaspoon freshly ground pepper
- ¼ teaspoon ground ginger
- ¼ cup dried apricots
- ½ cup pitted prunes
- 1 large cooking apple, cut into 1-inch chunks
  Hot cooked noodles

In a Dutch oven, sauté the pork cubes and onions in oil until browned. Add the chicken broth, salt, pepper, and ginger, stirring to combine, and bring to a boil. Reduce heat, cover, and simmer for 30 minutes. Add the apricots, prunes, and apple and simmer covered 20 minutes longer, or until the pork is fork-tender. Serve the stew in a deep platter, surrounded with noodles.

Veal Stew

Makes 6 servings

- 1 cup water
- 1 medium onion, cut up
- 1 carrot, pared and cut up
- 3 sprigs parsley
- ½ cup all-purpose flour
- 1 teaspoon salt
- ¼ teaspoon ground cloves
- ¼ teaspoon dried thyme
- ¼ teaspoon pepper
- 1 bay leaf
- 2 pounds veal shoulder, cut in 1-inch cubes
- 12 small white onions, peeled
- ½ pound button mushrooms
- ½ cup heavy cream
- 2 egg yolks
- 2 teaspoons lemon juice
  Chopped parsley (optional)

Put water, onion, carrot, parsley, flour, salt, cloves, thyme, pepper, and bay leaf into blender container. Cover; blend at medium speed until vegetables are chopped. Put veal and small white onions into large kettle or Dutch oven; add blended mixture. Cover; simmer 1 hour, stirring occasionally. Wipe mushrooms with damp cloth and add to stew. Simmer covered 30 minutes, stirring occasionally. Put cream, egg yolks, and lemon juice into blender container. Add about ½

cup hot liquid from veal. Cover; blend at high speed until smooth. Stir into liquid in kettle. Cook over low heat, stirring constantly, about 3 minutes or just until sauce bubbles. Do not allow sauce to boil. Sprinkle with chopped parsley, if desired.

Indonesian Lamb Stew

Makes 6 servings

- 2 pounds lamb shoulder neck slices
- 2 tablespoons vegetable oil
- 2 medium-size onions, sliced
- 1 clove garlic, minced
- 1 can (16 ounces) stewed tomatoes
- 1½ teaspoons salt
- 1 teaspoon chili powder
- 1 teaspoon turmeric
- ½ teaspoon ground ginger
- ¼ teaspoon ground cinnamon
- ¼ teaspoon crushed red pepper
- ¼ teaspoon freshly ground black pepper
- 2 tablespoons cider vinegar
- 1 large cooking apple, peeled and chopped
- ½ cup Sun-Maid® Seedless Raisins
- 1 can (20 ounces) white kidney beans, undrained

In a Dutch oven, brown the meat on all sides in oil. Remove from the pot and add the onions and garlic. Sauté until the onions are soft but not browned. Return the meat to the pot and add the remaining ingredients except the beans; bring to a boil. Reduce heat, cover, and simmer for 1½ hours, or until the meat is fork-tender. Add the beans and simmer 10 minutes longer.

Flemish Carbonnades

Makes 4 to 6 servings; 1 cup gravy

- 1½ pounds round steak, sliced ¾ inch thick
- 2 tablespoons shortening
- ¾ cup beer
- 1 can (10½ ounces) Campbell's Condensed French Onion Soup
- 2 teaspoons sugar
- 1 tablespoon all-purpose flour mixed with ¼ cup water

Cut meat into serving-size pieces; pound with meat mallet. In a skillet, brown meat in shortening; pour off fat. Add beer; stir to loosen browned bits in pan. Add soup and sugar. Cover; cook over low heat for 1 hour, stirring occasionally. Stir flour mixture into pan. Slowly cook, stirring constantly, until thickened and smooth.

Ranchero Supper Stew (page 25). Photo courtesy of Thomas J. Lipton, Inc.

Hungarian Goulash

Makes 4 servings
  ¼ **cup cooking oil**
  1 **large Spanish onion, chopped**
  2 **pounds beef chuck, cut into 1½-inch cubes**
  ¾ **cup hot beef stock or bouillon**
  2 **teaspoons paprika**
    Salt and pepper
  1 **cup diced raw potatoes**
  1 **cup diced raw carrots**
  ¼ **cup tomato juice**
  1 **package (8 ounces) wide egg noodles**

Heat the cooking oil in Multi-Cooker Frypan to 350°F. Sauté the onion until soft and transparent, but not browned. Add beef cubes and brown. Add stock, paprika, salt, and pepper to taste. Cover, reduce heat to 250°F., and simmer 1 hour. Add potatoes, carrots, and tomato juice; simmer 30 minutes longer, or until beef is tender and vegetables are cooked. Meanwhile, cook noodles according to package directions. Serve goulash over noodles.

Beef and Cabbage Casserole

Makes 4 servings
  1 **pound lean ground beef**
  1 **medium-size onion, chopped**
  3 **cups finely shredded cabbage**
  1 **can (8 ounces) tomato sauce**
  ½ **cup uncooked long grain rice**
  2 **packets Sweet 'N Low**
  1¼ **cups water**

Preheat oven to 350°F. In medium-size non-stick skillet, brown beef and onion; drain fat. Transfer beef and onion to 2½-quart casserole and combine with remaining ingredients. Bake covered about 45 minutes. **Note:** If you don't own a non-stick skillet, you can spray your skillet with a non-stick coating agent.

Ham and Cheese Casserole

Makes 4 servings
  1 **cup milk**
  10 **soda crackers**
  ½ **pound cooked ham, cut in 1-inch pieces**
  ½ **pound Swiss cheese, cut in 1-inch pieces**
  5 **eggs**
  1 **teaspoon Worcestershire sauce**
    Sweet Sour Mustard Sauce (recipe follows)

Warm milk in saucepan. Put crackers in milk; set aside. Assemble Food Grinder with fine disc. Grind ham and cheese into small mixer bowl. Assemble Mixer. In large mixer bowl, beat eggs at High until light and thick (about 5 minutes). Add cracker mixture, ham-cheese mixture, and Worcestershire sauce; fold with rubber spatula until evenly mixed. Pour into a greased 2-quart casserole. Bake at 350°F. for 30 minutes. Reduce temperature to 275°F. and bake an additional 30 minutes. Serve hot, plain, or with Sweet Sour Mustard Sauce.

Sweet Sour Mustard Sauce

Makes 1 cup
  ½ **cup sugar**
  ½ **teaspoon salt**
  2 **teaspoons dry mustard**
  1 **egg**
  ¼ **cup milk**
  ¼ **cup vinegar**

Assemble Blender. Put all ingredients into blender container. Cover and process at Liquefy until blended. Pour into small saucepan and heat, stirring constantly, until sauce begins to thicken and boil. Serve warm.

Beef and Eggplant Casserole

Makes 6 servings
  1 **pound eggplant**
  3 **eggs, divided**
  ½ **cup fine dry bread crumbs**
  1½ **teaspoons salt, divided**
  4 **tablespoons oil, divided**
  ⅓ **cup chopped onion**
  1 **pound lean ground beef**
  ½ **cup diced tomato**
  2 **tablespoons Lea & Perrins Worcestershire Sauce**
  1 **tablespoon cornstarch**
  ½ **cup milk**

Cut eggplant into ¼-inch slices. Lightly beat 1 egg. Combine bread crumbs with ½ teaspoon salt. Dip eggplant into the egg, then into the bread crumbs. In a large skillet, heat 2 tablespoons oil. Sauté eggplant, a few slices at a time, about 1 minute on each side; remove and set aside. Wipe skillet with paper towels. Add remaining 2 tablespoons oil to the skillet. Add onion; sauté until tender, about 5 minutes. Skim off excess fat. Blend in tomato, Lea & Perrins, and remaining 1 teaspoon salt. Simmer uncovered for 5 minutes. In a small saucepan, mix cornstarch with milk. Cook and stir until thickened. Lightly beat remaining 2 eggs; slowly stir into the hot milk mixture. Arrange half of the eggplant slices in a 10x6x1½-inch baking pan. Spoon all of the meat mixture over the eggplant. Arrange remaining eggplant over the meat. Pour egg mixture over all. Bake in a preheated moderate oven (350°F.) for 30 minutes.

Bean-Lamb Casserole

Makes 8 to 10 servings

- 3 cups dried white beans
- 3 tablespoons olive oil
- 2 cups chopped onions
- 1 piece boneless lamb, about 3 pounds, cubed
- 1 tablespoon salt
- ¾ teaspoon black pepper
- 1½ bay leaves
- 2¼ cups peeled and chopped tomatoes
- 3 cloves garlic, minced
- 3 tablespoons finely snipped parsley

Wash the beans, cover with water, and bring to a boil. Cook 5 minutes, remove from heat, and let stand 1 hour. Drain. Add fresh water, cover, bring to a boil, and simmer over low heat for 1½ hours. Drain. Heat the oil in a flameproof casserole; brown the onions in it. Add lamb and cook until browned. Add beans, 1¾ cups boiling water, salt, pepper, bay leaves. Cover and cook over low heat 1 hour. Add tomatoes and garlic; re-cover and cook 1 hour longer, or until beans and lamb are tender. Sprinkle with parsley.

Helpful to know: This dish improves on standing. Make the day before; heat in the oven to serve.

Stews

As generally recognized, the term means a concoction of small pieces of meat or poultry or fish plus vegetables in a savory gravy. Most stews are long-cooking foods, because they are generally made of the more economical but less tender cuts of meat and a long cooking period is necessary to make them tender.

In some cases, the meat is browned in fat before liquid is added. Flavoring vegetables—such as onion (often stuck with three or four cloves) and celery—are added at the beginning of the cooking period; vegetables to be eaten as part of the stew and other ingredients—pasta, for example—are added toward the end of the cooking period, so that they will be just done but not overcooked when the stew is served. Or these ingredients may be cooked separately and incorporated into the stew just before serving. This is often done with carrots, parsnips, or turnips by people who don't like the sweet taste they impart to the stew when cooked in it.

Almost any vegetable is proper material for a stew, other than beets, which turn the mixture a sickly pink. Some stews traditionally call only for certain vegetables—but feel free to break with tradition if the fancy moves you.

Beef stews.   These are generally hearty, cold-weather fare. Although no law (community or culinary) says you must brown the meat, the stew will be both more flavorful and better looking if you do. Kidneys are traditional with beef stews; include them if your family enjoys them. After browning, add liquid—generally water, sometimes tomato juice or stock for fine flavor, just to cover the meat. Tuck in an onion studded with three cloves, a bay leaf if you like the flavor. Toward the end of cooking time, add vegetables in any combination you like: carrots, tomatoes, small whole onions, green beans, lima beans, potatoes. Check seasoning and correct it if necessary—and the choice is yours—thicken with flour-water paste if you wish.

Lamb stews.   Here the flavor will be less affected by browning or not browning the meat. Again, add an onion for flavoring along with the liquid. Thyme, marjoram, or rosemary are delicious with lamb. Or you may flavor your stew with curry powder near the end of cooking time. Appropriate additions: potatoes, peas, tomatoes, eggplant, turnips, celery, small onions. Onions and potatoes only are traditional in Irish stew. Rice, tomatoes, and green peppers go into a Spanish lamb stew.

Veal stews.   The best-known is *blanquette de veau,* in which the meat is not browned. Small white onions and mushroom caps are the vegetables; the gravy is flavored with lemon juice, thickened with eggs and cream. Garnish with parsley, serve with noodles for an entrancing meal. There are other veal stews as well, but however you use the veal, do not brown it or brown only very lightly. Sour cream is delicious added to a veal stew gravy. Peas, parsnips, carrots, celery, and snow peas are appropriate.

Pork stews.   The most-often-served pork stew in this country is American chop suey, a blend of cut-up pork (browned or not) with celery and onions, sometimes water chestnuts, bean sprouts and/or bamboo shoots. But flavorful pork can find a place in a stew with sweet potatoes or yams and corn, with lima beans and carrots, or with almost any combination of vegetables you wish.

All-American Ground Meat Favorites

Your family always appreciates the savory goodness of ground meat—delicious meat loaves, stroganoffs, meat pies, casseroles, and more. Why not serve one tonight?

Old-Fashioned Meat Loaf

Makes 6 servings

    1   pound ground chuck or round
    ½   pound ground pork
    ½   pound ground veal
    5   slices bread
    ¼   cup milk
    1   small onion, cut up
    ½   green pepper, seeded and cut up
    ¼   cup catsup
    1   teaspoon Worcestershire sauce
    1   egg
    2   teaspoons salt
    ¼   teaspoon pepper

Heat oven to 350°F. Combine chuck, pork, and veal in large bowl. Tear two slices of bread into blender container. Cover; blend at medium speed until crumbled. Add to meat. Repeat process until all bread is crumbled. Put remaining ingredients into blender container in order listed. Cover; blend at medium speed until vegetables are chopped. Pour over meat; mix gently but thoroughly. Pack meat mixture into greased 9x5x3-inch loaf pan. Bake 1¼ hours. Serve hot or cold.

Rita's Glazed Meat Loaf

Makes 6 servings

    1½ pounds lean ground beef
    1   cup crushed gingersnaps
    ½   cup chopped onion
    ¼   cup chopped parsley
    ¼   cup chopped walnuts
    2   eggs, lightly beaten
    ⅓   cup evaporated milk
    2   tablespoons Lea & Perrins Worcestershire Sauce
    1½ teaspoons salt
    ¼   teaspoon ground allspice
        Orange Glaze (recipe follows)

In a large bowl, combine beef with remaining ingredients except Orange Glaze. On a jelly roll or shallow baking pan shape meat into a rectangle, about 9x5 inches. Bake in a preheated moderate oven (350°F.) for 45 minutes. Brush Orange Glaze over meat loaf. Bake 15 minutes longer.

Orange Glaze

In a small saucepan, combine ⅓ cup orange marmalade, 1 tablespoon lemon juice, 1 teaspoon Lea & Perrins, and ½ teaspoon ground allspice. Heat gently for 2 minutes.

About Mixing

When you incorporate other ingredients—eggs, crumbs, seasonings, liquids, whatever—into ground meat for loaves or patties or meatballs, use a light hand. Mix only until blended. Overmixing will give a tough, heavy result.

Mini Meat Loaves Hawaiian

Makes 6 servings

    1½ pounds lean ground beef
    ¾   cup soft bread crumbs
    ½   cup minced onion
    1   can (8 ounces) tomato sauce
    1   egg, lightly beaten
    4   teaspoons Lea & Perrins Worcestershire Sauce, divided
    1½ teaspoons salt
    ½   cup drained canned crushed pineapple

In a large bowl, combine beef with bread crumbs, onion, tomato sauce, egg, 3 teaspoons Lea & Perrins, and salt. Shape into 6 individual meat loaves. Place in a shallow baking pan. Bake in a preheated moderate oven (350°F.) for 25 minutes. Increase oven temperature to hot (425°F.). Mix pineapple with remaining teaspoon Lea & Perrins. Spoon on top of each meat loaf. Return to hot oven; bake 15 minutes longer.

Mini Meat Loaves Hawaiian. Lea & Perrins

Meat Loaf Parmesan

Makes 6 to 8 servings

  1½ pounds lean ground beef
   1 cup rolled oats
   1 cup tomato juice
   ½ cup Sun-Maid® Seedless Raisins
   ¼ cup minced onion
   ¼ cup grated Parmesan cheese
   1 egg
   1 teaspoon oregano
  1½ teaspoons salt
   ¼ teaspoon freshly ground pepper
   1 large tomato, sliced
      Tomato sauce

Preheat oven to 350°F. Place all the ingredients except the tomatoes in a large bowl and mix with your hands until very smooth. Shape the mixture into an 8x4-inch oval and place in a 13x9x2-inch baking pan, overlapping the tomato slices on top of the loaf. Bake for 1 hour; remove from the oven and let stand 5 minutes before placing on a warmed serving platter. Slice the meat loaf and serve it with tomato sauce and additional grated Parmesan cheese.

Good idea: Round out the menu with noodles and buttered broccoli.

Italian Stuffed Meat Loaf

Makes 6 to 8 servings

   2 pounds lean ground beef
   ½ cup soft bread crumbs
   1 cup finely chopped onions, divided
   1 can (8 ounces) tomato sauce
   3 eggs, divided
   3 teaspoons Lea & Perrins Worcestershire Sauce,
        divided
  1¾ teaspoons salt, divided
   ⅛ teaspoon ground black pepper
   1 tablespoon butter or margarine
   2 tablespoons chopped green pepper
   1 cup cooked rice
   ½ cup chopped tomato
   ¼ cup shredded sharp cheddar cheese
   1 tablespoon chopped pitted green olives
   ¼ teaspoon Italian seasoning
   ⅛ teaspoon garlic powder

In a large bowl combine beef, bread crumbs, ¾ cup onions, tomato sauce, 2 eggs, 2 teaspoons Lea & Perrins, 1¼ teaspoons, and black pepper. Mix well, but do not overmix. Place ¾ of the meat mixture into a 9x5x3-inch loaf pan. Pat gently; make a well running

lengthwise in the center of the meat. In a medium skillet melt butter. Add remaining ¼ cup onion and green pepper; sauté until tender, about 5 minutes. Stir in rice. Lightly beat remaining egg; add, together with the remaining 1 teaspoon Lea & Perrins and ½ teaspoon salt and the remaining ingredients; mix well. Spoon rice mixture into the well formed in the meat. Top with remaining meat mixture; pat gently. Bake in a preheated moderate oven (350°F.) until done, about 1½ hours. Let stand in pan for 10 minutes before turning out. Slice and serve.

Meat Loaves Plain and Fancy

No law requires that a meat loaf be baked in a loaf pan, or even that it be loaf shaped. Try a 9-inch square pan for 6 meat rectangular servings. If you have individual bread-loaf pans, they can be used for meat loaf, too. Or bake the meat loaf mixture in large muffin pans or custard cups for individual servings. Or bake the mixture in a deep ring mold.

Borrow grandma's trick of burying hard-cooked eggs in a line down the center of the loaf—that way, each serving has a neatly centered slice of egg. Or hide a cube of cheddar or a ball of blue cheese in the center of each meatball. To extend a meat loaf, pat out the prepared mixture into a rectangle on a sheet of wax paper. Spread with a well-seasoned bread stuffing or with not-too-soft mashed potatoes (with grated cheese folded in, if you like), roll up jelly roll fashion, and—using the wax paper to help you—transfer to a baking pan. Or frost a meat loaf after baking with hot mashed potatoes, sprinkle lightly with paprika or with grated Parmesan, and broil for a moment or two to brown; or skip the browning and sprinkle lightly with snipped parsley.

A meat loaf of plain beef is neither as tasty nor as juicy as one made with pork and veal as well. Good proportions are 1½ pounds of beef to ½ pound each of veal and pork. A lamb loaf is a nice change of pace; make it all lamb, or a quarter as much veal as lamb. Tomato and lamb are good partners—make a lamb loaf, using a half of an 8-ounce can of tomato sauce as all or part of the liquid in the loaf. Season the remaining half can of sauce with a little salt, a speck of sugar, a few drops of garlic juice, and ½ teaspoon of basil or oregano, and pour over the lamb loaf before you put it in to bake.

Country French Meat Loaf

Makes 6 to 8 servings

 2 pounds ground beef
 1 cup soft bread crumbs
 ½ cup finely chopped onion
 1 egg
 1 teaspoon salt
 ¼ cup Wish-Bone Sweet 'n Spicy French Dressing

Preheat oven to 350°F. In large bowl, combine all ingredients. In shallow baking pan, shape into loaf and bake 1 hour, or until meat loaf is done.

Know Your Ground Beef

Not too long ago, when you bought a package labeled "hamburger" or "ground beef," you had no way of knowing what you were getting. You paid your money and you took your chances, or you picked out a nice piece of chuck or round steak and had it ground to order, paying the marked price for the meat and, sometimes, a little extra for the grinding. Then the USDA took a hand, setting standards for ground beef according to fat content and the beef cut from which the meat came. Here are those standards.

Hamburger: A package labeled hamburger contains ground beef from an unspecified cut, and can be up to 30 percent fat. Extra fat may be added, since beef usually does not carry this much fat.

Ground beef: This may also contain up to 30 percent fat, but no extra fat may be added; only the fat attached to the beef may be ground with it. In practice, this generally means that meat labeled ground beef contains only 20 to 25 percent fat. No extenders may be added—nonfat dry milk, soy protein, cereals, or water.

Ground chuck: This must be meat from the chuck primal cut; it contains 15 to 25 percent fat and will be more expensive per pound than either hamburger or ground beef.

Ground round: Meat must come from the round, generally contains only about 11 percent fat, and is accordingly more expensive per pound than ground chuck.

Ground sirloin: It is not the lower fat content but the cut that makes this the most expensive ground beef. Sirloin steaks and roasts are tender and have excellent flavor; most people prefer to eat sirloin in those forms, using ground beef from lesser cuts.

Special Meat Loaf

Makes 8 servings

 2 pounds boneless lean beef chuck, cut in 1-inch
    pieces
 ½ pound boneless pork, cut in 1-inch pieces
 1 small onion, quartered
 2 slices white bread, torn in pieces
 2 eggs, lightly beaten
 1 cup milk
 1 tablespoon prepared horseradish
 1 teaspoon salt
 ¼ teaspoon pepper
 2 slices bacon

Assemble Food Grinder with fine disc. Grind beef, pork, onion, and bread into large bowl. Add remaining ingredients except bacon to bowl and mix until combined. Pack into a 9¼x5¼x2¾-inch loaf pan. Top with bacon slices. Bake at 350°F. for 1½ hours, or until meat is well browned and shrinks from sides of pan.

Curried Meat Loaf

Makes 8 servings

 2-pounds lean ground beef
 ½ cup fine cracker crumbs
 1 can (5⅓ ounces) evaporated milk
 ¼ cup finely chopped green bell pepper
 ⅓ cup minced onion
 ⅓ cup chili sauce
 2 teaspoons salt
 ¼ teaspoon pepper
 1 can (8¾ ounces) crushed pineapple, drained
 ½ teaspoon curry powder

Preheat oven to 325°. Mix together all ingredients except pineapple and curry. Shape into a 10- x 5-inch loaf and place on rack in open roasting pan. Combine pineapple and curry and spread over top of loaf. Bake 1½ hours.

About Hamburgers

For truly gourmet burgers, start with high-quality meat—home-ground sirloin is great. Season lightly with fresh-ground pepper (hold the salt) and a few drops of garlic juice. Mix with ice water—yes, ice water—adding just enough so that the mixture holds together. Remember to use a light hand. Shape patties and broil or grill until medium rare. Meanwhile, sauté slices of sourdough bread briefly in butter. Serve burgers on this bread, topped with a sprinkling of crumbled blue cheese.

Souperior Meat Loaf. Photo courtesy of Thomas J. Lipton, Inc.

Souperior Meat Loaf

Makes about 8 servings

   1 **envelope Lipton Onion or Beef Flavor Mushroom Recipe Soup Mix**
   2 **pounds ground beef**
1½ **cups soft bread crumbs**
   2 **eggs**
 ¾ **cup water**
 ⅓ **cup catsup**
     Lipton Onion Gravy (recipe follows)

Preheat oven to 350°F. In large bowl, combine all ingredients except Lipton Onion Gravy. In shallow baking pan, shape into loaf (or pack into 5-cup ring mold and invert onto jelly roll pan). Bake 1 hour, or until done. Serve with Lipton Onion Gravy.

Lipton Onion Gravy

Makes about 2¾ cups

   2 **cups water**
   1 **envelope Lipton Onion Recipe Soup Mix**
4 to 6 **tablespoons all-purpose flour**
   1 **cup water**

In medium saucepan, bring 2 cups water to a boil, then stir in Lipton Onion Recipe Soup Mix. Simmer covered 10 minutes. Combine all-purpose flour (depending on consistency desired) with 1 cup water and gradually stir into soup. Bring to a boil; then simmer, stirring frequently, until gravy thickens, about 5 minutes.

Idea: Try this tasty gravy on leftovers, on open-face meat sandwiches, or on other main dishes.

Barbecued Meat Loaf

Makes 12 servings

 ¼ **cup molasses**
 ¼ **cup prepared mustard**
 ¼ **cup vinegar**
   1 **can (8 ounces) tomato sauce**
   2 **eggs**
   3 **cups soft bread**
   1 **medium onion, quartered**
   8 **sprigs parsley**
   1 **tablespoon salt**
 ½ **teaspoon thyme**
   3 **pounds ground beef**

Combine molasses, mustard, and vinegar in a small bowl. Add ½ cup of this mixture to the tomato sauce and eggs in a large mixing bowl. Beat with Mixmaster Hand Mixer or Mixmaster Mixer until well blended. Tear a slice of fresh bread into pieces and put into Oster

Blender. Cover and process at Crumb. Empty bread crumbs into a measuring cup. Repeat process until 3 cups have been made. Put into mixing bowl with tomato mixture. Place onion and parsley in blender. Cover and process at Chop. Put into the mixing bowl. Add salt, thyme, and ground beef. Mix well. Form into a loaf in a shallow baking pan. Brush with part of the remaining molasses mixture. Bake in a preheated 350°F. oven 1½ hours, brushing with remaining mixture.

> *Q. How can I prevent my meat loaf from sticking to the bottom of the pan?*
> *A.* Put a strip or two of partially cooked bacon in the bottom of the pan (you won't taste the bacon, however). Or, bake the loaf on a rack in a small roasting pan (and add the bacon on the top, if you like to add the flavor).

Meat Loaf Under Wraps

Makes 8 servings

   1 **can (6 ounces) Hunt's Tomato Paste**
1½ **cups water**
1½ **pounds lean ground beef**
   1 **cup fine cracker crumbs**
  ½ **cup *each* finely chopped onion and green pepper**
   2 **eggs, separated**
  ½ **teaspoon salt**
  ¼ **teaspoon pepper**
   3 **cups hot prepared mashed potatoes**
  ¼ **cup shredded cheddar cheese**
   1 **tablespoon butter**
   2 **tablespoons firmly packed brown sugar**
   2 **tablespoons Worcestershire sauce**
   2 **tablespoons mushroom stems and pieces**

Blend together Hunt's Tomato Paste and water in small saucepan; set aside. Combine in a bowl ½ cup tomato paste mixture, ground beef, cracker crumbs, onion, green pepper, egg whites, salt and pepper; mix well. Shape mixture into a loaf in a shallow baking dish. Bake at 350°F. 45 minutes. Meanwhile, in a saucepan, combine hot prepared mashed potatoes, cheese, butter, and egg yolks. Stir and heat 2 to 5 minutes to melt cheese. Drain fat from meat loaf; frost with potato mixture. Bake 15 to 20 minutes longer. Add brown

sugar, Worcestershire sauce and mushrooms to saucepan of remaining tomato paste mixture; heat 3 to 5 minutes. Serve over slices of meat loaf.

Meat Loaf Under Wraps. Beatrice/Hunt-Wesson Foods

Pork and Apple Loaf

Makes 8 servings

 1½ pounds lean ground pork
 1 medium-size onion, finely chopped
 1 clove garlic, crushed
 ⅓ cup coarsely chopped walnuts
 1 teaspoon grated lemon peel
 2 medium-size apples, peeled, cored, and finely chopped
 2 tablespoons lemon juice
 1½ cups cubed fresh whole wheat bread, crusts removed
 ½ cup chicken-flavored bouillon
 2 eggs, beaten
 1 teaspoon salt
 1 packet Sweet 'N Low
 ¼ teaspoon rosemary
 ¼ teaspoon sage
 ¼ teaspoon thyme
 ⅛ teaspoon ground nutmeg
 Chopped fresh parsley

Preheat oven to 350°F. In large bowl, combine pork, onion, garlic, walnuts, and lemon peel. In separate bowl, toss apples in lemon juice and add to pork mixture. Soak bread in bouillon. Add to pork with eggs, salt, Sweet 'N Low, and seasonings. Thoroughly mix all ingredients, mold into 12-inch loaf, and place in shallow roasting pan. Bake uncovered 1 hour to 1 hour and 15 minutes, or until loaf is brown and juices run clear when pricked. Let stand 10 minutes. Pour off fat. Sprinkle top with parsley.

Mrs. Cowden's Ham Loaf with Cherry Sauce

Makes 6 to 8 servings

 1½ pounds ground ham
 1 pound ground fresh pork
 2 eggs, lightly beaten
 1 cup wheat flakes
 2 tablespoons chopped green pepper
 2 tablespoons chopped onion
 ½ cup milk
 1 can (12 ounces) Solo Cherry Filling
 1 tablespoon prepared mustard
 ¼ teaspoon ground cloves
 ⅛ teaspoon ground allspice
 ¼ cup cherry liqueur

Preheat oven to 350°F. Combine ground ham and pork in a mixing bowl and blend well. Add eggs, wheat flakes, green pepper, onion, and milk; blend well. Pat mixture into a 9½x5½x3-inch loaf pan.

Combine cherry filling, mustard, cloves, and allspice. Spread ¼ cup of this mixture over the top of the meat. Bake 1 hour and 30 minutes. Remove from oven and let loaf cool. Drain off excess fat. Refrigerate loaf until well chilled. At serving time, combine cherry liqueur with remaining cherry mixture and heat, but to not boil. Serve hot sauce with very cold slices of ham loaf.

Mini Meat Loaves

Makes 6 servings

 1½ pounds lean ground beef
 1 cup fresh bread crumbs
 ½ cup Sun-Maid® Zante Currants
 1 small onion, minced
 3 tablespoons soy sauce
 ½ teaspoon ground ginger
 ½ teaspoon salt
 2 eggs
 1 cup sliced scallions (including lots of the green)

Preheat the oven to 375°F. Place all the ingredients except the scallions in a large bowl. Add ½ cup water and mix with your hands until the mixture is very smooth. Shape into six small oval loaves. Place in 13x9x2-inch baking pan. You may brush the loaves with additional soy sauce. Bake for 30 minutes. Remove the loaves from the pan with a slotted pancake turner and drain briefly on paper towels before placing on a warmed platter. Garnish loaves with sliced scallions.

Good idea: Mini meat loaves team well with rice and a stir-fry of Chinese vegetables.

Monterey Beef Rice Skillet

Makes 4 to 6 servings

 1 pound ground beef
 1 cup Uncle Ben's® Converted® Brand Rice
 2½ cups water
 2 teaspoons water
 1 cup chopped onion
 1 package (3 ounces) cream cheese, cubed
 1 can (15 ounces) tomato sauce
 1 teaspoon chili powder

Brown beef in 10-inch skillet; drain. Stir in rice, water, salt, and onion. Bring to boil. Reduce heat, cover, and cook over low heat until water is absorbed, about 25 minutes. Stir in cubed cheese until it softens. Combine tomato sauce and chili powder; pour over rice mixture. Cover and heat 5 minutes, or until hot.

Variations

Stir in ⅓ cup sliced ripe olives after adding cheese.

Add 1 tablespoon diced canned green chiles to cheese-rice mixture and omit chili powder.

Veal-Chicken Patties with Asparagus Sauce

Makes 4 servings

    1 whole chicken breast, skinned and boned
 ½ pound ground raw veal
    1 cup soft white bread crumbs
 ½ cup heavy cream
    1 small onion, chopped
 ½ teaspoon salt
 ¼ teaspoon pepper
 ⅛ teaspoon ground nutmeg
 ¼ cup butter
    1 can (10½ ounces) Campbell's Condensed
       Cream of Asparagus Soup
 ½ cup light cream

Chop raw chicken very fine and mix with veal, bread crumbs, heavy cream, onion, salt, pepper, and nutmeg. Shape mixture into 4 patties. Fry patties in ¼ cup butter until golden brown on both sides. Add soup and light cream and simmer slowly until mixture is heated through, but do not allow the sauce mixture to boil.

Greek Moussaka

Makes 8 to 10 servings

    3 medium-size eggplants
    1 cup butter, divided
    3 large onions, finely chopped
    2 pounds ground lamb or beef
    3 tablespoons tomato paste
 ½ cup red wine
 ½ cup snipped parsley
 ¼ teaspoon ground cinnamon
       Salt to taste
       Freshly ground black pepper to taste
    6 tablespoons all-purpose flour
    1 quart milk
    4 eggs, beaten until frothy
       Ground nutmeg
    2 cups ricotta or cottage cheese
    1 cup fine, dry bread crumbs
    1 cup freshly grated Parmesan cheese

Peel the eggplants and cut them into slices about ½ inch thick. Brown the slices quickly in ¼ cup butter. Set aside. Heat ¼ cup butter in the same skillet and cook the onions until they are browned. Add the ground meat and cook 10 minutes. Combine the tomato paste with the wine, parsley, cinnamon, salt, and pepper. Stir this mixture into the meat and simmer

over low heat, stirring frequently, until all the liquid has been absorbed. Remove the mixture from the heat. Make a white sauce by melting ½ cup butter and blending in the flour, stirring with a wire whisk. Meanwhile, bring the milk to a boil and add it gradually to the butter-flour mixture, stirring constantly. When the mixture is thickened and smooth, remove it from the heat. Cool slightly and stir in the beaten eggs, nutmeg, and ricotta cheese. Oil an 11x14-inch pan and sprinkle the bottom lightly with bread crumbs. Arrange alternate layers of eggplant and meat sauce in the pan, sprinkling each layer with Parmesan cheese and bread crumbs. Pour the ricotta cheese sauce over the top and bake in a preheated 375°F. oven for 1 hour, or until top is golden. Remove from the oven and cool 20 to 30 minutes before serving. Cut into squares and serve.

Helpful to know: The flavor of this dish improves on standing one day. Reheat before serving.

Freezing Ground Meat

If you come upon a sale of ground meat at a good price, you can avail yourself of the bargain if you have a freezer in which to store it. Ground meats do not have as long a freezer life as other meat cuts, but you can safely freezer-store them for 2 to 3 months.

Portion the meat into meal-size packages for freezing. If the meat is to be cooked as patties, shape it that way before freezing, stacking patties in meal-size numbers, separating them with pieces of plastic wrap. Portion meat not to be used as patties in recipe quantities—enough for a meat loaf, enough for spaghetti sauce, enough for your favorite casserole dish, and so on. Patties can be conveniently frozen in round plastic freezer containers or freezer-weight plastic bags. Other portions of ground meat should be tightly enclosed in moisture/vaporproof wrappings—heavy-duty foil, or other freezerwrap material. Be sure to date packages and observe the first-in/first-out rule.

In recipe-size portions, ground meat will thaw readily in the refrigerator or, if the package is waterproof, under cold running water. Do not thaw at room temperature. Do not season ground meats or add other recipe ingredients—bread or cracker crumbs, eggs or milk—before freezing. However, the dish may be completely prepared, cooked (preferably somewhat undercooked), and then frozen, needing only reheating (about one and one-half times as long as the original cooking time) for serving.

Splendid Beef Specialties

Beef: Americans eat more of it than anyone. The reason is choice—you can serve the perfect roast, a gourmet specialty, or an exotic beef combination. The choice is yours.

California Pot Roast

Makes 8 servings

- 1 3-pound chuck roast, trimmed of excess fat
- 2 tablespoons all-purpose flour
- 1 teaspoon salt
  Freshly ground pepper to taste
- 1 tablespoon vegetable oil
- 1 large onion, quartered
- 2 large carrots, sliced in 1-inch pieces
- 1 tablespoon Worcestershire sauce
- 2 cloves garlic, crushed
- 2 packets Sweet 'N Low
- 1 bay leaf
- 1 cup water

Dredge meat in flour, salt, and pepper. Brown in oil in heavy saucepan or Dutch oven. Add remaining ingredients. Cover and simmer very slowly over low heat, about 3 hours, or until meat is very tender.

Pot Roast with Vegetables

Makes 6 to 8 servings

- 2 tablespoons fat
- 1 4- to 5-pound boneless beef pot roast
- 1½ teaspoons salt
- ¼ teaspoon pepper
- 1 large onion, peeled and sliced
- 6 medium carrots, scraped and cut in half
- 4 medium potatoes, peeled and cut in half
- ¾ cup sliced celery

Preheat Multi-Cooker Frypan to 360°F. Melt fat and brown pot roast on all sides. Add ¼ cup water. Season with salt and pepper. Turn dial to E in Simmer; add onion. Cover and cook until meat is tender, 2½ to 3 hours. About 45 minutes before meat is done, add carrots, potatoes, and celery. Set dial at 320°F. until mixture comes to a boil; reduce heat again to Simmer. Cover and finish cooking. If desired, remove meat and vegetables, add 1½ cups of water to pan, and thicken gravy.

Bountiful Beef Pot Roast

Makes 1 pot roast

- ¼ cup all-purpose flour
- ¾ teaspoon salt
- ⅛ teaspoon pepper
- 3½ - to 4-pound boneless beef chuck cross-rib pot roast
- 2 tablespoons cooking fat
- ¾ cup water
- 1 cinnamon stick, broken in half
- 2 teaspoons brown sugar
- ⅛ teaspoon ground allspice
- 8 small onions
- 5 whole cloves
- 16 pitted prunes, plumped
- 2 cooking apples, cored and quartered
  Water

Combine flour, salt, and pepper; dredge pot roast. Reserve leftover flour. Brown pot roast in cooking fat in large frying pan or Dutch oven. Pour off drippings. Add water, cinnamon, brown sugar, and allspice. Cover tightly and cook slowly, 2½ to 3 hours. Stud 5 onions with cloves. Add onions; continue cooking covered, 10 minutes. Remove pot roast to warm platter. Add prunes and apples to frying pan and continue cooking covered 12 to 15 minutes, or until apples are done. Remove onions and fruits to platter. Remove cinnamon stick. Add water, if necessary, to cooking liquid to make 1½ cups. Combine reserved flour with ¼ cup water, add to cooking liquid and cook, stirring until thickened. Reduce heat and cook slowly 3 to 5 minutes. Serve gravy with roast.

Bountiful Beef Pot Roast, Carrot-Stuffed Idaho Potatoes (page 49). Idaho Potato Commission

BEEF ROASTING CHART

Cut of beef	Weight	Cooking Time Minutes per Pound★
Rib Roast, Large End	4 to 8 pounds	23–32 rare 27–38 medium 32–42 well-done
Rib Roast, Large End, Boneless	4 to 6 pounds	28–30 rare 32–35 medium 37–40 well-done
Round Rump Roast, Bone-less	4 to 6 pounds	28–30 rare 32–35 medium 37–40 well-done
Rib Eye Roast	4 to 6 pounds	18–20 rare 20–22 medium 22–24 well-done
Rib Roast, Small End	3 to 5 pounds	30 rare 35 medium 40 well-done
Loin Tender-loin Roast	4 to 5 pounds	10 rare

(If you don't like rare beef don't buy fillet!) Rare beef should register 140° on the meat thermometer; medium beef, 160°; well-done, 170°. Fillet should register 140°.

★ *Meat at refrigerator temperature at start of roasting.*

Polynesian Pot Roast

Makes 8 servings

  1 **can (8½ ounces) pineapple tidbits**
  2 **tablespoons brown sugar**
 ½ **teaspoon ground ginger**
 ½ **cup chopped onion**
 ⅓ **cup cider vinegar**
  3 **tablespoons soy sauce**
  2 **tablespoons oil**
  1 **tablespoon Lea & Perrins Worcestershire Sauce**
  1 **5-pound beef chuck arm pot roast**
  1 **can (10½ ounces) condensed beef broth**
1½ **teaspoons salt**
  3 **cups peeled sweet potato chunks**
  2 **tablespoons cornstarch**
  2 **tablespoons cold water**

Combine pineapple, brown sugar, ginger, onion, vinegar, soy sauce, oil, and Lea & Perrins. Place beef in a snug-fitting bowl or doubled plastic bag. Pour pineapple mixture over meat. Cover or fasten. Refrigerate for 12 hours, mixing or turning once. Place beef and the pineapple marinade in a large saucepot or Dutch oven. Add broth and salt. Bring to boiling point. Reduce heat and simmer covered for 1½ hours. Add sweet potatoes. Simmer covered for ½ hour. Remove beef to a warm platter. Blend cornstarch with water. Stir into liquid in saucepot. Cook and stir until sauce thickens. Serve hot with the pot roast.

Spiced Pot Roast

Makes 8 to 10 servings

  2 **tablespoons all-purpose flour**
  1 **teaspoon salt**
 ⅛ **teaspoon pepper**
  2 **tablespoons fat or vegetable oil**
  4 **to 5 pounds boneless chuck, rump, or round, rolled and tied**
1½ **cups water**
 ½ **cup vinegar**
  2 **medium onions, cut up**
  2 **carrots, pared and cut up**
  2 **stalks celery, cut up**
  2 **cloves garlic, halved**
  2 **tablespoons brown sugar**
  1 **bay leaf**
 ¼ **teaspoon ground cinnamon**
 ¼ **teaspoon ground cloves**
 ½ **cup seedless raisins**
  8 **gingersnaps**

Mix flour, salt, and pepper together. Rub meat well with mixture. Heat fat in Dutch oven; add beef and brown on all sides. Put water, vinegar, onions, carrots, celery, garlic, and brown sugar into blender container. Cover; blend at medium speed just until vegetables are chopped. Pour over meat. Add bay leaf, cinnamon, and cloves. Cover; cook over low heat 2 hours. Add raisins. Continue cooking about 1 hour, or until meat is tender. Remove bay leaf. Break gingersnaps into blender container. Add 1 cup gravy from pot roast. Cover; blend at high speed until smooth. Pour into Dutch oven; heat to serving temperature.

Slicing Pot Roast and London Broil

The edible parts of meat are the muscles, which are composed of long, thin fibers packed close together. Before you begin to slice, look carefully to see in what direction these fibers run. If you cut across these fiber-that is, "against the grain"—you will produce neat slices. Even more important, because you have cut the long fibers into small pieces, the meat will be tender. If you cut with the grain, you'll get stringy, fall-apart pieces that are likely to be tough.

Beef Chart

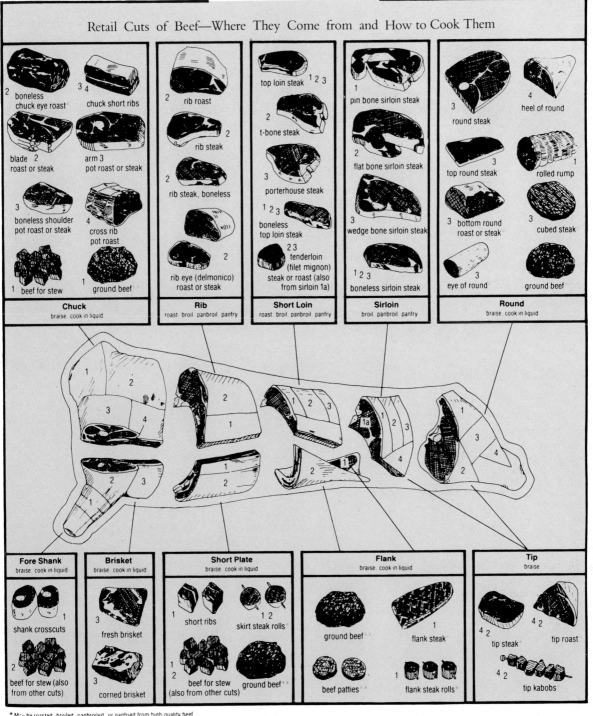

Retail Cuts of Beef—Where They Come from and How to Cook Them

Chuck
braise, cook in liquid

2 boneless chuck eye roast
3 4 chuck short ribs
blade 2 roast or steak
arm 3 pot roast or steak
3 boneless shoulder pot roast or steak
4 cross rib pot roast
1 beef for stew
ground beef

Rib
roast, broil, panbroil, panfry

2 rib roast
2 rib steak
2 rib steak, boneless
2 rib eye (delmonico) roast or steak

Short Loin
roast, broil, panbroil, panfry

top loin steak 1 2 3
2 t-bone steak
3 porterhouse steak
1 2 3 boneless top loin steak
2 3 tenderloin (filet mignon) steak or roast (also from sirloin 1a)

Sirloin
broil, panbroil, panfry

1 pin bone sirloin steak
2 flat bone sirloin steak
3 wedge bone sirloin steak
1 2 3 boneless sirloin steak

Round
braise, cook in liquid

3 round steak
4 heel of round
3 top round steak
1 rolled rump
3 bottom round roast or steak
3 cubed steak
3 eye of round
ground beef

Fore Shank
braise, cook in liquid

1 shank crosscuts
2 beef for stew (also from other cuts)

Brisket
braise, cook in liquid

3 fresh brisket
3 corned brisket

Short Plate
braise, cook in liquid

1 short ribs
1 2 skirt steak rolls
1 2 beef for stew (also from other cuts)
ground beef **

Flank
braise, cook in liquid

ground beef **
1 flank steak
beef patties **
1 flank steak rolls *

Tip
braise

4 2 tip steak *
4 2 tip roast *
4 2 tip kabobs *

* May be roasted, broiled, panbroiled, or panfried from high quality beef
** May be roasted, baked, broiled, panbroiled, or panfried

Sauerbraten. Campbell Soup Company

Hearty Meeting House Supper

Makes 6 to 8 servings
  2 tablespoons oil
  1 3- to 4-pound boneless beef pot roast (rump, chuck or round)
  1 envelope Lipton Onion Recipe Soup Mix
  1 cup water
  ¾ teaspoon caraway seed
  2 jars (16 ounces each) red cabbage, drained, or 1 can (27 ounces) sauerkraut, drained
  2 medium apples, chopped

In large skillet, heat oil and brown beef; add Lipton Onion Recipe Soup Mix blended with water and caraway seed. Simmer covered 2 hours, or until beef is tender. Add red cabbage and apples; simmer covered an additional ½ hour. Garnish, if desired, with an additional apple cut into wedges or rings.

Citrusbraten

Makes 8 to 10 servings; 5 cups gravy
  1 5-pound boneless bottom round, chuck, or rump roast
  1 can (6 ounces) frozen Florida grapefruit juice concentrate, reconstituted
  1 cup dry red wine
    Brown sugar
  1 tablespoon mixed pickling spices
  2 teaspoons peppercorns
  2 bay leaves
  1 medium onion, sliced
  ½ cup gingersnap crumbs
  ½ cup raisins
  ½ cup sour cream
    Florida grapefruit sections

Place meat in earthenware, glass, or enamelware bowl. Combine grapefruit juice, wine, ¼ cup packed brown sugar, pickling spices, salt, peppercorns, bay leaves, and onion in medium saucepan and bring to a boil. Pour over meat; cool. Cover and marinate in refrigerator 2 to 4 days, turning twice a day.

Remove meat from marinade; pat dry with paper towels. Brown meat on all sides in deep kettle, fat side down first. Add marinade. Cover and cook 3 to 3½ hours, or until meat is tender, turning occasionally. Remove meat to heated platter; keep warm. Strain marinade; return to kettle and bring to boil. Blend in gingersnap crumbs, 3 to 4 tablespoons packed brown sugar, and raisins. Cook, stirring constantly, until slightly thickened. Remove from heat; blend in sour cream. Turn into heated gravy boat. Slice meat, garnish with grapefruit sections, and serve with gravy.

German Pot Roast

Makes 12 servings
  1 5-pound bottom round of beef, well trimmed
  1 cup sliced onions
  1 teaspoon minced garlic
  1 can (12 ounces) unsweetened pineapple juice
  ½ cup wine vinegar
  ¼ cup Lea & Perrins Worcestershire Sauce
  ¼ cup water
  1 tablespoon salt
  1 tablespoon oil
  2 bay leaves
    All-purpose flour

Place meat in a large bowl or a doubled plastic bag. Add onions and garlic; set aside. Combine pineapple juice, vinegar, Lea & Perrins, water, and salt; pour over meat. Cover or fasten; place in refrigerator for at least 24 hours. Remove meat from marinade; wipe dry. In a large saucepot or Dutch oven, heat oil. Add meat; brown well on all sides, about 15 minutes. Meanwhile, strain onions and garlic from marinade; add to saucepot; sauté for 5 minutes. Add 2 cups of the marinade and the bay leaves. Bring to boiling point. Reduce heat and simmer covered until meat is tender, about 2½ hours. Remove meat from saucepot. Strain gravy; remove excess fat; measure gravy into saucepot. For each cup of gravy, blend 1½ tablespoons flour with 2 tablespoons cold water. Add to gravy; cook and stir until thickened. Slice meat; serve with gravy.

Sauerbraten

Makes 6 to 8 servings
  2 cans (10¾ ounces each) Campbell's Condensed Old Fashioned Vegetable Soup
  1 cup red wine vinegar
  1 tablespoon sugar
  ½ teaspoon pepper
  4 whole cloves
  4 peppercorns
  2 bay leaves
  3 pounds round steak
  8 or 10 gingersnaps, crushed

In a large bowl, combine soup, vinegar, sugar, pepper, cloves, peppercorns, and bay leaves. Place beef in soup mixture. Cover; store in refrigerator 4 days. On fifth day, drain meat. Brown on all sides; add a little shortening if necessary. Add marinade liquid. Remove bay leaves. Cover. Cook over low heat about 3 hours, or until tender. Remove meat to warm serving platter. Force broth through a wire strainer. Remove fat from gravy. Add gingersnaps; cook until thickened. Serve with meat.

Gourmet Skillet Steak

Makes about 6 servings

- ½ cup Wish-Bone Italian Dressing
- 1 2-pound chuck steak, 1 inch thick, cut into serving pieces
- 1 can (16 ounces) whole tomatoes, undrained
- 1 envelope Lipton Onion-Mushroom Recipe Soup Mix

In large shallow baking dish, pour Wish-Bone Italian Dressing over beef. Cover and marinate in refrigerator, turning occasionally, 4 hours or overnight. Remove beef, reserving marinade. In large skillet, heat 2 tablespoons marinade; brown beef. Add tomatoes and Lipton Onion-Mushroom Recipe Soup Mix blended with remaining marinade; simmer covered 1½ hours, or until beef is tender.

Idea: Serve topped with grated Parmesan cheese. Serve with hot cooked spaghetti or rice.

Rolled Flank Steak

Makes 6 servings

- 5 eggs
- ⅓ cup grated cheddar cheese
- 2 tablespoons butter or margarine
- 1 3-pound flank steak
- ½ teaspoon salt
- ½ teaspoon pepper
- 1 small pimiento, diced
- ½ cup cooked green peas
- 6 cups beef broth

Using Mixmaster Hand Mixer, set at medium speed, beat eggs and cheddar cheese together. Preheat Multi-Cooker Frypan to 300°F. Melt butter, add egg mixture, and cook, stirring constantly until eggs are dry. Remove from Frypan. Sprinkle flank steak with salt and pepper. Cover with cooked eggs, pimiento, and peas. Roll from the short side and sew. Wrap in cheesecloth and sew again. Place in Frypan and add broth. Turn dial to 300°F. and bring to a boil. Skim if necessary. Turn Frypan dial to Simmer. Cover and cook 1½ to 2 hours, or until tender. Remove steak from stock; press with a heavy object and refrigerate. Serve cold, cut into slices.

Good to know: Fiambre, as this is known in its native Montevideo, is usually served with an assortment of vegetables marinated in a vinaigrette sauce.

Mandarin Beef

Makes 4 to 6 servings

- 2 tablespoons olive oil
- 2 pounds flank steak, cut across grain into thin strips
- ¼ teaspoon garlic powder
- ½ teaspoon salt
- ⅛ teaspoon pepper
- ¼ teaspoon ground ginger
- ¼ cup soy sauce
- ½ teaspoon sugar
- 2 tomatoes, quartered
- 2 green peppers, cut into chunks
- 1 can bean sprouts, drained
- 1 tablespoon cornstarch

Heat Multi-Cooker Frypan to 380°F. Place oil in Frypan and add beef, garlic powder, salt, pepper, and ginger. Brown beef quickly. Turn Frypan to Simmer. Add soy sauce and sugar. Cook covered 5 minutes. Add tomatoes, pepper, and bean sprouts. Bring to a boil, cover, and cook 5 minutes. Combine cornstarch and ¼ cup water; add to beef mixture. Cook, stirring until slightly thickened.

Carpetbag Steak

Makes 4 to 6 servings

- 2½ pounds boneless sirloin, 1½ inches thick
- 1 teaspoon salt
- ¼ teaspoon pepper
- 1½ dozen oysters
- 2 tablespoons cooking oil
- 1 tablespoon finely chopped onion
- 2 teaspoons lemon juice
- ½ teaspoon paprika
- 1 tablespoon parsley
- 2 tablespoons sherry

Trim surplus fat from steak. With a sharp knife, cutting through the side of the steak, make a large pocket. Season pocket with salt and pepper. Fill pocket with oysters and fasten with toothpicks or sew with coarse thread. Combine oil, onion, lemon juice, and paprika. Place steak in shallow dish and pour oil mixture over. Marinate at least 1 hour, turning occasionally. Preheat Multi-Cooker Frypan to 380°F. and grease lightly. Place steak in Frypan and cook 6 to 7 minutes per side for rare, 8 to 10 minutes for medium rare, turning once without piercing meat. Remove steak from Frypan; keep warm. Pour marinade into Frypan; bring to a boil. Stir in parsley and sherry and pour over steak.

Chicken-Fried Steak

Makes 4 servings

  3 tablespoons all-purpose flour
  ½ teaspoon salt
  ¼ teaspoon pepper
  1 pound round steak, ¾ inch thick
  2 tablespoons shortening
  ½ cup milk

Combine flour, salt, and pepper. Pound this mixture into both sides of meat. Preheat Multi-Cooker Frypan to 350°F. Melt shortening; brown meat on both sides. Lower heat to 260°F. and cook 10 minutes longer, turning occasionally. Remove steak to hot platter. Add milk to skillet slowly, stirring constantly. Cook until slightly thickened; pour over steak.

Steaks

Whatever cut you choose, leave steak unseasoned during cooking—seasonings draw out and waste the juices, make the steak less tender and juicy than it could be. Add seaonings by topping each serving with a slice of steak butter. Make steak butter in advance, creaming together softened butter or margarine with finely snipped herbs of your choice—parsley, basil, oregano, or thyme are all good with beef—or with minced garlic or scallions, or with grated Parmesan, Romano, or sapsago cheese. Form the seasoned butter into a roll about 1½ inches in diameter, wrap in foil or plastic, and refrigerate. Slice to serve. The hot steak melts the butter, spreading it and the good flavor it carries over each serving of the steak.

Ropa Vieja

Makes 4 servings

  1 large onion, chopped
  1 clove garlic, minced
  2 tablespoons vegetable oil
  1 pound beef flank steak
  ⅓ cup Sun-Maid® Seedless Raisins
  2 tablespoons cider vinegar
  1 teaspoon salt
  ¼ to ½ teaspoon crushed red pepper
  2 large tomatoes, chopped
  1 small green pepper, seeded and chopped
  ¼ teaspoon ground cinnamon
  ⅛ teaspoon ground cloves

In a large skillet, sauté the onion and garlic in oil until soft but not browned. Add the flank steak, 1½ cups water, and the remaining ingredients. Bring to a

boil, reduce heat, cover, and simmer for 1 to 1½ hours, or until the meat is very tender. Place the meat on a cutting board. Holding one end of the meat firmly with a heavy fork, "comb" it lengthwise into strings with a table fork. Turn and repeat on other end of meat. Return shredded meat to skillet and reheat.
Idea: Serve this dish over steamed rice and decorate with strips of pimiento. Accompany it with refried beans and a salad of avocado and watercress. Flambéed bananas end the dinner on a high note.

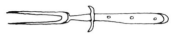

Stuffed Steak Chilean

Makes 8 servings

  2 flank steaks, 2 pounds each, butterflied
  3 tablespoons Lea & Perrins Worcestershire Sauce, divided
  1 clove garlic, minced
  1 teaspoon salt
  ½ teaspoon chili powder
  ½ pound fresh spinach
  2 cups carrot sticks
  1 cup onion rings
  2 tablespoons oil
  2 beef bouillon cubes
1½ cups boiling water
  2 tablespoons all-purpose flour

Open steaks; place long side of one steak over long side of second steak, overlapping by about 2 inches (shingle fashion). Pound the joined ends together to seal. Brush with 1 tablespoon Lea & Perrins. Combine garlic, salt, and chili powder; sprinkle over steaks. On steaks place spinach in one layer; arrange carrots lengthwise with the grain; top with onion rings. Carefully roll steaks with the grain, jelly roll fashion. Tie with loops of string. In a large shallow roasting pan place oil. Add the meat roll; brown in a preheated very hot oven (475°F.) for 15 minutes. Remove pan with meat from oven. Reduce oven heat to moderate (350°F.). Spoon off excess fat from pan. Dissolve bouillon cubes in water; stir in remaining 2 tablespoons Lea & Perrins. Pour into pan. Cover securely with heavy-duty foil. Return pan to moderate oven; roast until beef is tender, about 2 hours. Remove meat to a large cutting board; let stand for 20 minutes. Meanwhile, pour pan juices into a large measuring cup; spoon off excess fat. Add additional water or dry red wine, if necessary, to make 2 cups. In a medium saucepan, blend flour with pan juices. Cook and stir until mixture boils and thickens. Slice beef roll and serve with gravy.

Savory Swiss Steak

Makes about 6 servings

1 **2-pound chuck or round steak, about 1 inch thick**
1 **envelope Lipton Onion or Beef Flavor Mushroom Recipe Soup Mix**

Preheat oven to 375°F. On heavy-duty aluminum foil (about 18x18 inches), place steak on foil; sprinkle both sides with Lipton Onion Recipe Soup Mix. Wrap foil loosely around steak, sealing edges airtight with double fold. Bake 1 hour, or until steak is tender.

> **Q.** *How many servings can I estimate per pound of meat?*
>
> **A.** 4; ¼ pound per serving.
>
> It's not difficult to estimate the number of servings meat will yield if you remember this rule: Ground meat and any other boneless meat will yield 4 servings to the pound; meat with a small-to-moderate amount of bone, 2 to 3 servings to the pound; meat with large amounts of bone, 1 serving to the pound.

Italian Steak and Vegetables (page 50). Photo courtesy of Thomas J. Lipton, Inc.

Variation

Top uncooked steak with chunks of peeled potatoes, carrots, and celery; dot with butter.

Citrus Swiss Steak

Makes 4 servings

¼ **cup all-purpose flour**
1 **teaspoon salt**
¼ **teaspoon pepper**
2 **pounds round steak, 1½ inches thick**
3 **tablespoons shortening**
2 **medium onions, sliced**
1 **tablespoon brown sugar**
1 **cup grapefruit juice**

Season flour with salt and pepper. Place steak on a board and pound half of flour mixture into each side. Reserve any leftover flour. Cut meat into 4 servings. Preheat Multi-Cooker Frypan to 350°F. Melt shortening and brown meat on all sides. Remove meat. Add onions; brown lightly. Make a paste of reserved flour, brown sugar, and a small part of grapefruit juice. Stir into onions; gradually stir in remaining grapefruit juice. Return steak to Frypan. Turn dial to first M in Simmer; cover and cook 1½ hours, or until steak is tender.

Our Secret Steak

Makes 4 to 6 servings

¼ **cup Lea & Perrins Worcestershire Sauce**
2 **tablespoons lemon or lime juice**
2 **tablespoons oil**
¼ **cup instant minced onion**
¾ **teaspoon salt**
½ **teaspoon instant minced garlic**
1 **3-pound beef loin sirloin steak, 1½ inches thick**
2 **tablespoons butter or margarine**
1 **tablespoon chopped parsley**
1 **teaspoon Lea & Perrins Worcestershire Sauce**

In a small bowl, combine ¼ cup Lea & Perrins with lemon juice, oil, onion, salt, and garlic; mix well and set aside. Place steak in snug-fitting pan. Pour Lea & Perrins mixture over steak. Cover and refrigerate for 2 hours. Remove steak from marinade. Place steak on a rack over hot charcoal. Grill for 7 to 10 minutes on each side, or until done as desired, brushing occasionally with leftover marinade. Remove steak to serving plate. In a small saucepan, melt butter. Stir in parsley and 1 teaspoon Lea & Perrins. Pour over steak. Or, if desired, arrange steak on a rack in a broiler pan. Place under a preheated hot broiler; follow preceding directions for cooking.

Citrusbraten (page 43). Florida Department of Citrus

Beef Roulades with Roquefort

Makes 6 servings

    6 cubed beefsteaks, about 1½ pounds
    1 teaspoon salt
    ¼ teaspoon pepper
    ½ cup crumbled Roquefort cheese, packed
    1 can (3 ounces) mushroom pieces
    1 tablespoon minced onion
    2 tablespoons all-purpose flour
    2 tablespoons shortening
    1 can (12 ounces) vegetable juice cocktail
    1 tablespoon Worcestershire sauce

Sprinkle steaks with half of the salt, pepper, and Roquefort. Drain mushrooms, reserving juice. Combine mushrooms, onion, and remaining salt and pepper. Divide mixture over Roquefort on steaks. Roll up steaks and fasten with wooden toothpicks or tie with string. Dredge rolls in flour. Preheat Multi-Cooker Frypan to 340°F. Melt shortening in hot Frypan and brown rolls well on all sides. Pour off as much fat as possible from Frypan. Combine juice drained from mushrooms, vegetable juice cocktail, and Worcestershire sauce. Pour mixture around beef. Cover Frypan. Reduce heat to Simmer and cook 40 minutes to 1 hour, or until tender. Remove roulades to a heated platter. Remove toothpicks or strings. Stir remaining Roquefort into drippings in Frypan. Cook, stirring to bring up browned bits from bottom of pan. Pour sauce over roulades.

Idea: This goes particularly well with broad noodles, buttered and sprinkled with poppy seeds.

Quick Wine Steaks

Makes 6 servings

    1 package (1 ounce) beef gravy mix
    1 cup beef bouillon
    1 cup dry red wine
    1 tablespoon red currant jelly
    6 thin, tender steaks, ¾ inch thick
    1 teaspoon salt
    ¼ teaspoon pepper
    ¼ cup butter or margarine

Prepare beef gravy mix according to directions on the package, using 1 cup beef bouillon. Stir in wine and jelly. Heat and stir until jelly dissolves. Sprinkle steaks with salt and pepper. Preheat Multi-Cooker Frypan to 420°F. Heat butter in hot Frypan. Brown steaks very quickly in hot butter. Pour wine sauce over steaks, lower heat to 380°F., and cook 3 to 4 minutes, or until steaks are cooked to desired degree of doneness. Serve at once.

Steak Orientale

Makes about 8 servings

    1 cup (8 ounces) Wish-Bone Italian Dressing
    ¼ cup soy sauce
    2 tablespoons brown sugar
    1 2- to 2½-pound steak (your favorite cut)
    1 green pepper, cut into chunks
    1 onion, sliced
    ½ teaspoon ground ginger (optional)

In large shallow baking dish, blend Wish-Bone Italian Dressing, soy sauce, and brown sugar; add beef, green pepper, and onion. Cover and marinate in refrigerator, turning occasionally, 4 hours or overnight. Remove beef and vegetables, reserving marinade. Broil steak, turning and basting frequently with reserved marinade, until done. During the last 20 minutes of cooking, add vegetables.

Steak Marcia

Makes 6 servings

    6 strip or shell steaks
    1 can (10½ ounces) Campbell's Condensed
        Consommé
    1 clove garlic, minced
    3 tablespoons A-1 sauce
    3 tablespoons oil
    2 tablespoons honey
    ½ cup red wine
    ½ teaspoon salt
    1 tablespoon cornstarch
    ¼ cup water

Place steaks in a shallow glass or enamel pan. Add remaining ingredients except cornstarch and water. Marinate for 2 hours at room temperature. Drain steaks and reserve marinade. Broil steaks to desired doneness. In a saucepan, combine cornstarch and water. Gradually stir in reserved marinade. Cook over low heat, stirring constantly, until sauce bubbles and thickens. Serve over hot broiled steaks.

Beef Roulades

Makes 8 servings

2½ **pounds round steak, cut ⅛ inch thick**
¾ **pound ground pork**
1 **teaspoon poultry seasoning**
¾ **teaspoon salt**
½ **clove garlic, crushed**
2 **tablespoons minced onion**
¼ **cup soft bread crumbs**
8 **slices bacon**
3 **tablespoons butter or margarine**
8 **small onions, peeled**
⅓ **cup all-purpose flour**
1 **can (10 ounces) beef bouillon**
2½ **cups dry red wine**
1 **pound fresh mushrooms**
1 **bay leaf**

Cut round steak into 8 equal-size pieces. Combine ground pork, poultry seasoning, salt, garlic, onion, and bread crumbs. Toss lightly. Place about 2 tablespoons of mixture on each piece of beef. Roll up. Wrap each with a slice of bacon and tie with heavy thread. Preheat Multi-Cooker Frypan to 360°F. Melt butter in hot Frypan. Add beef rolls and brown on all sides. Remove meat from Frypan. Add onions and brown lightly. Remove onions. Stir flour into Frypan. Gradually stir in bouillon and wine. Lower heat to 300°F. and cook, stirring constantly until mixture comes to a boil. Return meat and onions to Frypan. Add mushrooms and bay leaf. Simmer covered about 1 hour, or until meat is tender. If sauce gets too thick during cooking time, thin with a little more red wine. Before serving, remove bay leaf and thread from beef rolls. Serve with onions, mushrooms, and gravy from pan.

Meat Cookery

Tender cuts of meat should be cooked by a dry-heat method—roasted, broiled, fried, pan-broiled without added fat—and will be ready to eat in a relatively short time. Tough cuts, on the other hand, require moist-heat methods—braising, boiling, simmering, stewing—and need long, slow cooking.

For the Meat-and-Potatoes Family

Many diners feel that a tender cut of beef is not complete without a baked potato to accompany it. Whether the choice is a simple, but perfect, baked potato or a more elaborate stuffed variety, we know you will enjoy one of the following recipes.

Perfect Baked Potatoes

Makes 4 servings
4 **medium baking potatoes**

Scrub the potatoes gently under running water with a vegetable brush or kitchen sponge. Dry. Pierce each potato several times with the tines of a fork before baking. (This allows steam to escape and ensures that the potatoes won't burst. Don't wrap in aluminum foil—that steams them instead of baking.) Place in preheated 400°F. oven and cook for 45 minutes to an hour. (Potatoes will tolerate any temperature from 325° to 450°F., so if you are cooking something else in the oven, simply adjust the time to suit.)

Carrot-Stuffed Idaho Potatoes

Makes 4 servings
4 **Idaho® potatoes**
¼ **cup butter or margarine**
1 **large onion, chopped (1 cup)**
1½ **cups shredded carrot**
¼ **cup milk**
4 **teaspoons lemon juice**
1 **teaspoon prepared mustard**
½ **teaspoon salt**
¼ **teaspoon pepper**
¼ **cup chopped parsley**

Scrub potatoes, dry, and prick with a fork. Bake in a 425°F. oven 55 to 65 minutes, until soft. Reduce oven temperature to 350°F. Cut a slice from top of each potato. Carefully scoop out pulp without breaking skin. Set skins aside. Meanwhile in medium saucepan melt butter; sauté onion and carrot until soft. In large bowl, whip potatoes. Add milk, lemon juice, mustard, salt, and pepper; beat until smooth. Stir in sautéed vegetables and parsley. Spoon potato mixture into reserved potato skins. Bake in a 350°F. oven 20 to 30 minutes, until potatoes are heated through.

Italian Steak and Vegetables

Makes about 6 servings
- 1 cup (8 ounces) Wish-Bone Italian Dressing
- 1 2-pound boneless chuck steak, 1 inch thick
- 1 can (16 ounces) whole tomatoes
- 1 pound fresh green beans
- 1 medium eggplant, cut into ½-inch slices
- 1 pound fresh mushrooms, sliced

In shallow baking dish, pour ½ cup Wish-Bone Italian Dressing over beef; cover and marinate in refrigerator, turning occasionally, at least 3 hours. Repeat procedure with remaining Italian Dressing and vegetables. In large skillet, brown beef; add beef marinade and simmer covered 45 minutes. Add tomatoes, beans, and vegetable marinade and continue simmering covered 40 minutes. Add eggplant and simmer covered 20 minutes. During last 10 minutes of cooking add mushrooms.

Steak Royal

Makes 8 servings
- 2 tablespoons butter or margarine
- 2 tablespoons all-purpose flour
- 1 cup milk
- 1 cup whipping or heavy cream
- 1 envelope Lipton Onion-Mushroom or Onion Recipe Soup Mix
- 2 tablespoons brandy (optional)
- 8 tenderloin steaks (filet mignon), bacon-wrapped
- 8 toast rounds

In medium saucepan, melt butter and stir in flour. Blend in milk, cream, Lipton Onion-Mushroom Recipe Soup Mix, and brandy. Simmer, stirring constantly, until sauce is thickened, about 5 minutes. Meanwhile, grill or broil steaks until done. Serve, if desired, on toast rounds; top with sauce.

Variation

Serve sliced, cooked London broil (2 to 3 pounds) on toasted French bread, topped with sauce.

Idea: Serve with side dishes of tiny red beets and French-style green beans. Cherries jubilee makes the perfect dessert.

Glazed Corned Beef (page 61). Photo courtesy of Thomas J. Lipton, Inc.

Mushroom Steaks

Makes 6 servings

1 pound stew meat or chuck roast, cut in 1-inch
    pieces
2 slices white bread
1 small onion
¼ green pepper
1 clove garlic, minced
½ teaspoon dry mustard
½ teaspoon salt
½ teaspoon pepper
    Mushroom Sauce (recipe follows)
    Buttered cooked noodles

Assemble Food Grinder with fine disc. Grind meat,
bread, onion, and green pepper, alternating ingredients. Combine with seasonings. Shape into 6 patties,
using ⅓ cup for each. Pan-fry over medium heat until
brown, turn, and cook other side. Spoon Mushroom
Sauce over patties; cover and heat on low 10 minutes.
Serve over buttered noodles.

Mushroom Sauce

½ small onion
¼ pound fresh mushrooms
3 tablespoons butter or margarine
1¼ cups water
3 tablespoons all-purpose flour
1 beef bouillon cube
¼ teaspoon bottled browning sauce
    Dash pepper

Assemble Salad Maker with French fry cutter disc
and large bowl. Process onion and mushrooms. Move
meat patties to one side of pan. Melt butter and sauté
onion and mushrooms until tender. Assemble Blender.
Place all remaining ingredients in blender container.
Cover and process at Blend. Pour over mushrooms.
Stir and cook until thickened.

About Meat Thermometers

Q. *How do I use an internal meat thermometer?*
A. Insert meat thermometers into the thickest part of
the meat, making sure   the bulb at the business end
of the gadget does not rest in fat or against bone. Cook
the meat until the internal temperature reaches 5° be-
low the doneness you desire. Remove the meat to a
warmed platter and let it stand 15 to 20 minutes, which
will bring it up to temperature, firm it slightly, and
make carving much easier. If juices run off the meat
during the standing time, incorporate them into gravy.

New England Boiled Dinner (page 52). Photo courtesy of
Thomas J. Lipton, Inc.

New England Boiled Dinner

Makes 6 to 8 servings
    1 3- to 3½-pound boneless beef pot roast (rump, chuck, or round)
    2 envelopes Lipton Beef Flavor Mushroom or Onion Recipe Soup Mix
1½ quarts water
    4 medium potatoes, quartered
    4 medium carrots, quartered
    ½ medium head cabbage, cut into wedges

In Dutch oven, add roast and Lipton Onion Recipe Soup Mix blended with water. Bring to a boil, then simmer covered 2 hours. Add vegetables; continue cooking covered an additional 20 minutes, or until beef and vegetables are tender.

Juicy Tidbit

Jus is the French word for the natural, unthickened juices of meat or fowl. Meat served *au jus* is accompanied by these juices. *Jus lié* is, in French, thickened gravy.

Steak Roll-Ups

Makes 6 servings
    2 tablespoons oil, divided
    ½ cup minced carrots
    2 tablespoons minced onion
    2 tablespoons minced green pepper
1½ cups chopped mushrooms
    2 tablespoons Lea & Perrins Worcestershire Sauce, divided
1¼ teaspoons salt, divided
    6 individual (2 pounds) beef cubed steaks or chuck top blade steaks
    3 tablespoons water
    1 tablespoon catsup

In a large skillet, heat 1 tablespoon of the oil. Add carrots, onion, and green pepper; sauté for 3 minutes. Add mushrooms; sauté for 3 minutes. Stir in 1 tablespoon Lea & Perrins and ½ teaspoon of the salt; set aside. Blend remaining 1 tablespoon Lea & Perrins with the remaining ¾ teaspoon salt. Brush ½ teaspoon of this mixture over one side of each steak; turn steaks over. Spoon about 1 tablespoon mushroom mixture on narrow side of each steak. Roll; secure with toothpicks. Repeat. In the same skillet, heat remaining 1 tablespoon oil. Add meat rolls; brown well on all sides, about 10 minutes. Remove to serving platter. Add water and catsup to skillet; stir to loosen browned particles from the bottom of the pan. Heat until hot. Spoon over steaks and serve.

Swiss Steak

Makes 4 to 6 servings
    2 pounds boneless round or chuck, ½ inch thick
    ½ teaspoon salt
    ⅛ teaspoon pepper
    2 tablespoons fat or vegetable oil
    ½ pound mushrooms, sliced
    1 large onion, cut up
    1 green pepper, seeded and cut up
    1 clove garlic, halved
    1 can (8 ounces) tomato sauce
    1 cup water
    1 to 2 tablespoons all-purpose flour (optional)

Cut meat into serving-size pieces. Sprinkle with salt and pepper. Heat fat in heavy skillet; add beef and brown on all sides. Remove meat; set aside. Add mushrooms to fat remaining in skillet; cook, stirring occasionally, until lightly browned. Return meat to skillet. Put remaining ingredients except flour into blender container in order listed. Cover; blend at high speed until smooth. Pour over meat and mushrooms in skillet. Cover; simmer 1½ hours, or until meat is tender. Remove meat to heated platter. Skim fat from gravy and discard. If a thicker gravy is desired, blend 1 to 2 tablespoons flour and a small amount of water to a smooth paste. Stir into gravy; cook, stirring constantly, until thickened.

Herbed Steak Italiano

Makes about 6 servings
    1 cup red wine
    ½ cup Wish-Bone Italian Dressing
    1 envelope Lipton Onion Cup-a-Soup
    2 teaspoons ground thyme
    1 teaspoon ground marjoram
    ¼ teaspoon pepper
    1 clove garlic, finely chopped
    1 2- to 3-pound round steak, 2 inches thick
    1 cup cold water
    1 tablespoon all-purpose flour

In oblong baking dish, combine wine, Wish-Bone Italian Dressing, Lipton Onion Cup-a-Soup, thyme, marjoram, pepper, and garlic; add steak. Cover and marinate in refrigerator, turning occasionally, at least 5 hours. Remove steak, reserving marinade. In medium saucepan, blend water with flour; add marinade. Heat, stirring constantly, until sauce is lightly thickened. Meanwhile, grill or broil steak 30 minutes, turning once. Serve steak with sauce.

Carving Beef

Meat should stand for a time between coming out of the oven and being carved ("rest a spell," was grandma's term for it). This sets the juices and firms the meat, making it easier to carve. In general—although there are some exceptions—carve all meats across the grain, all fowl with the grain. Move with reasonable speed, with broad—not short, choppy—strokes of the knife, to ensure attractive, even portions.

Properly handled in the cooking, beef is tender and succulent. Properly handled in the carving, it is juicy and delectable. Here are the ways with the usual cuts.

Standing rib roast: Place the roast with the meaty, flat side down on a platter large enough to hold the juices that carving will release. It should be positioned so that the ends of the bones are to the carver's left. Trim off excess fat, but bear in mind that some people think that the fat is the best part of the meat. Anchor the meat firmly by piercing it between ribs with a carving fork. With the carving knife, slice the meat toward you, from the outside of the roast toward the bones, parallel to the platter, making the slices of whatever thickness you like. (Very thin slices are called "English-cut," very thick ones "pub-cut.") When you have carved as many slices as you wish, cut down, from top to bottom, along and as close as possible to the rib bones—this frees the slices from the bones.

Rolled roast: Stand the roast up on the platter, with the meat side up, the tying strings parallel to the platter. Anchor firmly with the carving fork. Slice, toward you, as thickly or thinly as desired, starting at the top. Although it may seem as if it would be simpler to place the roast on its side and slice as you'd slice a loaf of bread, the position described keeps juices in the roast, instead of allowing them to run out on the platter.

Steaks, sirloin, and porterhouse: It's not necessary, of course, to carve a single-portion steak—that's the individual diner's problem. But when a steak is large and thick, it will serve a number of people and must be carved. Place steak flat on a platter, anchor firmly with carving fork. With the tip of the carving knife (a shorter one is better here), cut closely around the bone. Lift out bone and lay aside. Carve across the steak, including in each slice meat from either side of the bone. Cut the slices slightly on the diagonal, across the grain. Cut the tail of the steak in slightly diagonal slices across the width.

Blade pot roast: Place meat flat on a platter. Anchor with the carving fork. With (short) carving knife, cut between muscles and around bones to remove meat one solid piece at a time. Turn the cut-out piece of meat so that its fibers (grain) are parallel to the platter. Holding the piece with the fork, slice down, across the grain. Repeat with remaining pieces.

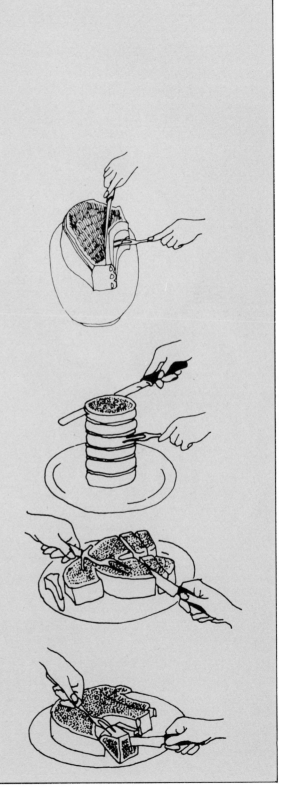

Tournedos Royale. Campbell Soup Company

Tournedos Royale

Makes 4 servings

 ¼ cup butter
 ½ cup chopped onion
 ⅓ cup dry bread crumbs
 1 teaspoon paprika
 1 teaspoon capers
 1 teaspoon minced truffles
   Pinch thyme
 ½ cup finely chopped cooked sweetbreads
 4 canned artichoke bottoms
 4 filets mignons, 10 ounces each
   Garlic
   Salt and pepper
   Sauce Béarnaise (see index)

Heat butter and sauté onion until tender and golden. Add bread crumbs, paprika, capers, truffles, thyme, and sweetbreads. Cool. Shape mixture into 4 balls. Place 1 ball in each artichoke bottom. Rub filets with garlic and sprinkle with salt and pepper. Broil to doneness desired. Top with stuffed artichoke bottom. Spoon Sauce Béarnaise over stuffed artichoke bottoms and filets mignons.

Tenderloin of Beef Stroganoff with Wild Rice

Makes 6 servings

 6 slices beef tenderloin, about 1 inch thick
 ⅓ cup butter
 1 carrot, finely chopped
 ½ cup finely chopped celery
 1 tablespoon finely chopped onion
 ½ teaspoon dill seed
 3 tablespoons all-purpose flour
 1 can (10½ ounces) Campbell's Condensed Beef
   Broth or Consommé
 1 tablespoon catsup
 ¼ cup sauternes wine
 ½ cup sour cream
 4½ cups cooked wild rice

Sauté beef slices in butter until medium rare. Place on a platter and keep warm. To drippings in pan add carrot, celery, onion, and dill. When vegetables are tender, stir in flour. Gradually stir in beef broth, catsup, and wine. Cook over low heat, stirring constantly, until sauce bubbles and thickens. Press sauce through a sieve or whirl in a blender. Reheat and stir in sour cream. Heat but do not boil. Spoon sauce over meat slices, which have been placed over hot wild rice.

Grenadine of Beef Tenderloin

Makes 8 servings

 8 slices filet mignon, 1 inch thick
 8 long strips sliced bacon, ½ inch wide
   Salt and pepper
 16 small mushrooms
 1½ cups Sauce Chasseur (see index)
 1 cup Sauce Béarnaise (see index)

Pound beef until like scallopini. Using a larding needle, insert 1 strip of bacon in each piece of beef. Sprinkle meat on both sides with salt and pepper. Melt butter and sauté beef until the desired degree of doneness. Add mushrooms and sauté until golden brown. Heat Sauce Chasseur and spoon onto a platter. Top with beef slices and mushrooms. Spread meat with Sauce Béarnaise and place under broiler for 1 minute. Serve at once.

Beef Tips Basquaise

Makes 6 to 8 servings

 4 pounds tenderloin or sirloin tips
   Salt and pepper
 ½ cup butter or margarine (may use oil or shortening)
 ⅓ cup finely chopped shallots or green onions
 ½ cup diced green pepper
 ¼ pound mushrooms, sliced
 1 cup red wine
 1 can (10½ ounces) Campbell's Condensed Beef
   Broth
 2 teaspoons Worcestershire sauce
 1 can (11 ounces) Campbell's Condensed Bisque
   of Tomato Soup
   Watercress

If tips are tenderloin they can be cut into thin slices, sprinkled with salt and pepper, and broiled until medium rare. If the tips are from a tougher cut of beef, they can be roasted or braised until tender, then thinly sliced. In a skillet, melt butter, add shallots, green pepper, and mushrooms. Sauté until tender but not brown. Pour off fat. Add red wine, beef broth, and Worcestershire sauce. Bring to a boil and boil gently until liquid is reduced to half its original volume. Add bisque of tomato and simmer until sauce thickens slightly. Spoon sauce over beef tips. Garnish with watercress.

Tournedos Rossini with Madeira Mushroom Sauce

Makes 6 servings

    6 filets mignons, 1 inch thick
 ½ cup butter
    Salt, pepper
    6 slices toast, trimmed to fit meat
    1 can (4¾ ounces) pâté de foie gras, cut into 6 slices
    1 truffle, cut into 6 slices
    6 large mushroom caps sautéed in butter
    Watercress
    Madeira Mushroom Sauce (recipe follows)

Brown filets in butter until the desired degree of doneness. Season to taste with salt and pepper. Place each tournedo on toast slice and top with slice of pâté and slice of truffle. Top with mushroom cap. Spoon hot Madeira Mushroom Sauce over tournedos and serve garnished with watercress.

Madeira Mushroom Sauce

Makes 2 cups

 ½ pound mushrooms, sliced
    1 tablespoon butter
    2 tablespoons all-purpose flour
    1 tablespoon minced shallots or white onions
    1 can (10½ ounces) Campbell's Condensed Beef Broth
 ¼ cup Madeira
 ¼ cup sherry
    1 teaspoon minced parsley
    Salt and pepper

Sauté mushrooms in butter. Sprinkle flour and onions. Gradually stir in beef broth, Madeira, and sherry. Cook, stirring, until sauce bubbles and thickens. Add parsley, salt, and pepper to taste.

Tenderloin en Brochette

Makes 8 servings

    8 slices filet mignon, 1 inch thick
    4 green peppers
 ½ pound thick-sliced bacon
    Salt and pepper
    Olive oil
    Sauce Chasseur (see index)

Cut meat into 2-inch squares; cut green peppers into 1½-inch squares; cut bacon into 2-inch pieces. Alternate filet, pepper, and bacon on skewers. Sprinkle with salt and pepper. Brush with olive oil. Broil to desired degree of doneness. Serve with Sauce Chasseur.

Filets of Beef with Marsala Sauce

Makes 4 servings

    4 filets mignons, 1 inch thick
    Salt and pepper
 ¼ cup butter
 ½ cup Marsala
    1 cup Brown Sauce (strained without pressing vegetables through sieve) (see index)
 ¾ cup Sauce Béarnaise (see index)
    2 tomatoes, chopped and sautéed in 2 tablespoons butter and seasoned with salt
    2 tablespoons finely chopped truffles
    4 slices bread, crusts trimmed and cut into triangles
 ¼ cup oil

Season filets with salt and pepper. Melt butter and sauté filets about 4 minutes on each side. Remove filets and add Marsala and Brown Sauce to pan drippings. Simmer 2 to 3 minutes, scraping pan. Replace filets in sauce and spread ½ cup of the Sauce Béarnaise over tops of filets. Spoon hot tomatoes over Béarnaise Sauce. Sprinkle with truffles. Simmer 10 minutes. Sauté bread triangles in oil until golden brown on both sides. Place filets on a platter and surround with bread triangles. Beat remaining Béarnaise Sauce into sauce in pan. Serve this sauce with the filets.

A Taste of Old Vienna

Makes 4 to 6 servings

    1 cup water
    2 tablespoons oil
    1 envelope Lipton Beefy Onion Recipe Soup Mix
    2 tablespoons paprika
    2 teaspoons grated lemon peel
 ¼ teaspoon caraway seed
1½ pounds beef cubes
    2 tablespoons all-purpose flour
 ½ cup cold water
    Hot buttered noodles

In Dutch oven, combine water, oil, Lipton Beefy Onion Recipe Soup Mix, paprika, lemon peel, and caraway seed; add beef. Bring to a boil, then simmer covered, stirring occasionally, 1½ hours or until beef is tender. Add flour blended with cold water; bring to a boil, then simmer, stirring occasionally, an additional 15 minutes, or until gravy is slightly thickened. Serve, if desired, with hot buttered noodles.

Savory Sauce Sampler

Quick White Sauce

Makes 1 cup

  2 tablespoons butter
  1½ to 2 tablespoons all-purpose flour
  1 cup milk, milk and light stock, light stock, or
    light stock and cream
    Seasonings to taste (celery salt, nutmeg, ½ tea-
      spoon Worcestershire sauce, 1 teaspoon sherry,
      1 teaspoon onion juice, 2 tablespoons chopped
      parsley, or 2 tablespoons chopped chives)

Over low heat, melt butter and add flour, stirring about 3 or 4 minutes, or until well blended and raw-flour taste is gone. Slowly stir in milk and seasonings. Simmer and stir sauce with wire whisk until it has thickened and is smooth and hot. Combine with other ingredients just as it boils. Do not let it become watery.

Bordelaise Sauce

Makes 2 cups

  ¼ cup beef marrow, diced★
  2 tablespoons minced shallots
  1 tablespoon butter or margarine
  ¾ cup red wine
  1 teaspoon salt
  ⅛ teaspoon freshly ground pepper
  1½ cups brown gravy
  2 teaspoons lemon juice
  2 teaspoons minced parsley

Gently simmer beef marrow in water a few minutes. Drain and set aside. In a large skillet, sauté shallots in butter until soft but not browned. Add wine, salt, and pepper. Simmer until reduced by half. Add brown gravy. Stir and simmer 5 minutes longer. Add beef marrow, lemon juice, and parsley and heat thoroughly. Serve over steaks or beef patties.

★To prepare beef marrow: Have beef marrow bones sliced by butcher. Wrap in foil and bake 30 minutes. Scrape out marrow in one piece. This can be done ahead of time and kept in refrigerator until ready to use.

Sauce Béarnaise

  1 clove garlic, mashed
    Salt and pepper
  1 can(10½ ounces) Campbell's Cream of Chicken
    Soup
  ¼ cup melted butter
  1 to 3 teaspoons tarragon vinegar
  2 tablespoons drained capers
  ¼ cup finely chopped parsley

Combine all ingredients and heat until bubbly.

Brown Sauce
A Base for Other Sauces

Makes about 1 quart

  2 pounds veal-shank bones
  2 large onions, coarsely chopped
  2 carrots, scraped and chopped
  1 cup chopped celery
  2 tablespoons all-purpose flour
  2 cans (10½ ounces each) Campbell's Condensed
    Consommé
  1 can (12 ounces) "V-8" juice
  2 quarts water

Preheat oven to 500°F. Place bones in a 6-quart Dutch oven or other casserole. Brown bones for 20 minutes. Add onions, carrots, and celery and brown another 10 minutes. Sprinkle with flour and brown another 10 minutes. Add consommé, "V-8," and water. Replace in oven and continue cooking until stock begins to boil. Lower heat to 400°F. and cook for 1½ hours. Remove from oven and let cool. Remove bones. Strain broth and chill. When cold, take off the top layer of fat. Discard and use broth underneath as a base for any sauce requiring Brown Sauce.

Sauce Chasseur

Makes about 4 cups

  ½ pound small mushrooms, sliced
  1 tablespoon butter
  1 tablespoon olive oil
  1 teaspoon chopped shallot or white onion
  1 small clove garlic, minced
  ⅓ cup white wine
  ⅓ cup Marsala
  2 cups Brown Sauce(see above)
  1 can (10½ ounces) Campbell's Condensed
    Consommé
  ½ cup chopped ripe tomatoes
  1 tablespoon minced parsley
  1 bay leaf

Sauté mushrooms in butter and oil. Add shallot and garlic and sauté for another 5 minutes, or until pale golden brown. Add white wine and Marsala. Cook at a boil until half its original volume, about 15 minutes. Add Brown Sauce, consommé, tomatoes, parsley, and bay leaf. Simmer 15 minutes. Remove bay leaf.

Golden Mushroom "Sir-Loin" Beef Tips

Makes 6 servings
- 2 pounds beef, cut into 1-inch cubes
- ¼ cup butter or margarine
- ¾ cup sherry
- 1 medium clove garlic, minced
- 2 cans (10½ ounces each) Campbell's Condensed Golden Mushroom Soup
- 1 tablespoon finely chopped onion or shallot
- ½ cup water
  Cooked noodles

In skillet, brown beef in butter. Add remaining ingredients. Cover and cook over low heat 2 hours, or until tender. Stir occasionally. Serve over noodles.

Beef and Beer

Makes 6 servings
- 2 pounds onions
  Butter or margarine
- 3 pounds chuck or round steak, cut into cubes
  All-purpose flour
  Salt and pepper
- 3 cloves garlic
- 1 cup beer

Peel onions. Slice with Sunbeam Knife. Preheat Multi-Cooker Frypan to 300°F. Melt 4 tablespoons butter. Add onions and cook until soft and lightly browned. Remove onions. Dust meat cubes with a little flour. Melt 4 tablespoons butter in Frypan. Add meat and brown. Return onions to Frypan. Season with salt and pepper. Add garlic and beer. Bring to a boil. Reduce heat to Simmer. Cover and cook about 1¼ hours, or until meat is tender.

Tenderloin Tips with Wild Rice

Makes 4 to 6 servings
- 1½ to 2 pounds beef tenderloin strips
- 6 tablespoons butter or margarine
- 1 package (6 ounces) Uncle Ben's® Original Long Grain & Wild Rice
- 1 can (10¾ ounces) beef gravy
- 1¼ cups water
- 1¾ cups chopped onion
- 1⅓ cups green pepper

Cut beef into very thin 2- to 3-inch strips. Brown in 3 tablespoons butter. Add contents of both packets of Long Grain & Wild Rice, beef gravy, and water. Bring

Golden Mushroom "Sir-Loin" Beef Tips. Campbell Soup Company

to boil. Cover and cook over low heat until water is absorbed, about 25 minutes. Meanwhile, sauté onion and green pepper in 3 tablespoons butter for 3 minutes. Do not overcook. Add to cooked rice and beef.

Beef Stroganoff

Makes 6 to 8 servings
- ¼ cup butter or margarine
- 2 pounds beef tenderloin or sirloin, cut in thin strips
- 1 can (4 ounces) mushrooms, drained
- 1 large onion, sliced
- 2 tablespoons all-purpose flour
- 1 teaspoon salt
- ¼ teaspoon pepper
- 1 clove garlic, halved
- 1 can (10½ ounces) condensed beef broth
- ½ cup dry white wine
- 1 cup sour cream
- 1 tablespoon chopped parsley

Heat butter in large skillet; add beef and brown well on all sides; remove; set aside. Add mushrooms and onion to fat remaining in skillet and cook over medium heat, stirring occasionally, until onion is tender. Put mushroom-onion mixture, flour, salt, pepper, garlic, beef broth, and wine into blender container. Cover; blend at high speed until smooth. Return meat to skillet; pour blended mixture over meat. Cover; simmer 15 minutes, or until meat is tender, stirring occasionally. Stir in sour cream; heat just to boiling, stirring constantly. Sprinkle with chopped parsley.
Note: Stroganoff is a good make-ahead dish. Simply prepare it up to the point before the sour cream is added. When you are ready to serve, reheat, stir in the sour cream, and bring just to boiling.

Q. *We like stir-fry beef dishes, and also stroganoff, both of which call for thin slices of raw beef. I use a very sharp knife, but it's difficult to get uniform slices as thin as I'd like them. Is there a trick to it?*
A. There is. Freeze the meat before you cut it. It does not have to be frozen solid—even partially frozen beef cuts more easily than meat at room or refrigerator temperature.

Beef à la Deutsch

Makes 6 servings

     2 tablespoons butter
   ½ cup sliced fresh mushrooms
   ¼ cup sliced green pepper
  1½ pounds beef tenderloin, cut into ¼-inch-thick
       slices
     2 tablespoons all-purpose flour
     1 can (10½ ounces) Campbell's Condensed
       French Onion Soup
  1½ cups sour cream
     3 tablespoons diced pimiento
       Hot cooked green noodles

Melt butter and sauté mushrooms and green pepper until tender. Remove vegetables and brown meat slices in drippings. Add vegetables and sprinkle with flour. Stir in onion soup. Cook, stirring, until soup bubbles. Stir in sour cream and pimiento. Reheat but do not boil. Serve spooned over hot cooked green noodles.

Meat Tenderizers

These kitchen helpers fall into three classes: natural, chemical, and mechanical. The *natural* tenderizers are acidic—wine, and lemon, orange, lime juice, sometimes tomato and lemon juices in combination. These are essential ingredients in any marinade meant to make meat more tender. Keep in mind, however, that these are the least effective tenderizers; although they are great for enhancing flavor, they contribute only a little toward making the meat more tender. *Chemical* tenderizers are generally available in powder form to be sprinkled over moistened meat and, if the meat is thick, encouraged to do their work if you plunge a two-tined fork into the meat at close intervals. The working ingredient of such tenderizers is papain, an enzyme extracted from papaya—which should assure you that you needn't shy away from the "chemical" label. If you follow package directions, this type of tenderizer works very well. *Mechanical* tenderizers are small machines made with a handle on one end and a number of razor-sharp pointed projections at the other. Place the machine on the meat and press down. A spring mechanism drives the sharp points deep into the meat. The deep penetration, plus the fact that the tenderizer's teeth are set close together, guarantees breakup of the meat's long fibers and assures tenderness.

Boeuf Bourguignon

Makes 8 servings

     4 pounds boneless chuck or round, cut in 1½-
       inch cubes
   ½ cup all-purpose flour
     1 teaspoon salt
   ½ teaspoon pepper
   ½ cup fat or vegetable oil
     3 cups Burgundy
     1 bay leaf
     1 can (10½ ounces) Campbell's Condensed Beef
       Broth
     2 teaspoons tomato paste
   ¼ cup parsley sprigs
     1 large onion, cut up
     2 carrots, pared and cut up
     2 cloves garlic, halved
   ½ teaspoon dried thyme
    12 to 16 small white onions, peeled

Dredge beef in mixture of flour, salt, and pepper. Reserve remaining flour mixture. Heat fat in heavy skillet or Dutch oven. Add meat; brown well on all sides. Add wine and bay leaf. Heat oven to 325°F. Put beef broth, tomato paste, parsley, onion, carrots, garlic, and thyme in blender container. Cover; blend at medium speed just until vegetables are chopped. Pour over meat; cover. Cook in oven 1½ hours. Add small white onions. Continue cooking 1½ hours, or until beef is tender.

Skillet Delight

Makes 6 servings

     1 cup uncooked rice
   ½ cup chopped onion
   ½ cup chopped green pepper
     2 tablespoons salad oil
     1 can (12 ounces) corned beef, cut in chunks
     1 can (4 ounces) Vienna sausages, cut in chunks
     2 large tomatoes, peeled and cut in chunks
   ½ pound mushrooms, sliced
     1 can (8½ ounces) peas, drained
   ½ cup sliced pitted ripe olives

In a skillet brown rice, onion, and green pepper in oil. Add corned beef, Vienna sausages, tomato chunks, mushrooms, and 1½ cups water. Cover and simmer 20 minutes. Stir in peas and olives. Cover and continue to cook 10 minutes, or until rice is done.

Tamale-Chili Casserole

Makes 6 servings

 1 can (15 ounces) Hormel Chili with Beans
 1 can (15 ounces) Hormel Tamales
 3 tablespoons chopped onion
 ½ cup grated cheddar cheese

Spread chili in 11x7-inch baking pan. Remove paper from tamales; place tamales on chili. Sprinkle with onion and cheese. Bake in 350°F. oven 30 minutes.

Filet of Beef Elysian

Makes 8 servings

 1 filet of beef, about 3½ pounds, well trimmed
 1 can (8 ounces) pâté de foie gras
 1 can (⅞ ounce) truffles, sliced
   Salt and pepper
   Suet in thin sheets to wrap around filet
 1 carrot, chopped
 1 onion, chopped
 ½ teaspoon crumbled thyme
 1 bay leaf
 1 clove garlic, chopped
 1 cup Marsala
 1 cup Brown Sauce (see index)
 8 pieces endive, braised
 ⅓ cup grated Parmesan cheese
 1 cup button mushrooms, sautéed in butter
   Watercress

Cut filet crosswise into 8 slices, cutting all the way through. Cut pâté into 8 slices and stuff one slice into each cut. Add truffle slices. Sprinkle filet with salt and pepper. Wrap meat with suet and tie with string. Roast in a shallow pan in a preheated 450°F. oven for 30 minutes. Add carrot, onion, thyme, bay leaf, and garlic. Roast another 5 minutes. Remove from pan and keep warm. Add Marsala and Brown Sauce to pan and bring to a boil, scraping to loosen all bits in pan. Simmer for 10 minutes. Remove suet from meat and place meat on a platter. Surround with endive sprinkled with Parmesan cheese and button mushrooms. Strain sauce and spoon sauce over meat and vegetables. Cut slices of filet between slashes stuffed with pâté. Garnish with watercress.

Glazed Corned Beef

Makes 4 to 6 servings

 ½ cup Wish-Bone Russian Dressing
 2 tablespoons brown sugar
 1 tablespoon prepared mustard
 1 teaspoon prepared horseradish
 ½ teaspoon Worcestershire sauce
 ½ teaspoon ground cloves
 1 3- to 4-pound cooked corned beef

Preheat oven to 350°F. In small bowl, combine Wish-Bone Russian Dressing, brown sugar, mustard, horseradish, Worcestershire sauce, and cloves. In shallow baking pan, place meat, fat side up; score if desired. Brush glaze over meat; bake about 20 minutes. Heat remaining glaze and serve over meat.

How to Buy and Store Beef

How to buy: Fresh beef is available all year around, is most plentiful—and therefore likely to be least expensive—between January and April. Quite often, large cuts cost less per pound than small cuts. If you see a bargain, buy it. Cut it yourself, or have it cut, into sizes useful for your family. For example, the tenderloin—fillet mignon—is likely to be cheaper whole than cut, and is easy to slice into pieces of the exact thickness you prefer. A large pot roast can be cut into a smaller pot roast, slices to use for Swiss steak, and cubes to make a stew. A large rib roast will yield a roast and rib steaks, as well as short ribs. (In all cases, don't forget to salvage any bones for stock or soup.) Be guided by the USDA grade mark—ask questions about beef that does not carry the mark, and don't buy it if the answers aren't satisfactory.

How to store: If your refrigerator has a meat keeper, store the meat in it, unwrapped. If not, remove or loosen the store wrappings, store loosely wrapped in the coldest part of the refrigerator. Raw ground meat and stew meat can be stored in the refrigerator for 1 to 2 days; steaks and other smaller cuts, 2 to 4 days; roasts, 3 to 6 days. Cooked meat should be cooled slightly and stored tightly covered (meat and gravy separately) in the coldest part of the refrigerator no more than 4 days.

Sukiyaki

Makes 4 to 5 servings

- 4 medium carrots, cut in thin strips
- 2 medium onions, thinly sliced
- 2 bunches green onions, diagonally sliced in 1-inch pieces
- 2 cups celery, diagonally sliced in ½-inch pieces
- 1 cup sliced fresh mushrooms (about 4 ounces)
- 2 cans (5 ounces each) sliced bamboo shoots, drained
- Salad oil
- 2 pounds sirloin, sliced very thin
- ¼ pound silver noodles (bean threads), soaked in warm water, cut in 3-inch pieces
- 2 squares tofu (bean curd), cut into 12 cubes (optional)
- 4 cups spinach torn in pieces (about 4 ounces)

Sauce
- 1 can (10½ ounces) Campbell's Condensed Chicken Broth
- 1 cup soy sauce
- ¼ cup sugar
- 3 tablespoons sherry
- Cooked rice

Divide first 6 ingredients in half. Add each in order listed to 2 large skillets and cook in oil until just tender. Push vegetables to one side; divide the meat between the 2 skillets and brown on both sides. Prepare sauce by combining all ingredients; stir 1 cup sauce into each skillet; divide and add noodles and tofu; top with spinach. Cook 5 minutes. Serve Sukiyaki with cooked rice and remaining sauce.

Szechuan Beef Stir-Fry

Makes 4 servings

- 1 pound boneless tender beef steak
- 2 tablespoons cornstarch
- 3 tablespoons Kikkoman Soy Sauce, divided
- ½ teaspoon sugar
- ½ teaspoon crushed red pepper
- 1 large clove garlic, minced
- 1½ teaspoons cornstarch
- 3 tablespoons vegetable oil, divided
- ¼ pound green onions and tops, cut into 1½-inch lengths, separating whites from tops

Cut beef across grain into thin slices, then into strips. Combine 2 tablespoons *each* cornstarch and soy sauce with sugar, red pepper, and garlic; stir in beef. Let stand 20 minutes. Meanwhile, blend together remaining soy sauce with 1½ teaspoons cornstarch and ⅔ cup water; set aside. Heat 2 tablespoons oil in large skillet or wok over high heat. Add beef and stir-fry 1 minute; remove. Heat remaining oil in same pan; add white part of green onions and stir-fry 1 minute. Stir in beef, soy sauce mixture, and green onion tops; bring to boil. Cook and stir only until sauce thickens. Serve immediately.

Beef Teriyaki

Makes 6 servings

- 2 pound loin tenderloin steak
- ½ cup mirin (sweet saké) or dry sherry
- 1 cup soy sauce
- 2 teaspoons powdered ginger
- 2 cloves garlic, minced
- 1 medium onion, minced
- 2 tablespoons sugar
- Hot mustard
- Parsley

Cut meat into ½-inch-thick strips. Combine all ingredients except meat. Blend well and pour over meat. Allow to stand two hours. Broil or grill close to heat in broiler, or on hibachi about 1 minute on each side. Serve with very hot mustard and garnish with parsley.

Stir-Fry
Stir-fry cooking is a marvelous way to cook food very quickly. Food is usually cooked in a wok, a metal cooking vessel with a round bottom and high sloping sides. Stir-fry cooking needs your undivided and uninterrupted attention because food cooks in seconds and must be kept constantly in motion. It is especially important to have everything organized, prepared for cooking, and within easy reach before you start.

Sukiyaki. Campbell Soup Company

Beef 'n' Cheese Strata

Makes 6 servings
   ½ cup finely chopped onion
   ½ cup finely chopped celery
   2 tablespoons butter or margarine
  12 white bread slices, crusts trimmed
   1 can (12 ounces) Armour Star Chopped Beef,
       sliced into 12 slices
   1 cup (4 ounces) shredded cheddar cheese
   3 eggs, beaten
  1½ cups milk
   1 teaspoon salt
       Dash pepper

Heat oven to 350°F. Cook onion and celery in butter 5 minutes. In a greased 12x8-inch baking dish, layer bread, chopped beef slices, onion and celery mixture, and cheese; repeat. Mix together eggs, milk, and seasonings; pour over casserole. Bake at 350°F. for 40 minutes. Let stand 5 minutes.

Mexicale Casserole

Makes 4 to 6 servings
   ½ cup chopped celery
   ¼ cup chopped green pepper
   2 tablespoons butter or margarine
   1 can (15 ounces) Hormel Tamales
   1 can (15 ounces) Hormel Chili–No Beans
   ½ cup shredded cheddar cheese
   1 package (8½ ounces) corn muffin mix

In a small skillet, sauté celery and green pepper in butter until tender. Remove papers from tamales and slice into bite-size pieces. Combine tamales, chili, celery, and green pepper. Pour half of mixture into 8- or 9-inch square baking dish. Sprinkle with cheese and top with remaining mixture. Prepare corn muffin mix according to package directions; drop batter by spoonfuls over top of mixture. Bake in 375°F. oven 25 minutes.

Oven Chili

Makes 6 servings
   1 pound lean ground beef
   1 medium-size onion, chopped
   ⅓ cup chopped green pepper
   1 can (29 ounces) tomato sauce
   1 can (30 ounces) red kidney beans, drained and
       rinsed
   ½ teaspoon salt
   1 to 2 teaspoons chili powder
       Corn bread or crackers

Preheat oven to 400°F. Crumble ground beef evenly over the bottom of a shallow 11x14-inch baking pan. Brown in oven for 10 minutes; stir twice to break up meat. Reduce heat to 325°F. Add all other ingredients to pan and stir well. Bake for 1 hour and 45 minutes. Serve hot with corn bread or crackers. This chili is thick and delicious.
Note: This recipe can easily be doubled.

Ways to Prepare Liver

To braise, whole or large pieces: Dredge in seasoned flour, brown in fat. If desired, add vegetables such as onions and carrots. Add ½ cup liquid, cover tightly, and cook over low heat, allowing 30 minutes per pound.

To braise slices: Follow above directions, but use only ¼ cup liquid, allowing 20 minutes total cooking time.

To broil: Use slices ½ to ¾ inch thick. Dip in melted bacon drippings or butter. Broil at moderate temperatures just long enough to brown lightly, about 3 minutes each side.

To pan-fry: Dredge in seasoned flour; brown on both sides in small amount of cooking fat. Liver should be sufficiently cooked when brown—overdone liver is tough.

To deep-fat fry: Have liver cut in long, thin strips. Dredge in seasoned flour; fry in deep fat at 350°F. until nicely browned. If desired, the liver strips may be dipped in beaten egg, then in crumbs, before frying.

Liver that is to be used for a loaf, a pâté, or such must be ground. Don't attempt to grind raw liver. Partially cook it first—about 5 minutes on each side—in cooking fat.

Chili Monterey Style

Makes 8 to 10 servings
   2 pounds boneless beef chuck, cut in 1-inch pieces
   1 clove garlic
   2 large onions, quartered
   ½ green pepper, seeded
   2 tablespoons vegetable oil
   3 tablespoons chili powder
   2 teaspoons ground cumin
   1 cup beef broth
   1 can (28 ounces) tomatoes, undrained
   3 cans (16 ounces) red kidney beans, undrained
   1 teaspoon salt
   1 cup uncooked spaghetti, broken in 1-inch pieces

Assemble Food Grinder with fine disc. Grind meat, garlic, onion, and green pepper in bowl. Heat oil in Dutch oven or saucepan over medium heat; sauté beef, onion, and green pepper. Add chili powder, cumin, beef broth, tomatoes, kidney beans, and salt. Simmer covered for 1 hour. Add spaghetti; simmer covered for 30 minutes.

Shepherd's Pie

Makes about 4 servings

    2 tablespoons butter or margarine
    1 medium onion, chopped
    1 package (10 ounces) frozen mixed vegetables
    2 cups cut-up cooked beef
    1 envelope Lipton Beef Flavor Mushroom Recipe
        Soup Mix
    1 tablespoon all-purpose flour
    1½ cups water
    2 to 3 cups hot mashed potatoes

In large skillet, melt butter and cook onion until tender; add mixed vegetables, beef, and Lipton Beef Flavor Mushroom Recipe Soup Mix and flour blended with water. Simmer, stirring occasionally, 10 minutes, or until vegetables are tender. Turn into 1½-quart casserole; top with potatoes and broil until browned.

Variation

Top casserole with grated cheddar cheese before browning.

German Beef 'n' Beer Crêpes

Makes about 4 servings

    1 envelope Lipton Onion-Mushroom Recipe
        Soup Mix
    1 tablespoon brown sugar
    ½ teaspoon caraway seed
    1 cup beer
    ½ cup water
    1 pound boneless round steak, cut into ½-inch
        cubes
    1½ tablespoons all-purpose flour
    ⅓ cup (about 1½ ounces) shredded Swiss cheese
    8 crêpes

In medium skillet, blend Lipton Onion-Mushroom Recipe Soup Mix, sugar, ½ teaspoon caraway, beer, and ¼ cup water; add beef. Bring to a boil, then simmer covered 40 minutes, or until beef is tender. Stir in flour blended with remaining water. Bring to a boil, then simmer, stirring constantly, until sauce is thickened, about 5 minutes. Preheat oven to 350°F. Equally top center of crêpes with beef mixture; roll up and place in greased 2-quart oblong baking dish. Top with cheese and remaining caraway. Bake 20 minutes, or until heated through.

Creole Liver

Makes 4 servings

    3 slices lean bacon
    2 tablespoons all-purpose flour
    ½ teaspoon salt
    ¼ teaspoon pepper
    1 pound beef liver, thinly sliced
    1 cup vegetable juice cocktail
    1 medium onion, thinly sliced

Place bacon slices in Multi-Cooker Frypan. Turn dial to 340°F. and cook bacon until crisp. Remove and reserve. Combine flour, salt, and pepper and use for dredging liver slices. Brown liver in a small amount of bacon fat. Add vegetable juice cocktail, onion, and crumbled bacon. Turn Frypan to simmer and cook covered about 10 minutes, or until liver is tender.

Glorious Liver

Makes 4 servings

    1 pound calves' liver
      All-purpose flour
      Salt and pepper
      Paprika
    2 tablespoons butter
    2 tablespoons salad oil
    1 clove garlic, minced
    ½ cup dry white wine
    2 tablespoons snipped parsley
    ¾ cup sour cream
      Buttered cooked noodles or rice

Cut liver into thin strips about ½ inch thick. Dredge with flour seasoned with salt, pepper, and paprika. Preheat Multi-Cooker Frypan to 340°F. Add butter and oil, and heat. Add strips of liver and garlic and cook very quickly, turning so that all the liver strips become browned and cooked. This should take about 2 to 4 minutes. Remove liver to a hot platter and keep warm. Pour off most of the fat from Frypan. Add wine and parsley and cook, stirring, so that browned bits are brought up from bottom of pan. Add sour cream and heat, but do not boil. Taste and add more seasoning if necessary. Return liver strips to pan and heat and stir. Serve immediately over buttered noodles or hot cooked rice.

Plenty of Pork

If you thought you were limited to only chops or Easter hams, look again, and find juicy stuffed loins, saucy Oriental dishes, dazzling fruit and pork combinations— all will please your palate.

Marinated Pork Chops

Makes 4 servings★

- 1 packet Butter Buds, mixed with ¼ cup hot water
- ¼ cup red wine
- 3 tablespoons chopped onion
- 2 teaspoons freshly squeezed lemon juice with pulp
- 1 bay leaf
- 1 large clove garlic, crushed
- ¼ teaspoon crushed rosemary
- ¼ teaspoon thyme
- ¼ teaspoon dry mustard
- ⅛ teaspoon freshly ground pepper
- 4 pork chops, about 1½ pounds

Combine all ingredients except pork chops and blend thoroughly. Pour into large, shallow glass bowl. Marinate pork chops, completely covered, 4 to 6 hours or overnight. Preheat oven to 350°F. Remove chops from marinade and bake in square baking dish 20 to 25 minutes or cook outdoors on charcoal grill.

★By using Butter Buds instead of vegetable oil in this recipe, you have saved 228 calories per serving.

Pork Chops Hawaiian

Makes 4 servings

- 4 pork chops, ½ inch thick
- 1 can (8 ounces) sliced pineapple in heavy syrup, drained (reserve syrup)
- 1 envelope Lipton Onion-Mushroom Recipe Soup Mix

In large skillet, brown chops. Mix reserved syrup with enough water to equal 1 cup; blend in Lipton Onion-Mushroom Recipe Soup Mix and add to skillet. Simmer covered, turning occasionally, 40 minutes; top with pineapple and heat through.

Variation

Add ½ cup diced green pepper, ¼ cup chopped pimiento, and ¾ cup slivered almonds.

Sherried Pork Roast (page 75). The Reynolds Wrap Kitchen

Peachy Pork Chops

Makes 6 servings

- 6 lean pork chops, about 2 pounds
- ½ teaspoon freshly ground pepper
- 1 can (1 pound) juice-packed peach halves
- 3 packets Sweet 'N Low
- 2 teaspoons lemon juice
- ¼ teaspoon ground cinnamon
- ¼ teaspoon ground ginger
- 3 whole cloves
- 2 teaspoons all-purpose flour

Carefully trim away any visible fat from chops. Season chops with pepper and brown in large non-stick skillet. Drain off fat. Drain peaches, reserving ½ cup juice. Pour over pork; cover tightly. Simmer gently over very low heat, about 45 minutes, or until pork is well cooked, turning chops once. Remove chops to serving platter and keep warm. Add peaches to liquid in skillet. Cover and heat through, about 5 minutes. Place one peach half on each chop. Mix flour with remaining juice and stir into pan juices. Heat and stir until sauce thickens, about 5 minutes. Remove cloves. Pour sauce over chops.

Pork Chops and Spanish Rice

Makes 4 servings

- 4 pork chops (about 1½ pounds)
- Salt and freshly ground pepper
- 1 large green pepper
- 1 cup long grain rice
- 1 onion, diced
- 1 can (8 ounces) tomato sauce

Place pork chops in shallow 2½-quart casserole. Sprinkle with salt and pepper to taste. Cut green pepper crosswise into 4 ½-inch thick rings. Dice remaining green pepper. Place 1 green pepper ring on each pork chop. Sprinkle rice over chops. Combine diced green pepper, onion, tomato sauce, 1½ cups water, and 1 teaspoon salt. Pour over chops and rice. Cover casserole. Bake at 350°F. 1 hour 15 minutes, or until rice is tender.

Pork Chops with Orange Dressing

Makes 4 servings

- **4 pork chops, each 1 inch thick**
- **2 tablespoons all-purpose flour**
- **2 teaspoons salt**
- **½ teaspoon paprika**
- **¼ teaspoon pepper**
- **1 tablespoon fat or vegetable oil**
- **6 slices bread, crusts removed**
- **Rind from one medium orange, cut up**
- **1 stalk celery, cut up**
- **1 small onion, cut up**
- **1 teaspoon sugar**
- **¼ teaspoon dried thyme**
- **½ cup orange juice**

Heat oven to 350°F. Dredge pork chops with mixture of flour, 1 teaspoon salt, paprika, and ⅛ teaspoon pepper. Heat fat in large, heavy skillet; add chops and brown on both sides. Tear one slice bread into blender container; add orange rind. Cover; blend at medium speed until bread is crumbed and orange rind is grated. Empty into bowl. Repeat process with remaining bread, one slice at a time; empty crumbs into bowl. Put celery and onion into blender container. Cover; blend at medium speed until chopped. Add to bread crumbs; add remaining 1 teaspoon salt, ⅛ teaspoon pepper, sugar, and thyme; mix lightly. Arrange chops in single layer in shallow baking dish. Heap one-fourth of the dressing on each chop. Pour orange juice into skillet; stir to dissolve any brown particles; pour liquid around chops. Cover baking dish. Bake 45 minutes. Uncover; bake 15 minutes, or until chops are tender.

Perfect Gravy Every Time

Good gravy complements a good roast, whether it's beef, pork, lamb, or veal. There's no mystery to producing the gravy. Just follow these simple steps:

1. Remove the roast to a warm platter; let it stand 15 to 20 minutes at room temperature.

2. Meanwhile, pour off fat from roasting pan. Return 3 tablespoons fat to the pan; discard the remaining fat or save for another purpose.

3. Place pan over medium heat. Add 2 cups of water. Cook about 2 minutes, stirring to dislodge browned bits that stick to the pan.

4. In a small bowl, stir together 3 tablespoons all-purpose flour and ¼ cup water to make a smooth paste.

5. Add gradually to liquid in pan, stirring constantly until mixture bubbles and is thickened. Cook 2 minutes longer. Season to taste with salt and pepper.

And there you have it—plain, simple, delicious meat gravy.

If you would prefer your gravy not quite so plain and simple, try any of these easy variations:

1. For 1 cup of the water, substitute 1 cup tomato juice if the roast is beef or lamb, 1 cup milk or half and half if the roast is veal or pork.

2. For all of the water, substitute 2 cups broth or stock, using chicken broth with veal or pork, beef broth with beef or lamb.

3. Stir 2 tablespoons tomato paste plus ¼ teaspoon sugar into beef or lamb gravy. And/or add ½ teaspoon onion powder, ¼ teaspoon garlic powder, or use onion or garlic juice in the same proportions.

4. For excellent flavor, season your gravy with herbs. Experiment on your own with your favorites, or try basil or oregano with beef, marjoram or rosemary with lamb, thyme or summer savory with veal, sage or cilantro with pork. Whichever you choose, add ¼ teaspoon of the dried herb, crumbled in your hand before adding. Stir and cook for a moment or two, then taste and add more of the herb if you wish.

Remember, gravy can be thickened with cornstarch rather than flour. Stir together 1½ tablespoons cornstarch and ¼ cup water to make a smooth paste; gradually stir into boiling liquid in pan. The difference between the two gravies? The one thickened with flour will be opaque, the one with cornstarch translucent.

No drippings with which to make gravy? Heat 1 can (about 15 ounces) of chicken or beef broth. While it heats, knead together 3 tablespoons soft butter and 3 tablespoons all-purpose flour until smooth. Stirring constantly, add bits of the butter mixture to the boiling broth until all is used. Cook two minutes; season to taste. (The butter-flour combination is *beurre manié*, a favorite French way to thicken sauces, soups, and stews.)

No time to make gravy? Open and heat a can or jar of commercial gravy, which can be had in a wide assortment of flavors. If the taste is a bit too timid, add any one or a combination of these: a dash or two of Worcestershire sauce, 1 tablespoon catsup, 1 teaspoon soy sauce, ½ teaspoon curry powder, or herbs as suggested above.

Hong Kong Pork Chops

Makes 6 servings

- 1 medium onion, halved
- 8 ounces fresh mushrooms
- 1 can (5 ounces) water chestnuts, drained
- ½ green pepper, seeded and halved
- 2 tablespoons vegetable oil
- 6 pork chops
- ¼ cup orange juice
- 2 tablespoons lemon juice
- ¼ cup soy sauce
- 1 clove garlic, mashed
- ½ teaspoon ground ginger
- 1 lemon, sliced

Assemble Salad Maker with thick slicer disc and large bowl. Process onion, mushrooms, and water chestnuts. Change disc to French fry cutter disc and process green pepper. Set aside. Heat vegetable oil in skillet and brown chops on both sides. Put all remaining ingredients except sliced lemon into skillet. Simmer covered for 30 minutes, or until chops and vegetables are tender. Garnish with lemon slices.

Bavarian Pork Chops

Makes 6 servings

- 6 pork chops, ¾ inch thick
- 1 cup chopped onion
- ½ cup chopped green pepper
- ½ cup sliced celery
- 1 envelope Lipton Beef Flavor Mushroom Recipe Soup Mix
- 1¼ cups water
- 2 tablespoons sherry

In large skillet, brown chops; remove. In drippings, cook onion, green pepper, and celery until tender; stir in Lipton Beef Flavor Mushroom Recipe Soup Mix blended with water and sherry. Return chops to skillet and simmer covered, turning occasionally, 45 minutes, or until chops are tender.

Variation

Add ¼ teaspoon dry mustard and 1 teaspoon cider vinegar.

Idea: Serve on a bed of hot cooked egg noodles or with red cabbage simmered in beer. Apple strudel is a wonderful way to cap the meal.

Pork Chops à la Jenni

Makes 6 servings

- 12 to 18 center-cut pork chops, sliced ¼ inch thick
  Salt and pepper
  All-purpose flour
- ½ cup butter
- 1 can (10½ ounces) Campbell's Condensed Cream of Mushroom Soup
- ½ cup grated Parmesan cheese
  Paprika

Season pork chops with salt and pepper. Dip chops into flour and shake off excess. Brown chops on both sides in butter in a large skillet. Place chops in overlapping rows in a shallow casserole. Spoon pan drippings over chops. Spread mushroom soup over chops. Sprinkle with Parmesan cheese and paprika. Bake covered in a preheated 350°F. oven 15 to 20 minutes.

Perfect Partners

Pork and fruit have carried on so long-lived a love affair it's practically a scandal. Pork and oranges. Pork and plums. Pork and apples. Pork and cranberries. Pork partners beautifully with sauces, jellies, herbs and spices and seeds, as well as applesauce (a good dash of cinnamon won't hurt a bit), cranberry or cranberry-orange or cranberry-raisin-walnut relish, cranberry or orange or currant jelly, curry, sage, caraway, anise, ginger, chili. And onions and garlic—pork's richly good flavor can take a lot of either, or of the two in combination.

Fill a crown roast of pork loin—either between individual chops or between the loin meat (it's easy to cut a pocket) and the ribs with a savory stuffing. Or heap individual chops or chops with a pocket cut in them with a stuffing, too—perhaps one boasting a liberal helping of chopped peanuts. Barbecue spareribs with a tomato-onion-molasses baste for an unbeatable treat.

Because pork gravy is so good, plan on something—mashed or riced potatoes, a simple pilaf, plain or caraway noodles, yams or sweet potatoes—that will complement it. And serve a vegetable that is particularly pork-happy, such as parsnips, sauerkraut, lightly panned cabbage, glazed onions or creamed onions and peas, egg-sauced creamed spinach, carrots in the Vichy style, turnips and rutabagas. Coleslaw makes a good pork go-with salad, so does carrot-and-raisin-and-nut, so does waldorf or pear-pecan waldorf. Apple or pumpkin desserts are particularly appropriate—but not if you've served apples or yams in the main part of the meal.

Danish Pork Chops

Makes 4 servings

    4 pork chops, cut ¾ inch thick
    1 tablespoon butter or margarine
    2 large apples, cored, peeled, and chopped
    ½ can (6 ounces) Solo Prune Filling
    ½ cup chicken bouillon
    ½ cup heavy cream
      Salt and pepper

Trim as much fat as possible from pork chops. Melt butter in a heavy skillet. Add pork chops and brown lightly on both sides. Add apples, prune filling, bouillon, and cream. Season lightly with salt and pepper. Cover and simmer 45 minutes, or until chops are tender. Stir sauce occasionally, and if sauce becomes too thick, add a little water. Remove chops. Skim off as much fat as possible from top of gravy and press through a sieve. Heat thoroughly and serve with chops.
Good Idea: Serve this very rich dish with mashed potatoes or noodles covered with the extra gravy.

Savory Skillet Pork Chops

Makes about 6 servings

    2 tablespoons oil
    6 pork chops, ½ inch thick
    1 medium onion, finely chopped
    ½ cup Wish-Bone Russian Dressing
    ½ cup water
    1 tablespoon lemon juice
    ½ teaspoon salt
    1 tablespoon cornstarch

In large skillet, heat oil and brown pork chops; add onion, Wish-Bone Russian Dressing, ¼ cup water, lemon juice, and salt. Simmer covered 45 minutes, or until chops are tender. Blend in cornstarch mixed with remaining water and cook, stirring constantly, until sauce is thickened, about 5 minutes.

Stuffed Pork Chops

Makes 4 servings

    4 Veribest Pork Loin Rib Chops, cut 1½ inches
       thick
    1 cup finely chopped apple
    1 cup soft bread crumbs
    ½ cup chicken broth
    ¼ cup chopped onion
    ¼ cup raisins
    2 tablespoons chopped parsley
    ½ teaspoon salt

Danish Pork Chops. Solo Food Products

Heat oven to 350°F. Make pocket in each chop by cutting between rib bones. Combine remaining ingredients; mix well. Stuff each chop with ½ cup stuffing mixture. Place in 12x8-inch baking dish. Bake at 350°F. for 1 hour and 15 minutes, turning once during baking.

Pork Chops in Vermouth

Makes 6 servings

    ¼ cup all-purpose flour
    1 teaspoon salt
    ½ teaspoon thyme
    ¼ teaspoon pepper
    6 pork chops, cut ½ inch thick
    2 tablespoons butter or margarine
    2 tablespoons salad oil
    ½ cup dry vermouth or dry white wine

Combine flour, salt, thyme, and pepper. Cut as much fat from pork chops as possible. Dust pork chops with flour mixture. Preheat Multi-Cooker Frypan to 340°F. Heat butter and oil in hot Frypan. Add pork chops and cook until golden brown on both sides. Drain off all fat from skillet. Add vermouth. Reduce heat to Simmer. Cover and cook 30 minutes, or until pork chops are tender. Add more wine during cooking time if necessary.

Q.   *I've been told that pork is hard to digest. Is this true?*
A.   That's another old wives' tale with no foundation in fact. Nor is pork excessively calorie laden. Today's porkers are raised to be less fat-burdened than yesterday's portly hogs.

Pork Chops and Spanish Rice (page 67). Caloric Corporation

Wild-Chinese Rice

Makes 6 servings
   1 package (6 ounces) Uncle Ben's® Original Long
      Grain & Wild Rice
   1 can (10¾ ounces) condensed cream of
      mushroom soup
1¼ cups water
   1 can (14 ounces) Chinese vegetables, drained
   6 lean pork chops
      Black pepper
      Chinese noodles
      Soy sauce

Mix contents of rice and seasoning packets, soup, and water in 2-quart casserole. Add Chinese vegetables. Arrange pork chops on top. Sprinkle with black pepper. Bake 1 hour and 20 minutes in 350°F. oven. Serve with Chinese noodles and soy sauce.

Variations

Veal chops or chicken may be substituted for the pork chops in this dish.

Sausage-Stuffed Pork Loin

Makes 10 servings
   1 4-pound boneless pork loin roast
   ½ pound bulk pork sausage
   1 onion, minced
   1 cup fresh bread crumbs
   1 package (32 ounces) sauerkraut
   1 cup dry white wine

Cut strings on pork roast and unroll. To increase surface of roast, slash "eye" of pork loin lengthwise and fold out flat. Brown sausage in skillet over moderate heat. Drain fat. Add onion and cook until tender. Remove from heat. Stir in bread crumbs. Spoon onto roast. Roll roast and retie with string. Rinse sauerkraut and place in large casserole. Place roast over sauerkraut. Pour wine over roast. Cover casserole. Bake at 350°F. for 2 to 2½ hours until internal temperature reaches 170°F. Let stand 10 minutes before slicing. Slice and serve with sauerkraut

Sweet-Sour Pork Tenderloin

Makes 6 servings
   ¼ cup butter
  12 slices pork tenderloin, well trimmed, ½ inch
      thick
      Salt and pepper
      Sweet-Sour Sauce (recipe follows)

Melt butter in a large skillet. Season pork with salt and pepper. Brown meat on both sides and sauté slowly, about 15 to 20 minutes, until meat is almost cooked. Add Sweet-Sour Sauce and simmer for another 15 minutes. Serve slices of pork with pan juices spooned over them.

Sweet-Sour Sauce

Makes about 2½ cups
   1 cup sugar
   ½ cup white vinegar
      Demi-Glacé Sauce (recipe follows)
   1 tablespoon cornstarch mixed with 2 tablespoons
      water

Add sugar to vinegar and stir to blend. Cook at a boil until liquid turns a golden brown. Slowly add Demi-Glacé Sauce. (Mixture will bubble violently.) Stir to blend. Stir in cornstarch mixture and cook, stirring, until sauce is thickened.

Demi-Glacé Sauce

Makes about 1½ cups
   1 can (10½ ounces) Campbell's Condensed Beef
      Broth
   ⅓ cup country-style tomato juice
   1 clove garlic, minced
      Pinch marjoram
      Pinch rosemary
   ½ bay leaf
   2 whole cloves
   ⅓ cup Madeira

Combine all ingredients and simmer for 15 minutes. Strain and store in the refrigerator for use as the base of most brown sauces.

Garnishing the Roast

Reluctant to send the meat to the table naked, many cooks stuff bits of parsley around the platter's perimeter and are satisfied. But an edible garnish can be both attractive and practical. For example, half-shells of oranges filled with fluffy whipped sweet potatoes complement a roast of pork excellently. Whole onions, glazed—after cooking, of course—in plenty of butter and a little sugar, go well with beef. Stuffed mushrooms are good partners for steak or lamb. Tiny peas, or purée of peas if you prefer, heaped into lemon shells, are perfect with veal. So are slices of herb-broiled eggplant crisscrossed with strips of pimiento. Use your imagination to make the dinner look—and taste—twice as good!

Pork Tenderloin Cordon Bleu à la Maria Christine

Makes 6 servings

  12 pork tenderloin slices, ½ inch thick, or thin-sliced center-cut pork chops, bone removed
   6 slices Emmenthaler cheese
   6 slices smoked ham
     All-purpose flour
   1 egg, well beaten
   2 tablespoons water
 1½ cups cracker crumbs
     Oil or shortening, 1 inch deep
   2 cans (10½ ounces each) Campbell's Condensed Golden Mushroom Soup
  ⅔ cup heavy cream

Pound meat slices until very thin. Top 6 of the slices with a slice of cheese and a slice of ham cut slightly smaller in size than the tenderloin. Top with remaining meat slices. Press together. Dip meat carefully into flour on both sides, then dip into egg beaten with water. Dip into crumbs, pressing firmly to make crumbs adhere. Fry slowly in oil or shortening, about 45 minutes, so pork has time to be thoroughly cooked and is richly browned. Drain on absorbent paper. In a saucepan combine soup and cream; heat until bubbly. Serve tenderloin topped with sauce.

Apricot Pork Roast

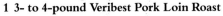

Makes 6 to 8 servings

   1 3- to 4-pound Veribest Pork Loin Roast
  ½ cup apricot nectar
  ¼ cup firmly packed brown sugar
   1 can (16 ounces) apricot halves, drained (reserve syrup)
   2 teaspoons vinegar

Heat oven to 325°F. Roast pork at 325°F. for 2 hours and 30 minutes, or until meat thermometer registers 170°F. Combine apricot nectar, brown sugar, apricot syrup, and vinegar. Brush pork with glaze during last 30 minutes of roasting time. Arrange apricots around roast on serving platter.

Pork Tenderloin in Cream

Makes 4 servings

   2 tablespoons shortening
   1 clove garlic
   2 whole pork tenderloins
     All-purpose flour
  ½ teaspoon salt
  ½ cup plus 2 tablespoons sour cream

Heat fat to 320°F. in Multi-Cooker Frypan. Sauté garlic until golden; remove. With Sunbeam Knife cut tenderloins into 2-inch pieces. Dip each piece in flour; brown on all sides in Frypan. Turn dial to Simmer. Add salt and ½ cup sour cream; simmer covered 40 minutes, or until tender. Just before serving, stir additional 2 tablespoons sour cream into gravy.

Pork Primer

How to store: Pork should be stored in the coldest part of the refrigerator, where the temperature falls just short of freezing. Plan on keeping fresh pork no more than 2 days before you cook it—it is the most perishable of the meats. Store in its wrappings if the meat was prepackaged, loosely in wax paper or foil if not. Cooked pork should be wrapped or covered and refrigerated in the coldest area up to 3 days. To calculate the number of servings, count on ⅓ pound per serving for boneless cuts, ½ pound for cuts with a moderate amount of bone. Pork, ounce for ounce, is the food richest in the B vitamin niacin, and it is also a good source of iron.

Freezing and thawing pork: Freeze fresh pork from the market as soon and as rapidly as possible, properly wrapped, labeled, and dated for freezing. Before you put it in the freezer, cut into portion or recipe sizes, separating chops and ground-pork patties from one another so that they can be easily parted while still frozen. Wrap well, pressing out all air. Roasts, chops, and patties can be cooked from the frozen state, provided you allow sufficient time for thorough cooking, bearing in mind that pork must never be served in any condition other than well done. Store pork in the freezer at 0° or lower up to 9 months—pork does not keep for as long a time as other frozen meats; the fat tends to turn rancid after that maximum 9-month period.

Thaw pork in its original wrapper in the refrigerator, never at room temperature. A roast will take somewhere between 12 and 24 hours, smaller pieces a proportionately shorter time.

Cooking pork: Present-day pork has been bred to have less fat and to be cooked to an internal temperature of 170°F. rather than the 185° that used to be recommended—at this new temperature it is safe, juicier, and more flavorful. Also, less cooking time means less shrinkage. Insert the thermometer into the meat in the thickest part of the flesh, but well away from the bone. If you do not use a thermometer, allow 25 minutes per pound, plus an additional 25 minutes, all at an oven temperature of 350°F. Meat cooked by methods other than roasting is done when it is completely fork-tender.

Pork Tenderloin Cordon Bleu à la Maria Christine (page 73). Campbell Soup Company

Glazed Roast Pork with Almond Wild Rice

Makes 6 servings
- 1 4-pound pork loin roast
- 1 package (6 ounces) Uncle Ben's® Original Long Grain & Wild Rice
- ⅓ cup slivered almonds
- 1 jar (12 ounces) apricot preserves
- ¼ cup prepared mustard
- ¼ cup soy sauce
- 1 cup water, or as needed
- 2 tablespoons sugar

Place pork roast in shallow roasting pan. Roast at 325°F. for about 2½ hours, or until roast reaches an internal temperature of 170°F. Place contents of rice and seasoning packets in 1-quart baking dish. Add the 1 tablespoon butter called for on the package. Bring the 2½ cups water called for on the package to a boil. Pour over rice; cover and bake for 40 minutes. Combine ½ cup preserves, mustard, and soy sauce; stir. About 30 to 40 minutes before end of roasting time, pour excess fat from pan. Spoon glaze over roast several times, adding water to pan as needed to prevent sauce from burning. Remove roast; keep warm. Add water to glaze to make 1 cup; add remaining preserves and sugar. Stir almonds into hot cooked rice. Heat and serve sauce over rice and pork.

Roast Leg-O-Pork with Potato Medley

Makes 6 to 8 servings
- 1 4- to 5-pound Veribest Boneless Leg-O-Pork (Fresh Ham)
- 2 large yams, cut in ½-inch slices
- 3 large potatoes, peeled and quartered
- 3 cups water
- ⅓ cup cornstarch
- 1 cup cold water
  - Salt
  - Pepper

Heat oven to 325°F. Roast pork at 325°F. for 3 hours, or until meat thermometer registers 170°F. Cook yams and potatoes in boiling salted water for 8 minutes; drain. Peel yams. Arrange yams and potatoes around pork during last 30 to 40 minutes. For gravy, pour off all but ½ cup drippings. Add 3 cups water. Moisten cornstarch with 1 cup cold water. Add to drippings; cook, stirring constantly until thickened. Season with salt and pepper.

Sherried Pork Roast

Makes 4 to 6 servings
- 1 tablespoon all-purpose flour
- 1 3-pound pork loin roast, boned, rolled, and tied
- ½ cup plus 1 tablespoon soy sauce, divided
- ½ cup plus 2 tablespoons sherry, divided
- 1 clove garlic, minced
- 1 tablespoon dry mustard
- 1 teaspoon ground ginger
- 1 teaspoon thyme leaves
- 1 jar (10 ounces) currant jelly

Shake flour in large size 14x20-inch Brown-In-Bag; place in 12x8x2-inch baking dish. Place pork roast in bag. Combine ½ cup soy sauce, ½ cup sherry, garlic, mustard, ginger, and thyme. Pour in bag; close bag with nylon tie. Turn bag gently several times to moisten meat. Marinate 3 to 5 hours or overnight in refrigerator; turn bag several times. When ready to cook, preheat oven to 350°F. Make 6 half-inch slits in top of bag. Insert meat thermometer through bag into pork roast. Cook in oven 1½ hours, or until meat thermometer reaches 170°F. To make sauce, melt jelly in small saucepan; add 2 tablespoons sherry and 1 tablespoon soy sauce. Stir and simmer 2 minutes. Spoon on top of pork roast.

Mincemeat-Glazed Ham (page 77). Armour Food Company

Dressed-up Ham

Without a glaze, a whole or half or portion of baked ham looks forlorn. And though the good ham flavor will be there without a glaze, it will be enhanced and reinforced by one, particularly a substantial and colorful topping with a tasty bonus, such as pieces of fruit. Sometimes a sauce, used to baste the ham throughout its cooking time, stands in for a glaze.

Here are some tried-and-true ham sauces and glazes. Unless otherwise directed, spread glaze over ham 20 to 30 minutes before the end of baking time, return to the oven.

Orange Sauce: Baste ham with 1 can condensed frozen orange juice, thawed and combined with 1 cup brown sugar, ½ cup A1 Sauce.

Cider Baste: Combine 1 cup apple cider, 1 cup brown sugar. Decorate ham with spiced crab apples.

Apricot Sauce: Combine 1 cup apricot nectar, ½ cup honey; use to baste ham last hour of cooking.

Sherry Sauce: Pour 1 cup sherry over ham just before placing in oven. Half an hour before ham is done, sprinkle with brown sugar, baste with an additional 1 cup sherry.

French-style Ham: Pour over whole ham 1 cup Madeira wine; sprinkle on ½ cup each sliced onions and carrots, 1 sliced rib celery, several parsley sprigs, 1 bay leaf, ½ teaspoon thyme. Bake. Make Madeira Sauce when ham is almost done—combine pan juices, 1 cup beef broth, 1 cup madeira; thicken with 1½ tablespoons cornstarch dissolved in a little more Madeira; simmer 5 minutes. Score ham fat, sprinkle with brown sugar; return to oven for 10 minutes. Baste with 2 tablespoons of the Madeira Sauce, bake 5 minutes longer. Serve with remaining Madeira Sauce.

Honeyed Country Ham: Soak and simmer ham according to directions. When done, transfer to a baking sheet. Spread liberally with honey, sprinkle lightly with grated orange peel; bake until glazed.

Applesauce Glaze: Combine ½ cup corn syrup, 1 cup applesauce, 2 tablespoons prepared mustard.

Cherry Glaze: Combine ¼ cup sugar and 1 tablespoon cornstarch in saucepan; gradually add reserved liquid from 1 can (16 ounces) red sour pitted cherries. Cook, stirring constantly, over low heat until thickened; add cherries. Continue cooking until cherries are heated. Stir in ½ teaspoon almond extract.

Mustard-Sugar: Combine ¾ cup dark brown sugar, 2 teaspoons dry mustard, enough ham drippings to moisten.

British-pub glaze: Combine ½ cup dark brown sugar, ¼ cup dark beer, ½ teaspoon summer savory, ¼ teaspoon basil. Garnish the ham at serving time with thick sautéed tomato slices; serve with brussels sprouts.

Sugaring-off Glaze: Cut ham fat crisscross style; stud with cloves where cuts meet. Pat maple sugar thickly over surface. Garnish with sautéed pinepaple rings.

Midwest Glaze: Combine 1 cup orange marmalade, ¼ cup cider vinegar, ¼ teaspoon nutmeg; spread over ham.

Deep-South Style: Combine 1 cup peach nectar, ½ cup honey; spoon over ham. Garnish serving platter with brandied peaches.

Cumberland Glaze: Melt 1 glass tart currant jelly; add 1 teaspoon dry mustard, 2 tablespoons sherry, 1 teaspoon grated orange peel.

Grandma's Way: Glaze ham with a combination of 1 cup molasses, ½ cup cider vinegar. Garnish platter with whole baked apples stuffed with mincemeat.

Ham in Cream: Bake a 1½-inch slice of ham in 2 cups heavy cream at 300°F., turning over once during cooking. Fifteen minutes before it is done, spread top very lightly with apple butter.

Sometimes a ham—particularly a boneless or canned one— tastes fine, but doesn't look all that much like ham. Then dress it up by baking it in a jacket of pastry—ham en croute. Use pie crust mix, thawed and rolled-out frozen patty shells, or refrigerated crescent rolls, the edges of their "seams" pinched together. Make decorations of scraps of pastry, place on top, and brush the whole thing with 1 egg yolk beaten with 1 tablespoon cream. Garnish with lemon cups filled with currant jelly.

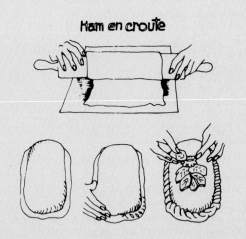

Ham en croute

Fruit Curried Ham Steak

Makes 6 servings
- 2 tablespoons butter or margarine, melted
- 2 tablespoons orange juice
- ¼ cup firmly packed brown sugar
- 1 teaspoon curry powder
- 1 teaspoon salt
- 2 bananas
- 2 peaches
- 1 can (8 ounces) pineapple chunks, drained
- 1 2-pound smoked ham center slice, cut 1 inch thick
- ¼ cup shredded coconut (optional)

Combine butter, orange juice, brown sugar, curry powder, and salt. Peel bananas and cut into 1-inch chunks. Peel and slice peaches. Add bananas, peaches, and pineapple to curry mixture. Stir to coat. Place ham in shallow baking dish. Spoon fruit mixture over ham. Sprinkle coconut over fruit. Bake at 350°F. for 35 minutes, or until ham and fruit are hot and coconut is lightly browned.

Rum-Raisin Glazed Ham

- 1 5- to 8-pound Armour Star Boneless Ham
- 2 tablespoons firmly packed brown sugar
- 1 tablespoon cornstarch
- ½ cup water
- 1 cup raisins
- ½ cup orange juice
- ⅓ cup currant jelly
- ¼ teaspoon rum extract
  Dash ground allspice
  Dash salt

Heat ham according to label instructions. Combine brown sugar and cornstarch; gradually add water, stirring until well blended. Add remaining ingredients; cook, stirring occasionally, until thickened. Spoon over ham during last 30 minutes of heating.

Frosted Easter Ham

- 1 package (8 ounces) cream cheese, softened
- ¼ cup plain yogurt
- 1 tablespoon lemon juice
- 1½ teaspoons prepared horseradish
- 1 teaspoon salt
- 1 5-pound Armour Star Ham
  Shredded carrot
  Parsley sprigs
  Orange slices
  Radish roses

Combine cream cheese, yogurt, lemon juice, horseradish, and salt. Beat with mixer until smooth. Remove excess gelatin from ham. Spread cream cheese mixture on top and sides of ham. Refrigerate several hours or overnight. Just before serving, garnish with carrot, parsley, orange slices, and radish roses.

Mincemeat-Glazed Ham

Makes 12 servings
- 1 5-pound Golden Star Ham by Armour
- 1 cup mincemeat
- 1 cup apple cider
- 2 teaspoons grated lemon rind
- 1 tablespoon cornstarch
  Lemons
  Mint sprigs

Heat ham according to label instructions. Combine mincemeat, ¾ cup apple cider, and lemon rind. Moisten cornstarch with ¼ cup apple cider; add to mincemeat mixture. Cook, stirring constantly, until thickened. Spoon mincemeat glaze over ham during last 30 minutes of heating time. Cut thin slice from end of each lemon. Starting at cut end, cut a thin spiral peel in a continuous motion. Curl peel to resemble a rose; secure with a wooden toothpick. Place heated ham on platter. Garnish with lemon-peel roses and mint.

The Wide, Wide World of Ham Leftovers

Nothing, not even a turkey, produces such bountiful and versatile leftovers as a ham. And when most of the meat is gone, use the bone and scraps for pea or bean or lentil soup, or chicken-ham chowder, or ham-corn soup.

Here is a random sampling of ham-leftovers ideas. Chicken breasts or thighs, boned, stuffed with ham. Ham and lima bean bake. Grilled ham and muenster sandwiches. French-fried ham and turkey (or chicken) sandwiches. Salad of fresh peach halves filled wtih ham-pickle relish-mayonnaise mixture. Old-fashioned ham and scalloped potatoes. For breakfast, split and buttered biscuits sandwiched with country ham, or ham and grits with red-eye gravy. Baked ham slices with sage-celery stuffing. Upside-down ham loaf with pineapple. Ham balls in sweet/sour sauce with dried apricots. Ham â la king in a corn bread ring. Ham croquettes with creamed peas and little onions. Ham shortcake made with buttermilk biscuits. Individual orange-glazed ham loaves. Corn fritters with slivers of ham. Molded ham-and-egg salad. Creamy scrambled eggs with frizzled ham. Ham soufflé. Ham-rice salad with pineapple chunks. Ham mousse. Ham creole over fluffy rice. Spaghetti with olive oil, grated cheese, ham chunks. Ham pie with cheddar crust. Ham succotash. Baked eggs with ham. Ham-stuffed cabbage. Ham-pecan waffles. Ham and eggs mollet in aspic. Well, you get the idea.

Pork Canton. Campbell Soup Company

Pork Canton

Makes 4 servings

  2 tablespoons peanut oil
  1 pound boneless, very lean, tender pork
  1 green pepper, seeded and cut into 1-inch triangles
  1 cup well-drained pineapple chunks
  1 cup diagonally sliced celery
  2 tablespoons catsup
  1 can (10½ ounces) Campbell's Condensed Chicken Broth
  ½ cup white vinegar
  ⅓ cup sugar
  2 tablespoons cornstarch
     Hot rice

In a large skillet, heat oil just until it starts to smoke. Add pork cut into ⅛-inch-thick strips. Stir quickly over high heat until pork is cooked, about 3 minutes. Add remaining ingredients except cornstarch. Cover and cook until vegetables are tender but crisp, about 6 minutes. Mix cornstarch and ¼ cup water; stir in quickly. Cook, stirring, until mixture bubbles and thickens. Season to taste with salt. Serve with hot rice.

Pork Sukiyaki

Makes 6 to 8 servings

  ¼ cup soy sauce
  ¼ cup water
  2 tablespoons sugar
  ½ cup Wish-Bone Italian Dressing
  2 pounds pork loin, sliced paper thin
  1 cup sliced celery
  2 cans (5 ounces each) bamboo shoots, drained
  1 can (4 ounces) sliced mushrooms, drained
  1 cup sliced green onions

In small bowl, combine soy sauce, water, and sugar. In large skillet, heat Wish-Bone Italian Dressing and brown meat well. Push meat to one side of skillet; pour half of soy mixture over meat. To other side of skillet, add celery, bamboo shoots, and mushrooms. Simmer 8 to 10 minutes. Add green onions and cover vegetables with remaining soy mixture. Cook an additional 5 minutes.

Saucy Spareribs

Makes 4 to 6 servings

  1 envelope Lipton Onion Recipe Soup Mix
  1½ cups water
  ⅓ cup honey
  ¼ cup soy sauce
  2 tablespoons sherry
  1 teaspoon ground ginger
  4 pounds spareribs, cut into serving pieces

In large shallow baking dish, combine all ingredients except spareribs; add spareribs. Cover and marinate in refrigerator, turning occasionally, at least 3 hours. Preheat oven to 350°F. Remove spareribs, reserving marinade. Place ribs on rack in foil-lined baking dish. Bake, turning and basting occasionally with marinade, 1¼ hours, or until spareribs are done.

Variation

Substitute 2 pounds chicken legs or pieces for 2 pounds of the spareribs.

Idea: Serve with crisp French fries and coleslaw or a dish of Oriental mixed vegetables.

Hawaiian Rice

Makes 4 to 6 servings

  1 pound boneless pork, cut in ¾-inch slices
  1 can (15¾ ounces) pineapple chunks
  ¼ cup vinegar
  1½ teaspoons salt
  ½ teaspoon garlic salt
  2 tablespoons sugar
  1 cup Uncle Ben's® Converted® Brand Rice
  1 green pepper, cut into small squares
  1 tomato, cut into thin wedges (optional)

Brown pork in cooking oil in 10-inch skillet; drain. Drain pineapple chunks, reserving liquid. Add water to liquid to make 2½ cups. Add liquid, vinegar, salt, garlic salt, and sugar to pork; stir. Bring to boil. Reduce heat, cover, and cook over low heat 20 minutes. Remove cover; stir in rice. Cover and continue cooking about 25 minutes, or until liquid is absorbed and pork tender. Stir in pineapple chunks, green pepper, and tomato wedges, if desired. Heat through.

Variation

Add water chestnuts and bamboo shoots at end of cooking.

Omit pork and substitute ham or cubed uncooked chicken.

Chop Suey

Makes 6 to 8 servings

    2 tablespoons peanut oil
    ¾ pound boneless lean pork shoulder, cut in ½-
      inch pieces
    ¾ pound boneless veal shoulder, cut in ½-inch
      pieces
    1 cup beef broth
    2 large sweet onions, quartered
    3 large stalks celery, cut in 4-inch pieces
    1 can (8 ounces) whole water chestnuts, drained
    ¼ cup soy sauce
    ½ teaspoon bead molasses
    2 tablespoons cornstarch
    1 can (4 ounces) mushroom pieces, drained
    1 can (16 ounces) bean sprouts, drained
    1 can (8 ounces) sliced bamboo shoots, drained
    4 cups cooked rice

Heat oil in a 5-quart Dutch oven or saucepan until hot. Add meat and brown quickly on all sides, stirring constantly. Add ½ cup beef broth; cover and simmer over medium-low heat for 20 minutes, or until meat is tender. Meanwhile, assemble Salad Maker with French fry cutter disc and large bowl. Process onion. Change disc to thick slicer disc and process celery and water chestnuts. Add processed vegetables to meat and stir to combine. Continue cooking covered for 15 minutes, or until celery and onion are crisp-tender. Mix soy sauce, remaining broth, molasses, and cornstarch. Pour into meat-vegetable mixture, add remaining vegetables, and stir well. Bring to a boil, reduce heat, and simmer for 10 minutes. Serve with rice.

Florentine Chopped Ham

Makes 6 servings

    ¼ cup butter or margarine
    ¼ cup all-purpose flour
    ½ teaspoon salt
      Dash pepper
    2 cups milk
    1 tablespoon prepared mustard
    1 can (12 ounces) Armour Star Chopped Ham,
      cubed
    1 package (10 ounces) frozen chopped spinach,
      cooked according to package directions
    1 jar (2½ ounces) sliced mushrooms, drained
    6 frozen patty shells, baked according to package
      directions

Melt butter; stir in flour, salt, and pepper. Slowly add milk, stirring until thickened. Stir in mustard, chopped ham, spinach, and mushrooms; heat thoroughly. Serve in patty shells.

Baked Ham and Asparagus Roll with Cheddar Cheese Sauce

Makes 4 servings

    24 fresh, frozen, or canned asparagus spears
    8 slices boiled ham, 4x6 inches
    2 cans (10¾ ounces each) Campbell's Condensed
      Cheddar Cheese Soup
    ¼ teaspoon paprika
    2 teaspoons prepared mustard
    ⅓ cup light cream
      Hash browned potatoes

Place 3 asparagus spears at the end of each slice of ham. Roll up and place rolls side by side in a shallow casserole. Combine remaining ingredients; blend well, spoon over asparagus. Bake in preheated 350°F. oven 30 minutes. Serve with hash browned potatoes.

Mexican Wild Rice Stir-Fry

Makes 6 servings

    1 package (6 ounces) Uncle Ben's® Original Long
      Grain & Wild Rice
    1½ cups cubed cooked ham
    1 tomato, coarsely chopped
    ¼ cup sliced green onions with tops
    ¼ cup sliced ripe olives
    2 teaspoons lemon juice
    1 avocado (optional)

Cook contents of rice and seasoning packets in a 10-inch skillet according to package directions. Stir in remaining ingredients except avocado. Cover and let stand 5 minutes. Peel and seed avocado; cut lengthwise into ½-inch slices. Arrange over rice mixture.

Ham with Honey Beer Basting Sauce

Makes 8 servings

    1 6-pound baked ham
    4 tablespoons coarse grain mustard
    ½ cup honey
    ½ cup Lowenbrau beer

Place ham in shallow roasting pan, fat side up. Score the fat. Combine mustard, honey, and Lowenbrau beer. Brush sauce on ham. Cook in 350°F. oven, basting every 10 minutes for 1 hour.

Carving Pork

Properly cooked—it is not necessary to burn the house down—pork is tender and juicy. Onion seasons pork excellently, and apples, sauerkraut or cabbage, and sweet potaotes go particularly well with it.

Crown roast: Carve in the manner of crown roast of lamb (see index).

Loin roast: First, remove the backbone, taking with it as little meat as possible. This can be done in the kitchen, before the roast is brought in, or by the carver. Then set the roast with the bone ends up and the concave side of the ribs facing you. You need only cut down between the ribs, separating the roast into chops for serving.

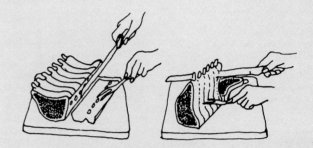

Rolled roast: Carve in the manner of boned-and-rolled shoulder of lamb (see index).

Whole ham: Position the ham on the platter with the fat side up and the shank bone to the carver's right. Anchoring the ham with the carving fork, cut 2 or 3 thin slices off the side nearest you if the ham is from a left leg, away from you if a right leg. Turn ham so that it rests on this cut, flat portion; slice straight down, from the top to the leg bone, making narrow, even cuts. Cut parallel and close to the leg bone beneath the slices to free them for serving.

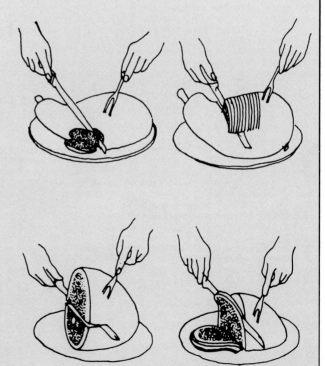

Shank-half ham: Position the meat on the platter so that the shank end is at the carver's left. This puts the thick "cushion" meat on top. Anchor ham with a carving fork; cut along and close to the leg bone. Lift off this all-meat top portion, and carve by cutting straight down through it in thin, even slices. Cut around the bone of the remaining piece; turn so that it rests on its flat side. Cut straight down into thin, even slices.

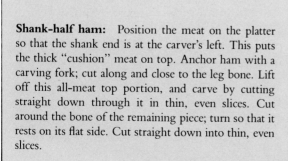

Lots of Lamb

From stately leg of lamb to traditional Irish stew, lamb has graced American tables for generations. Treat your family to great taste and good nutrition with a luscious lamb dish.

Butterflied Leg of Lamb

Makes 10 to 12 servings

- ½ cup lemon juice
- ½ cup vegetable oil
- ¼ cup chopped fresh dill or 2 tablespoons dried dill weed
- 1 large onion, minced
- 3 cloves garlic, minced
- ½ teaspoon freshly ground pepper
- 1 4½-pound boneless leg of lamb
  Cherry tomatoes, lemon wedges, and water-cress

Combine lemon juice, oil, dill, onion, garlic, and pepper in large glass bowl. Add lamb and turn to coat. Cover and refrigerate at least several hours or overnight, turning lamb occasionally. Place rack in third position from bottom in oven. Preheat broiler 3 minutes. Place lamb on broiler pan and broil 20 minutes. Turn lamb and broil 20 to 25 minutes, until lamb is done as desired. Garnish with cherry tomatoes, lemon wedges, and watercress.

Cranberry Shoulder Lamb Chops

Makes 4 servings

- 4 shoulder lamb chops, about ¾ inch thick
- ¼ cup all-purpose flour
- ½ teaspoon salt
  Freshly ground black pepper
- 1 tablespoon salad oil
- 1 clove garlic, halved
- ¾ cup pineapple juice
- 1 cup canned cranberries
- 2 tablespoons sugar
- 1 teaspoon salt
- ¾ teaspoon pepper
- 1 teaspoon Worcestershire sauce

Coat lamb with combined flour, salt, and pepper. Preheat Multi-Cooker Frypan to 360°F. Add oil; when hot, add chops and brown lightly on both sides. Place remaining ingredients plus ½ cup water in Oster Blender. Cover and process at Beat until smooth. Pour over lamb chops in Frypan. Cover and simmer 45 minutes, or until lamb is tender.

Grapefruit Marinade Lamb

Makes 6 to 8 servings

- 1 frozen leg of New Zealand lamb, about 5 pounds, thawed
- 3 cups Florida grapefruit juice
- ½ cup olive oil
- 2 teaspoons dried rosemary, crumbled
- 2 teaspoons dried leaf thyme, crumbled
- 3 cloves garlic, minced
- 1 tablespoon all-purpose flour
  Salt and pepper

With sharp knife, remove "fell" and fat from lamb. In medium bowl, combine grapefruit juice, olive oil, rosemary, thyme, and garlic; mix well. Place lamb in heavy plastic bag just large enough to hold lamb comfortably. Pour marinade over lamb. Press air out of bag. Seal bag. Turn bag to coat lamb with marinade. Refrigerate overnight. To cook, place lamb, meaty side up, on rack in roasting pan. Roast in a 325°F. oven 1 hour and 45 minutes, or until meat thermometer registers 140°F. for rare, 160°F. for medium, 170°F. for well done. Baste with marinade every 30 minutes during roasting. Remove meat to serving platter. Allow to "rest" 10 minutes before serving. Add flour to roasting pan. Stir over medium heat one minute. Gradually stir in remaining 1 to 1¼ cups grapefruit marinade. Cook until thickened. Gravy may be thinned if necessary with water or grapefruit juice. Season to taste.

Rack of Lamb with Truffle Sauce (page 91). Campbell Soup Company

Quick Curry of Lamb

Makes 4 servings

- ¼ cup butter
- ¾ cup finely chopped onions
- 2 tablespoons finely chopped crystallized or preserved ginger
- 2 teaspoons finely chopped fresh mint
- 1 tablespoon curry powder
- 1 can (10½ ounces) Campbell's Condensed Cream of Chicken Soup
- ½ cup grated fresh coconut
- 1 tablespoon lime juice
- ½ cup heavy cream
- 3 cups diced cooked lamb
  Hot cooked rice
  Chutney

In a saucepan, melt butter and sauté onions until golden and tender. Add ginger, mint, curry, soup, coconut, lime juice, and heavy cream. Simmer for 5 minutes, stirring constantly. Stir in lamb and reheat until just bubbly. Spoon curry over hot cooked rice. Serve with chutney.

Greek Lamb Kebabs

Makes 4 servings

- ½ cup tarragon vinegar
- ½ cup olive oil, divided
- ½ teaspoon basil
- 2 cloves garlic, crushed
  Freshly ground pepper
- 1½ pounds boned leg of lamb, cut into 1½-inch cubes
- ½ cup tomato juice
- 2 tablespoons lemon juice
- 2 tablespoons soy sauce
- ½ teaspoon crushed red pepper
- 1 large eggplant, unpeeled, cut into 1-inch cubes
  Rice or wheat pilaf

Combine vinegar, ¼ cup oil, basil, garlic, and pepper to taste. Add lamb and toss to coat. Cover and refrigerate at least 2 hours or overnight. Combine remaining ¼ cup oil, tomato juice, lemon juice, soy sauce, and red pepper. Add eggplant and toss to coat; cover and refrigerate at least 2 hours. Alternate lamb and eggplant on skewers. Broil for 30 minutes; serve hot with rice or wheat pilaf.
Note: Eggplant will be firm and crisp. If softer eggplant is preferred, parboil eggplant cubes in boiling salted water for 5 minutes before placing in marinade.

Spanish Lamb Stew

Makes 6 servings

- 1 tablespoon olive oil
- 2 pounds breast of lamb
- ⅓ cup all-purpose flour
- 1 teaspoon cider vinegar
- 1 bay leaf
- 3½ teaspoons salt
- ¾ cup chopped onion
- ½ cup chopped green pepper
- ½ cup rice
- 1 package (10 ounces) frozen peas, thawed
- 1 can (1 pound 3 ounces) tomatoes
- ½ teaspoon thyme
- 2 eggs
- 1 tablespoon olive oil

Preheat Multi-Cooker Fryer to 350°F.. Add olive oil. Cut lamb into 1½-inch pieces. Dredge lamb in flour and brown. Turn Fryer to R in Simmer. Remove lamb. Drain fat and oil from Fryer and replace lamb. Add vinegar, 3 cups hot water, bay leaf, and salt. Cover and cook about 1½ hours, or until lamb is almost tender. Add onion, green pepper, and rice. Cover; cook 20 minutes. Add peas, tomatoes, and thyme. Cover; cook 10 minutes. Combine eggs and oil; beat with a fork. Add to stew and cook, stirring until slightly thickened.

Irish Stew

Makes 4 servings

- 2 pounds lamb shoulder, cubed
- 2 onions, quartered
- 4 small whole carrots, scraped
- 8 small whole potatoes, peeled
- ½ head cabbage, coarsely shredded
- 3 tablespoons all-purpose flour
  Salt and pepper
- 1 cup hot cooked green peas

Place lamb, onions, and carrots in Multi-Cooker Frypan. Add water to cover. Turn dial to 300°F. and bring to a boil. Turn to first M in Simmer; cook covered, skimming off foam as it appears, until meat is tender. Add potatoes; when they are almost done, add cabbage. Mix flour with a little cold water and add, stirring until thickened. Season to taste. Serve on a hot platter with peas on top.

Leg of Lamb with White Beans

Makes 10 servings
- 1 pound dried navy pea beans
- ¼ cup butter or margarine
- 2 cloves garlic
- 2 pounds onions, thinly sliced
- Seasoned salt
- ½ teaspoon salt
- 1 teaspoon freshly ground pepper
- 1 teaspoon rosemary, divided
- 2 cans (1 pound each) Italian plum tomatoes
- 1 leg of lamb, about 6½ to 7 pounds

Place beans in Multi-Cooker Frypan. Cover with water. Turn dial to 400°F.; bring to a boil. Turn dial to Simmer and cook 2 minutes. Turn dial to Off. Cover and let stand about 1 hour. Turn dial to 300°F. and bring to a boil. Reduce heat to first M of Simmer and cook covered about 1 hour, or until beans are just tender. Check liquid during cooking period, adding water if necessary. Drain beans. Place beans in the bottom of a shallow roasting pan. Preheat oven to 325°F. Preheat Frypan to 300°F. Melt butter in hot Frypan. Crush 1 clove garlic and add to hot butter. Add onions and cook until golden brown, stirring occasionally. Add 2 teaspoons seasoned salt, salt, pepper, ½ teaspoon rosemary, and tomatoes. Blend thoroughly with the onion, then blend with beans in bottom of roasting pan. Split remaining clove of garlic and rub over entire surface of lamb. Sprinkle lamb with seasoned salt and remaining rosemary. Place lamb on top of beans. Insert a meat thermometer into heavy part of leg, being careful that it does not touch the bone. Roast uncovered about 3 hours, or until meat thermometer registers 150°F. Lamb should be slightly pink in the middle. Remove lamb to a carving board. Turn beans into a serving dish. Carve the lamb.

Accompaniments for Lamb
When you make a lamb curry (a perfect use-up for leftover lamb), send it to the table accompanied by halved underripe bananas lightly sautéed in butter, along with small dishes of chopped peanuts and thinly sliced scallions. These curry go-alongs are called sambals, and can be offered in as great a variety as you like. Other sambal ideas: thinly sliced olives, chopped cucumber, chopped hard-cooked egg, chutney (homemade or from a jar), *chilies en escabeche* (small, pickled peppers), anchovy fillets, quartered lemon slices marinated in vinaigrette. The list is virtually endless, and whether you serve 2 or 20, sambals add interest and flavor to a curry meal. Don't forget the rice!

Sherried Lamb Chops

Makes 4 servings
- 4 shoulder lamb chops, ¾ to 1 inch thick
- Salt and pepper
- ¼ cup salad oil
- 1 clove garlic
- ½ cup sherry
- 1 beef bouillon cube
- 8 small white onions, peeled
- 6 carrots, peeled and cut into chunks
- 4 small potatoes, peeled and halved

Sprinkle chops on both sides with salt and pepper. Preheat Multi-Cooker Frypan to 360°F. Add oil and garlic, and heat. Add chops and brown on both sides; remove garlic. Add sherry, ½ cup hot water, and bouillon cube. Cover, lower heat to Simmer, and cook 30 minutes. Add onions, carrots, and potatoes. Sprinkle lightly with salt and pepper. Cover and simmer 20 to 30 minutes, or until chops and vegetables are tender.

Selection of Lamb
Many Americans who do eat lamb never venture beyond a leg to roast, or loin or rib chops to broil, but there are many other possibilities.
Shanks: Meaty and tender, these can be roasted, but are at their juicy, flavorful best when oven-braised with vegetables in a small amount of liquid.
Chops: There are sirloin, loin, rib, and blade and arm shoulder chops to choose among; all can be broiled, but like the shank, meaty shoulder chops are best braised. There are also boneless chops, from the inside shoulder muscle.
Roasts: Leg of lamb can be purchased whole or, for smaller families, as the shank or butt half. There are also loin roasts, rib roasts (the elegant rack of lamb that many excellent restaurants feature), shoulder roasts, and boned shoulder (rolled, or with a pocket to accommodate a savory stuffing).
Steaks: The sirloin steak—because lamb is so small an animal—is usually considered a chop. Leg steaks are cut from the center of the leg when it is divided into two roasts.
Breast: The breast can be boned and rolled, or the breast bone removed to form a pocket for stuffing. Or the section may be cut into tasty lamb riblets.
And more: Ground lamb is available to serve as relief-from-beef patties, or to use in casseroles and for stuffing vegetables such as eggplant and peppers. Lamb stew meat, bone-in or boneless, is often cut from the neck and shoulders, but can come from any part of the carcass. And, of course, lamb supplies all the variety meats—brains, heart, kidneys, liver, sweetbreads, and tongue—for many kinds of good main dishes.

Lamb Kebabs. Anderson Clayton Foods

Lamb Kebabs

Makes 6 servings
- 2 cups Seven Seas Buttermilk Recipe Country Spice™ dressing
- ½ cup chopped onion
- 1½ teaspoons rosemary
- 1½ pounds lamb chunks, cut in 1½-inch squares
- 3 small tomatoes, cut in quarters
- 3 small onions, cut in quarters
- 12 large fresh mushroom caps
  Olive oil
- 4 cups cooked spinach noodles (4 ounces uncooked)

Combine dressing with chopped onion and rosemary. In a glass or enameled dish, place lamb chunks, tomatoes, and onion quarters. Pour dressing over all and marinate at least 1 hour or up to 1 day. Sauté mushroom caps briefly in olive oil and set aside. Thread meat and vegetables alternately on skewer and broil in oven or over charcoal. Serve over spinach noodles tossed with more dressing.

Crusted Rack of Lamb

Makes 4 to 6 servings
- 2 racks of lamb (about 2½ to 3 pounds each), ribs partially split
  Salt and pepper
- 1 garlic clove, cut in half
- 2 medium carrots, diced
- 2 celery ribs, diced
- 2 small onions, diced
- 2 garlic cloves, minced
- ¼ cup butter or margarine
- ½ cup dry bread crumbs
- 4 cups beef broth or stock
- 1 tablespoon tomato paste
- 2 bay leaves
- 1 teaspoon dried rosemary
- 1 tablespoon cornstarch

You will need: Corning Ware 12¼x10¼x2¼-inch open roaster; Corning Ware Menu-ette 6½-inch skillet

Trim excess fat from lamb. Rub lamb all over with salt, pepper, and halved garlic. Place in roaster, fat side up; surround with carrots, celery, onions, and minced garlic. Roast in 350°F. oven until meat is slightly under degree of doneness you prefer (25 to 30 minutes per pound for medium lamb). Meanwhile, melt butter in skillet. Add crumbs; toss over medium heat until lightly browned. Remove meat from oven; spread crumb mixture over fat side. Return to oven 5 minutes. Remove lamb from roaster; keep warm. Discard fat in roaster, then simmer vegetables over medium heat 10 minutes. Stir in broth, tomato paste, bay leaves, and rosemary. Bring to a boil. Reduce heat; simmer 10 minutes. Dissolve cornstarch in ¼ cup water, stirring until smooth. Add gradually to broth mixture, stirring constantly. Cook 5 minutes over low heat. Strain sauce into gravy dish.

Lamb 'n' Peaches Delight

Makes about 8 servings
- 2 tablespoons oil
- 2 pounds lamb cubes (about 1½-inch cubes)
- 1 can (16 ounces) sliced peaches, drained (reserve syrup)
- 2 envelopes Lipton Onion-Mushroom Recipe Soup Mix
- 1 teaspoon crushed mint flakes

In large skillet, heat oil and brown lamb; drain. Mix reserved syrup with enough water to equal 1¾ cups; blend in Lipton Onion-Mushroom Recipe Soup Mix and mint and add to skillet. Bring to a boil, then simmer covered 40 minutes; add peaches and simmer an additional 5 minutes.

Danish Roast Leg of Lamb (page 93). Campbell Soup Company

Savory Lamb Chops

Makes 4 servings

- 4 shoulder lamb chops, 1 inch thick
  Salt and pepper
- 2 tablespoons olive oil
- ¼ cup chopped onion
- ½ cup sliced carrots
- 1 cup peeled, quartered tomatoes
- ⅓ cup dry sherry
- 1 cup sliced mushrooms
- 2 tablespoons butter

Sprinkle chops with salt and pepper. Heat Multi-Cooker Frypan to 340°F. Brown the chops in the oil with the onions. Add carrots, tomatoes, and sherry. Turn dial to Simmer. Cover and cook 1 hour, or until tender. In a small skillet, sauté mushrooms in butter. Add to chops; cook 5 minutes longer.

Mandarin Lamb Shanks

Makes 6 servings

- 1 tablespoon salad oil
- 6 lamb shanks
  Salt and pepper
- 1 can (10½ ounces) condensed beef broth
- 1 cup uncooked rice
- 1 can (11 ounces) mandarin orange sections

Heat Multi-Cooker Frypan to 360°F. Heat oil. Add lamb shanks and brown well on all sides. Season with salt and pepper. Add 1 cup water. Cover and simmer 1½ hours. Remove lamb shanks. Pour liquid in pan into a measuring cup. Skim off fat from top. Add enough water to make 1 cup liquid. Pour into Frypan. Add beef broth, salt, and rice. Return lamb shanks to Frypan. Cover and simmer 25 minutes, or until rice is almost tender. Stir in undrained orange sections and simmer 5 to 10 minutes, or until rice is tender. Serve chops and rice piping hot.

Fruited Glazed Lamb Shanks

Makes 4 servings

- 4 lamb shanks, about 1 pound each
  Salt and pepper
- 2 tablespoons oil
- 1 can (16 ounces) fruit cocktail, drained (reserve syrup)
- 2 envelopes Lipton Onion Cup-a-Soup
- 2 cloves garlic, finely chopped
- 1¼ teaspoons crushed mint flakes
- ¾ cup Wish-Bone Russian Dressing

Season lamb with salt and pepper. In large skillet, heat oil and brown lamb shanks on all sides. Stir in reserved syrup with enough water to equal 1½ cups, Lipton Onion Cup-a-Soup, garlic, mint, and Wish-Bone Russian Dressing. Simmer covered over very low heat 1½ hours, or until lamb is tender. Add fruit cocktail and heat through.

Lamb Cashew Curry with Rice

Makes 6 servings

- 1 tablespoon cooking oil
- 1½ pounds boneless lamb cubes (about 1 inch)
- 2 medium onions, chopped
- 1 clove garlic, minced
- 1 tablespoon all-purpose flour
- 1½ teaspoons salt
- 1½ teaspoons tumeric
- 1½ teaspoons ground cumin seed
- ¼ teaspoon ground nutmeg
- 1 bay leaf
- 1½ cups apple juice
- 1 cup Uncle Ben's® Converted® Brand Rice
  Chopped salted cashews

Heat oil in 10-inch skillet. Add lamb; brown well on all sides. Add onions and garlic; stir well. Sprinkle with flour, salt, tumeric, cumin seed, and nutmeg; stir. Add bay leaf and apple juice. Cover and cook over low heat until meat is tender, about 1½ hours, stirring several times. Discard by leaf. Meanwhile, cook rice according to package directions. Serve with lamb and sprinkle with cashews.

Savory Lamb Casserole

Makes 4 to 6 servings

- 1 large onion, sliced
- 1 pound lean ground lamb or beef
- ⅔ cup medium-size precooked couscous, divided
- 1 can (10½ ounces) condensed chicken or beef broth, divided
- 1 teaspoon salt, divided
- ¼ teaspoon freshly ground pepper
- 3 tomatoes, diced
- 3 cups diced eggplant or zucchini
- ½ teaspoon coriander
- 1 small hot pepper, seeded and chopped
- 1 clove garlic, minced
- 1 small acorn squash, peeled, seeded, and cut into strips

Scatter onion in 3-quart casserole. Combine lamb, 2 tablespoons couscous, ⅓ cup chicken broth, ½ teaspoon salt, and pepper. Shape into 1-inch balls. Place over onion. Add remaining couscous, tomatoes, and eggplant. Combine remaining broth, coriander, hot pepper, garlic, and remaining ½ teaspoon salt. Pour over ingredients in casserole. Top with squash and cover. Bake at 375°F. for 1 hour and 30 minutes, or until vegetables are tender.

Londonderry Lamb Skillet

Makes about 4 servings

  2 pounds lamb riblets, cut into serving pieces
  1 envelope Lipton Onion-Mushroom or Onion Soup Mix
1½ cups water
  ½ teaspoon garlic salt
  ½ teaspoon pepper
  1 can (8½ ounces) peas, drained
  2 tablespoons diced pimiento

In medium skillet, brown lamb riblets; drain. Add Lipton Onion-Mushroom Soup Mix blended with water, garlic salt, and pepper; simmer covered 20 minutes. Add peas and pimiento; cook covered an additional 10 minutes, or until lamb riblets are tender.

Stuffed Crown Roast of Lamb

Makes 6 to 8 servings

  1 12- to 16-rib crown lamb roast (6 to 8 pounds)
  Salt and pepper
  Apple-Prune Stuffing (recipe follows)

Heat oven to 325°F. Wrap rib ends of roast with aluminum foil to prevent charring. Season meat with salt and pepper. Place roast, bone ends up, on rack in roasting pan. Spoon Apple-Prune Stuffing into center. Insert meat thermometer between ribs into center of thickest part of meat. Roast until thermometer registers 175°F. for medium done or 180°F. for well done (it will take about 35 to 40 minutes per pound). If you prefer lamb slightly pink, roast only until thermometer registers 170°F. Baste top of stuffing occasionally with pan juices. When roast is done, place on heated platter. Remove aluminum foil from ribs; top each rib with paper frill, if desired.

Note: Cover stuffing with aluminum foil if it begins to overbrown.

Apple-Prune Stuffing

Makes 4 servings

 12 slices bread
  2 large tart apples, pared, quartered, and cored
  1 cup stewed pitted prunes
  2 tablespoons liquid from prunes
  ¼ cup melted butter or margarine
  ½ teaspoon salt
  ½ teaspoon dried marjoram
  ½ teaspoon dried thyme

Tear 2 slices bread into blender container. Cover; blend at medium speed until coarsely crumbed. Empty into mixing bowl. Repeat process with remaining bread. Cut apple quarters into thirds. Put pieces into blender container. Add water to cover. Cover; blend at medium speed just until apples are chopped. Drain thoroughly in colander. Put remaining ingredients in blender container in order listed. Cover; blend at medium speed just until prunes are chopped. Add to bread crumbs, add apples, mix well.

Lamb Know-how

All lamb is sufficiently tender so that even the cuts usually braised are ready to eat in a much shorter time than, say, the less tender cuts of beef.

Wherever there is room for a difference of opinion, you can count on one to occur: There is considerable controversy among lovers of lamb as to whether the meat should be served rare, medium, or well done. There are fewer advocates of blood-rare lamb than there are of beef in the same condition, but most knowing lamb eaters cook or order the meat "pink"—medium, that is. Cook leg, loin, and shoulder roasts rare in a 300° to 325°F. oven to an internal (meat thermometer) temperature of 140°F.; the meat is medium—the desirable pink—at 160°, and well done at 175°. If the roast is frozen it need not be thawed, but one-third to one-half again the roasting time will be required.

Like beef, lamb roast will be juicier and more flavorful and will carve better if allowed to "rest" for 15 to 20 minutes after being removed from the oven. The parchmentlike fell, which covers the outer fat on lamb, should be left in place on roasts (it helps retain the juices) but removed from other cuts.

Lamb chops an inch or more thick can be broiled; those less than an inch are better panbroiled. This holds true for rib, loin, shoulder, sirloin, and leg chops—the last two often called steaks. These, too, can be served rare, medium or well done, although shoulder chops—more often braised, though they can be broiled or panfried—are generally served well done.

Because it is both tender and juicy, lamb lends itself well to cookouts. Boned and rolled legs and shoulders are ideal for spit-roasting, while thick chops and ground-lamb patties cook beautifully on the grill. A butterflied leg—boned, but not rolled—grill-cooks in a brief time; baste with lemon butter or with a combination of oil, dry vermouth, and summer savory. Cubes of boneless leg or shoulder, marinated in garlic-flavored oil and lemon juice, make great kebabs. Skewer with mushroom caps, cherry tomatoes, and squares of green pepper, and cook on the grill (or under the broiler).

Saddle of Lamb Marie Louise. Campbell Soup Company

Rack of Lamb with Truffle Sauce

Makes 4 servings
- 1 rack of lamb, about 4 pounds
- Salt and pepper
- Crumbled rosemary
- 4 medium Idaho potatoes
- ¼ cup butter
- 1 can (⅞ ounce) truffles
- ⅓ cup white wine
- 1 can (10½ ounces) Campbell's Condensed Beef Broth
- 2 tablespoons all-purpose flour mixed with ¼ cup water

Sprinkle lamb with salt, pepper, and crumbled rosemary. Roast on a rack in a shallow pan in a preheated 350°F. oven for 1 hour, or until lamb is just done. Slice potatoes very thinly and dry well. Melt butter in a large skillet. Arrange slices of potato in skillet in layers. Slice half the truffles and add to the potatoes. Cook until brown on one side, turn and brown on other side. In another skillet, combine remaining truffles, which have been chopped, white wine, and beef broth. Stir flour mixture into broth. Cook over low heat, stirring constantly, until sauce bubbles and thickens. Carve lamb into slices. Serve slices of lamb with hot sauce and potatoes.

Savory Leg of Lamb

Makes 8 to 10 servings
- 1 leg of lamb, 5 to 6 pounds
- 1 cup dry white wine
- 1 medium onion, cut up
- ⅔ cup olive oil
- 1 clove garlic, halved
- Thin strip lemon rind
- ½ teaspoon dried rosemary
- ½ teaspoon dried thyme
- ½ teaspoon salt
- ¼ teaspoon pepper

Place meat in deep glass or enamel baking dish. Put remaining ingredients into blender container in order listed. Cover; blend at medium speed until onion is finely chopped. Pour over meat. Cover; refrigerate at least 24 hours, turning meat occasionally. Heat oven to 450°F. Lift meat from marinade; let drain. Place lamb, fat side up, on rack in shallow roasting pan. Insert meat thermometer into thickest part of meat. Roast 15 minutes. Reduce oven temperature to 350°F. Pour marinade over meat. Roast until meat thermometer registers 170°F. for slightly rare, 175°F. for medium done, or 180°F. for well done. Baste roast frequently with marinade while cooking. Add a few tablespoons boiling water to pan during roasting if juices cook down too quickly.

Saddle of Lamb Marie Louise

Makes 6 servings
- 1 saddle of lamb, 4 to 5 pounds (7 to 8 pounds untrimmed)
- Salt and pepper, crumbled thyme, bay leaf, and tarragon
- 1 onion, chopped
- 1 cup Marsala
- 1 can (10½ ounces) Campbell's Condensed Beef Broth
- 1 can (10¾ ounces) Campbell's Condensed Tomato Soup
- 2 packages (9 ounces each) frozen artichoke hearts
- 1 cup button mushrooms, stems removed
- 12 small new potatoes, cooked
- ¾ cup butter or margarine
- 3 tomatoes, cut into halves
- ¼ cup grated Parmesan cheese
- 1 can (20 ounces) celery hearts
- Parsley

Trim saddle of lamb, removing skin, fat, and kidneys. Sprinkle meat with salt and pepper. Rub meat with crumbled herbs. Shape meat into a round piece and roast in a shallow pan on a rack in a preheated 450°F. oven for 35 to 45 minutes (lamb will be pink in the French manner). Remove lamb to a platter and keep warm. Drain excess fat from roasting pan. Add onion, Marsala, and beef broth to pan. Cook on top of range, scraping all particles. Bring to a boil and boil gently until liquid is half its original volume. Stir in tomato soup. Simmer until sauce is thickened. Sauté thawed artichoke hearts, mushrooms, and potatoes in ½ cup of the butter until golden. Sprinkle tomatoes with salt and pepper. Dot with remaining butter and broil until tomatoes are easily pierced. In small pan, heat celery hearts in broth from can. Drain, sprinkle with grated Parmesan cheese. Serve lamb on a platter surrounded by artichoke hearts, button mushrooms, potatoes, tomatoes, celery hearts. Garnish with parsley.

Q. *What is that dry, thin, papery covering on a leg of lamb? Should I cut it off or leave it in place?*
A. That parchmentlike membrane is called the "fell." It covers the exterior fat on all cuts of lamb, but is usually removed from all but the leg before the lamb is sold retail. The fell protects the meat, keeping the wholesale cuts fresh. The flavor of the lamb is not affected whether the fell is left in place or removed. However, if you are going to marinate the leg of lamb, it is best to cut away the fell or it will keep the marinade ingredients from penetrating the meat.

Stuffed Shoulder of Lamb

Makes 6 to 8 servings

  1 3- to 4-pound lamb shoulder roast with pocket
  1 teaspoon salt
⅛ teaspoon pepper
⅓ cup *each* diced celery and onion
  3 tablespoons butter or margarine
½ cup soft bread crumbs
¼ cup raisins
  1 teaspoon oregano
  1 clove garlic, crushed
  1 can (8 ounces) Hunt's Tomato Sauce

Sprinkle roast with salt and pepper. Cook celery and onion in butter in small skillet until transparent. Add bread crumbs and raisins; toss lightly. Stir oregano and garlic into Hunt's Sauce; add ⅓ cup to stuffing mixture. Use to fill pocket in roast; seal open edges with skewers or tie with twine. Roast on rack in shallow pan at 325°F. for 2 hours. Drain excess fat. Pour remaining Hunt's Sauce mixture over roast. Roast 30 to 40 minutes longer; baste often.

Note: For easier carving, have your butcher remove the blade bone from roast.

Chef Gérard Special Potted Lamb

Makes 6 servings

  1 boneless leg of lamb, about 3 pounds
¼ cup butter
  1 can (10½ ounces) Campbell's Condensed French Onion Soup
  1 can (11 ounces) Campbell's Condensed Bisque of Tomato Soup
  2 teaspoons caraway seed
  2 tablespoons chopped parsley
½ cup water

Brown lamb in butter in a Dutch oven on all sides. Add remaining ingredients, cover, and simmer for 1½ to 2 hours, or until lamb is tender. Stir occasionally and turn meat in sauce. Skim excess fat. Slice meat and serve with pan juices.

Carving Lamb

Young lamb (and most all available to us is young) is tender and juicy. Only roasts need carving; steaks—cross-cut slices of the leg—and chops are single-serving items.

Crown roast: The butcher who prepared the roast will have done all the hard work, making this the easiest of roasts to carve. It should be placed on the platter with the bone-ends up. All you need to do is steady it with the carving fork and use the knife to slice down through the ribs, cutting it into servings that are, in effect, chops. If the roast has been stuffed, add a spoonful of stuffing to each serving.

Leg of lamb, American style: Place the lamb on the platter with the leg bone to the carver's right. From the thin side of the leg, facing you, cut three thin lengthwise slices. Turn the roast so that it stands on this flat, cut surface. Starting at the point where the shank joins the thigh portion, cut ¼-inch slices perpendicular to the leg bone. Then loosen the slices by cutting under them, along the top of the leg bone.

Leg of lamb, French style: This is very simple, and more or less harks back to the Middle Ages carver. Hold the end of the leg bone with your hand, lifting it a little off the platter. Cut thin slices parallel to the leg bone.

Boned-and-rolled shoulder: Place the roast flat on the platter. Anchor with the carving fork, and cut neat, even, round slices, as if you were slicing bread.

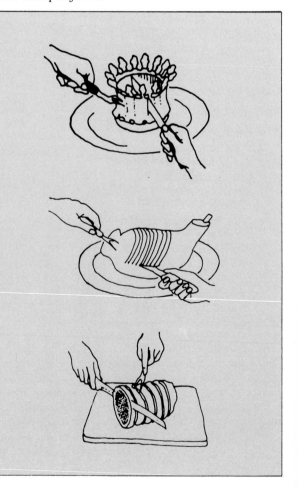

Braised Lamb Shanks Continental

Makes 4 servings
- 4 lamb shanks
- 1 clove garlic, slivered
- ¼ cup pure vegetable oil
- Salt and pepper
- 1 can (8 ounces) Hunt's Tomato Sauce with Onions
- ½ cup dry white wine
- ¼ cup water
- 1 tablespoon Worcestershire sauce
- 1 tablespoon firmly packed brown sugar
- ½ teaspoon basil
- Chopped parsley

With a sharp knife, cut several deep slits into meaty part of each lamb shank; insert slivers of garlic. Brown shanks lightly on all sides in oil in large skillet; drain excess fat. Sprinkle shanks on all sides with salt and pepper. Combine remaining ingredients, except parsley; pour over browned shanks. Cover; simmer gently about 1½ hours until fork-tender. Turn once or twice during cooking. Skim excess fat, if necessary. Sprinkle with parsley just before serving.

Braised Shoulder Chops

Makes 6 servings
- 2 tablespoons vegetable oil
- 6 shoulder lamb chops (about 2¼ pounds)
- 1 large onion, sliced
- 1 green pepper, seeded and sliced
- 1 clove garlic, minced
- 1 can (16 ounces) tomatoes, cut up (reserve liquid)
- 1 apple, cored and diced
- ½ cup raisins
- 4 to 5 teaspoons curry powder, or to taste
- 1 teaspoon salt
- Toasted sliced almonds
- Hot cooked rice (optional)

Heat oil in skillet. Brown chops lightly on both sides. Place in shallow casserole. Sauté onion, green pepper, and garlic in drippings in skillet. Spoon over chops. Combine tomatoes with liquid, apple, raisins, curry powder, and salt. Spoon over chops and vegetables; cover. Bake at 325°F. 2 hours, or until chops are tender. Check occasionally and add a little more liquid, if needed. Sprinkle with almonds and serve over hot rice, if desired.

Danish Roast Leg of Lamb

Makes 6 to 8 servings
- 1 leg of lamb, 6 to 8 pounds
- ½ pound salt pork
- Parsley sprigs
- 1 large head cauliflower
- 16 asparagus spears
- 1 pound small new potatoes, peeled
- ¼ cup butter
- 2 tablespoons sugar
- 1 can (10½ ounces) Campbell's Condensed Cream of Celery Soup
- 2 tablespoons lemon juice
- 2 tablespoons butter

Make about 6 slits in lamb. Stuff slits with small pieces of salt pork and parsley sprigs. Roast on a rack in a shallow pan in a preheated 325°F. oven for 3 to 4 hours for well-done lamb. Cook cauliflower, asparagus, and potatoes separately until tender. Heat butter and sugar in a skillet until mixture bubbles. Add well-drained new potatoes and keep turning over low heat until potatoes are richly browned. For sauce, whirl soup and lemon juice in a blender or press through a sieve. Add butter and simmer until hot. When meat is cooked, place on a large platter. Surround with vegetables. Spoon the hot sauce over the cauliflower and asparagus.

Larding

This procedure accounts for the fact that pot roasts in France are so much better—more juicily succulent—than they are in this country. Inserting long strips of fat into meat across the grain is called larding, a ploy that almost immeasurably increases the flavor, tenderness, and juiciness of the meat.

This requires a larding needle, obtainable at most hardware or housewares stores. It is a long metal device rather like a knitting needle, pointed at one end and with a gripper at the other to secure the lardoons—the long, thin strips of fat. Larding is not at all difficult to do, and once you've tried it, the improvement of the meat will be so great you'll kick yourself for not learning how long ago. Improve flavor even further by soaking the lardoons in brandy, then rolling them before using in a mixture of salt, pepper, finely chopped parsley, and a pinch of ground cloves.

A Variety of Veal

That tenderest of meats, veal, offers a taste and texture that are renowned. Although a little more expensive, veal goes a long way toward providing healthy and delicious dining.

Veal Ragout

Makes 6 servings
- 1½ pound veal shoulder roast boneless
- ½ cup diced onion
- 4 tablespoons butter or margarine, divided
- ½ teaspoon salt
- ⅛ teaspoon pepper
- 2¼ cups chicken broth, divided
- ½ cup diced carrots
- 1 stalk celery, sliced
- ½ medium green bell pepper, cut in thin strips
- ½ pound mushrooms, sliced
  Fresh parsley
- 2 tablespoons flour

Cut meat into 1-inch cubes. Sauté onion in dutch oven, in 2 tablespoons butter until soft but not browned. Add meat and sauté. Sprinkle with salt and pepper. Add 2 cups chicken broth, carrots, celery, green pepper, mushrooms, and 1 sprig parsley. Simmer, covered, for about 25 minutes or until veal is almost tender. In small saucepan, heat remaining butter and stir in flour until smooth. Stir in remaining chicken broth gradually. Add to veal and simmer until sauce is thickened. Garnish with chopped parsley and serve over rice.

Veal Normande

Makes 4 to 6 servings
- 1½ pounds veal cutlet
- 3 tablespoons butter or margarine
- 3 tablespoons brandy
- 1 can (10½ ounces) Campbell's Condensed Cream of Mushroom Soup
- ⅔ cup milk
- 1 apple, peeled and thickly sliced
  Cooked rice

Pound veal with meat hammer or edge of heavy saucer. In large skillet, brown veal in butter; remove from pan. Add brandy; stir to loosen browned bits. Stir in soup and milk. Add veal and apple; cook over low heat until tender, stirring occasionally. Serve with rice.

Veal and Peppers

Makes 4 to 6 servings
- 1½ pound veal for stew
- 2 tablespoons olive oil
- 3 tablespoons butter or margarine
- 1 large onion, sliced
- 4 large green bell peppers, cut in strips
- ⅔ cup dry white wine
- 1 can (16 ounces) stewed tomatoes
  Salt and pepper to taste

Brown veal in combination of olive oil and butter in large skillet. Remove and set aside. Sauté onion and green pepper in remaining oil and butter until soft but not browned. Remove and reserve. Drain off fat. Add wine to skillet and scrape up particles. Return meat, onion, and pepper to skillet. Add tomatoes and season with salt and pepper. Cover and simmer 20 minutes, or until meat is tender.

Veal Italienne

Makes 4 servings

    8 very thin veal cutlets
    4 thin slices Gruyère or Swiss cheese
    4 thin slices prosciutto
       Salt
       Freshly ground black pepper
       All-purpose flour
    2 tablespoons butter or margarine
    3 tablespoons olive oil
    ½ cup dry white wine
    ½ cup chicken bouillon

Place veal slices between 2 pieces of aluminum foil. Pound until very thin with the flat side of a cleaver. Place a slice of cheese and a slice of prosciutto on 4 pieces of veal. Top with remaining 4 slices of veal. Press edges of veal together to seal, or fasten securely with toothpicks. Season with salt and pepper. Dip in flour and shake off excess. Preheat Multi-Cooker Frypan to 380°F. Melt butter and oil in hot Frypan. Add veal and cook 2 or more at a time, turning gently until well browned on both sides. Remove veal to a heated serving platter. Discard most of fat from Frypan, leaving a thin film on the bottom. Pour in wine and bouillon and bring to a boil, stirring up any browned bits of veal on bottom. Return veal to Frypan. Reduce heat to Simmer. Cover and cook about 20 minutes, or until veal is tender. Turn veal over once during cooking period. Remove veal to a heated serving platter and pour sauce over the top.

Braised Shoulder of Veal

Makes 4 to 6 servings

    4 pounds veal shoulder
    2 cloves garlic, thinly sliced
    ¼ cup butter or margarine
    1 teaspoon salt
    1 teaspoon freshly ground pepper
    1 cup bouillon
    1 cup dry white wine
    1 teaspoon tarragon
    1 whole medium onion
    ½ bay leaf

Have butcher bone, roll, and tie veal shoulder. Be sure to take the bones with the meat. Make small incisions in the veal with a sharp knife and insert thin slivers of garlic. Preheat Multi-Cooker Frypan to 300°F. Melt butter. Add veal and brown well on all sides, turning often. Sprinkle with salt and pepper.

Add bouillon, white wine, tarragon, onion, and bay leaf. Add the veal bones. Cover and reduce heat to Simmer. Simmer gently about 2 hours, or until veal is tender. Remove veal to a hot serving platter. Remove strings and slice. Skim fat from juices in Frypan. Discard onion, bay leaf, and bones. Serve sauce with veal.

Veal Chops Marsala

Makes about 4 servings

    ½ cup Wish-Bone Italian Dressing
    4 veal chops (about 2 pounds), ¾ inch thick
    ¼ cup all-purpose flour
    ¼ pound mushrooms, sliced
    ¼ cup Marsala

In large shallow baking dish, pour Wish-Bone Italian Dressing over veal chops. Cover and marinate in refrigerator, turning occasionally, at least 3 hours. Remove chops, reserving marinade; coat chops with flour. In large skillet, heat 2 tablespoons marinade and brown chops; add remaining marinade and mushrooms. Simmer covered, stirring occasionally, 15 minutes. Add wine; simmer covered an additional 5 minutes, or until chops are tender.

Providential Veal au Gratin

Makes 4 servings

    1 pound boneless veal shoulder, cut in 1-inch
         pieces
    1 clove garlic, mashed
    1 teaspoon paprika
    ½ teaspoon thyme
    ¼ cup butter, at room temperature
    1 can (14½ ounces) asparagus spears, drained
    2 cups unseasoned croutons
    1 cup milk
    2 tablespoons all-purpose flour
    1 cup cheddar cheese cubes (1-inch)
    ¼ teaspoon salt
    ¼ teaspoon pepper
    ½ cup slivered almonds

Toss veal pieces with garlic, paprika, and thyme. Assemble Food Grinder with fine disc and small bowl. Grind seasoned veal. Shape veal into 4 patties. Melt 2 tablespoons butter in a large skillet over medium-high heat. Add patties and brown well on both sides. Cover skillet, reduce heat to medium-low, and cook until veal is done. Arrange asparagus spears in an 8x8x2-inch baking pan. Sprinkle with croutons. Top with the veal patties. Assemble blender. Put remaining butter, milk, flour, cheese, salt, and pepper into blender container. Cover and process at Chop until the cheese is finely chopped. Pour into a 2-quart saucepan and cook over medium-low heat, stirring constantly, until cheese is melted and sauce begins to thicken. Pour over meat and asparagus. Garnish patties with almonds. Bake at 350°F. for 30 minutes.

Veal Birds

Makes 6 servings

     6 slices veal for scallopini (1½ pounds)
     4 slices bread
     1 medium onion, cut up
     ½ teaspoon salt
     ¼ teaspoon pepper
     4 sprigs parsley
     ¼ cup melted butter or margarine
     1 can (10½ ounces) condensed beef broth
        All-purpose flour
     ¼ cup butter or margarine
     ½ teaspoon dried thyme
     ½ teaspoon dried oregano
     1 tablespoon all-purpose flour
     ½ cup water

Pound veal slices to ¼-inch thickness. Set aside. Tear two slices bread into blender container; add onion. Cover; blend at medium speed until onion is chopped. Empty into bowl. Tear remaining two slices bread into blender container; add salt, pepper, and parsley. Cover; blend at medium speed until bread is crumbed. Add to onion mixture. Stir in melted butter and ¼ cup beef broth. Divide mixture evenly among veal slices; roll up; tie with clean string in several places to hold together. Roll in flour; shake off excess. Heat ¼ cup butter in skillet; brown birds well on all sides; remove; keep warm. Stir thyme, oregano, and 1 tablespoon flour into fat in skillet. Add water and remaining beef broth. Stir to loosen browned bits on sides of pan; stir rapidly over medium heat until thickened and bubbly. Return birds to skillet. Cover; simmer over low heat 10 minutes. Snip string carefully from each bird.

Cold Veal with Tuna Sauce

Makes 8 servings

     2 or 3 tablespoons olive oil
     3 pounds boneless rolled leg or rump of veal
     2 medium carrots, pared and cut up
     2 stalks celery, cut up
     1 medium onion, cut up
     3 sprigs parsley
     1 clove garlic, halved
     2 bay leaves
     2 whole peppercorns
        Pinch dried thyme
     1 can (2 ounces) flat anchovy fillets, drained
     1 can (6½ or 7 ounces) tuna, drained and flaked
    1¼ cups dry white wine
     2 tablespoons capers, drained
     1 cup mayonnaise
        Capers and chopped parsley (optional)

Heat 2 tablespoons oil in Dutch oven. Add veal; brown lightly on all sides. Put carrots, celery, onion, parsley, and garlic into blender container. Add cold water to cover vegetables. Cover; blend at medium speed just until vegetables are chopped. Drain thoroughly in colander. Add to veal; cook about 10 minutes, stirring occasionally, until vegetables are tender. Add an additional tablespoon olive oil if necessary. Add bay leaves, peppercorns, thyme, anchovies, tuna, and wine. Cover; simmer 1¾ to 2 hours, or until veal is tender. Remove meat from Dutch oven; cool; wrap in aluminum foil; refrigerate. Measure sauce; if necessary, return sauce to pan and boil rapidly until reduced to 3 cups. Discard bay leaves and peppercorns. Chill sauce. When ready to serve, pour sauce into blender container; add 2 tablespoons capers and mayonnaise. Cover; blend at high speed until smooth. Slice veal; serve with sauce. Garnish with additional capers and chopped parsley, if desired.

Veal Know-how

Veal requires coddling. Cook it slowly and gently, whether by dry or moist heat. Roast veal at 300° to 325°F. (the lower temperature is preferable) until its interior temperature reaches 170°F. on a meat thermometer. If you braise veal or cook it in liquid, it will require a considerably shorter time than other meats. It is done when fork tender—don't cook it to death.

Cook stewing veal in liquid with a bay leaf (remove after 30 minutes), an onion stuck with three whole cloves, two diced ribs of celery, one whole sliced carrot, and a veal knuckle bone (ask the butcher). When it is very tender, remove veal and bone, strain stock, and boil it down until it is reduced by half. Shred the cooked veal into a loaf pan and pour the stock over, just to cover the meat. Cover, weight, and refrigerate— tomorrow, pressed veal for dinner.

Or stuff a breast of veal with well-seasoned cooked rice and peas; roast or braise. Or cook a veal roast; when cold, slice in ½-inch cuts, spread each slice with Duxelles, then a thick purée of cooked onions; reassemble the roast—it is now Veal Prince Orloff—for serving.

Freezing veal: Properly wrapped, all raw veal other than ground can be freezer-stored at 0°F. or lower up to 7 months; ground, up to 3 months. Cooked veal in a sauce or gravy may br freezer-stored up to 3 months.

Rosemary Veal Roast. Caloric Corporation

Deviled Veal Cutlets

Makes 4 servings
- 1 pound veal cutlets
- 2 tablespoons all-purpose flour
- ¾ teaspoon salt
- ¼ teaspoon pepper
- 2 tablespoons butter or margarine
- 1 carrot, pared and cut up
- 1½ cups water
- 1 stalk celery, cut up
- 1 medium onion, cut up
- 2 teaspoons prepared horseradish
- 1 teaspoon prepared mustard
- ½ cup plain yogurt

Pound cutlets to ¼-inch thickness; cut into serving-size pieces. Dredge pieces in mixture of flour, salt, and pepper; reserve remaining flour mixture. Heat butter in large skillet; add veal and brown well on all sides. Put carrot, celery, onion, and water into blender container. Cover; blend at medium speed just until vegetables are chopped. Add to veal in skillet; cover; simmer 25 minutes. Put horseradish, mustard, yogurt, and reserved flour mixture into blender container. Cover; blend at high speed until smooth. Pour into skillet with veal. Cook, stirring constantly, until thickened.

Rosemary Veal Roast

Makes 6 to 8 servings
- 2½ pounds boneless veal roast
- 3 cloves garlic, slivered
- 1 tablespoon butter or margarine
- 1 tablespoon vegetable oil
- 1 onion, sliced
- 1 can (16 ounces) tomatoes, cut up
- 1 cup chicken broth
- 2 teaspoons paprika
- ½ teaspoon rosemary
- 1½ teaspoons salt

Cut slits in roast with sharp knife. Insert garlic slivers in slits. Heat butter and oil in skillet and brown roast on all sides. Place roast in 2½-quart casserole. Sauté onion in drippings in skillet until transparent. Spoon over roast. Combine tomatoes, chicken broth, paprika, rosemary, and salt. Pour over roast. Add bay leaf. Cover casserole. Bake at 325°F. 1½ to 2 hours until internal temperature reaches 170°F. and roast is tender. Let stand 5 minutes before carving. Discard bay leaf. Serve with tomato mixture spooned over roast.

Stuffed Breast of Veal

Makes 6 servings

   1 **breast of veal with pocket (2½ to 3 pounds)**
   4 **tablespoons butter or margarine, divided**
   1 **small onion, finely chopped**
   2 **cups sliced mushrooms**
   1 **clove garlic, minced**
1½ **cups cooked rice**
  ½ **teaspoon oregano**
  ½ **teaspoon salt**
  ⅛ **teaspoon freshly ground pepper**
  ½ **cup dry white wine**
  ½ **cup chicken broth**

If necessary, cut pocket in veal. Loosen meat from rib bones along one side of veal with long sharp knife, leaving three sides uncut. Pull loosened edge up and continue cutting meat away from bones to within 1 inch of opposite side. Set aside. Heat 2 tablespoons butter in skillet. Sauté onion, mushrooms, and garlic until tender. Remove from heat. Stir in rice, oregano, salt, and pepper. Spoon into pocket of veal. Close opening with wooden toothpicks. Heat remaining 2 tablespoons butter in skillet. Brown veal lightly on both sides. Place in large casserole. Add wine, broth, and 1 cup water. Cover casserole. Bake at 300°F. for 2½ to 3 hours, or until tender. Check halfway through cooking and add a little more chicken broth or water, if needed.

> **Q.** *What should I look for when buying veal?*
> **A.** When purchasing veal, look for white meat with a slight greenish tinge, and white satiny fat that smells of milk. This means that the animal has been almost exclusively milk-fed. Meat with a reddish color indicates solid feeding; this veal will not be as tender as milk-fed veal.

Stuffed Breast of Veal. Caloric Corporation

Roast Veal with Sage Dressing

Makes 6 servings

      3 pounds boneless veal roast
        Salt and pepper
      1 onion, chopped
      1 carrot, chopped
      1 cup "V-8" juice
      ¼ cup all-purpose flour
      2 tablespoons butter
      1 can (10½ ounces) Campbell's Condensed
        Chicken Broth
      8 slices white bread, toasted and diced
      1 can (10½ ounces) Campbell's Condensed
        French Onion Soup
      1 teaspoon crumbled sage
      ¼ teaspoon pepper
      2 tablespoons melted butter
      2 eggs, well beaten

Season roast with salt and pepper. Place in shallow roasting pan with onion, carrot, "V-8." Roast in a preheated 350° F. oven for 3 hours or until brown and tender. Keep warm on a platter. Drain and strain pan juices. For sauce, combine flour and butter in a saucepan; gradually stir in strained pan juices and chicken broth; cook, stirring, until sauce bubbles and thickens. For dressing, combine remaining ingredients and place in a shallow greased 1-quart casserole. Roast with meat for additional 30 minutes. Slice meat and serve on dressing. Top with hot sauce.

Sliced Veal Steaks Bombay

Makes 4 servings

      1 1½-pound leg of veal, cut ½ inch thick
      ½ clove garlic, mashed
        Salt and pepper
        All-purpose flour
      3 tablespoons butter
      1 large onion, sliced
      1 can (10¾ ounces) Campbell's Condensed
        Tomato Soup
      1 teaspoon firmly packed brown sugar
      1 teaspoon curry powder
      1 teaspoon white wine
      1 teaspoon soy sauce
      1 can (1 pound) tomatoes, sliced, and their juice

Cut veal into 8 pieces, trimming meat. Rub meat with garlic. Sprinkle meat with salt and pepper. Dip meat into flour, coating slices completely. Melt butter in large skillet; brown meat and onions. Combine remaining ingredients; pour over meat. Cover; simmer, stirring occasionally, until the veal is tender, about 45 minutes.

Veal Cutlet Española

Makes 8 servings

      8 large veal scallopini, about 1½ pounds, Italian
        style or pounded thin
        Salt and pepper
        All-purpose flour
      2 eggs, well beaten
      2 cups dry bread crumbs
      ½ cup butter
      1 can (10¾ ounces) Campbell's Condensed
        Tomato Soup, heated
      2 ripe avocados, peeled and sliced
      8 ounces mozzarella cheese

Sprinkle veal on both sides with salt and pepper. Dip slices into flour, then into beaten eggs, then into crumbs. Press crumbs firmly against meat. Melt butter in a large skillet and brown meat on both sides. Place slices of veal side by side in a shallow broiler pan. Spoon hot soup on top of veal. Top with slices of avocado. Cover avocado with slices of cheese. Place under broiler and broil until cheese is melted and lightly browned.

Veal Piccata Pavilion

Makes 6 servings

     12 veal scallopini, pounded thin
      2 small zucchini squash, cut into ¼-inch slices
        Salt and pepper
      2 eggs, well beaten
      1 cup all-purpose flour
      ½ pound butter
      1 tablespoon cornstarch
      1 tablespoon sherry
      1 can (10½ ounces) Campbell's Condensed
        Chicken Broth
      2 tablespoons lemon juice
      2 tablespoons butter

Sprinkle veal and squash slices with salt and pepper. Dip veal and squash into eggs, then into flour. Melt part of the butter and sauté veal until golden brown, 5 to 6 minutes. Add squash and sauté on both sides, about 3 to 4 minutes. Add more butter as needed. Place veal on a platter; top each veal slice with 2 to 3 slices of zucchini. Keep warm. In a saucepan, combine cornstarch and sherry. Gradually stir in chicken broth. Cook over low heat, stirring constantly, until sauce bubbles and thickens. Spoon sauce over veal. Sprinkle lemon juice over meat. Melt 2 tablespoons butter; cook until golden brown. Spoon brown butter over veal.

Sweetbreads and Kidney, Old Style

Makes 4 servings

2 pairs sweetbreads
1 can (10½ ounces) Campbell's Condensed
    Chicken Broth
2 tablespoons butter
4 lamb kidneys, trimmed and diced into ½-inch
    cubes
1 can (⅞ ounce) truffles, finely chopped
1 cup chopped fresh mushrooms
¼ cup heavy cream
¼ cup Madeira
1 can (10½ ounces) Campbell's Condensed
    Cream of Chicken Soup
    Salt

In a saucepan, combine sweetbreads and chicken broth. Simmer until sweetbreads have turned white and firm. Drain and discard broth. Remove skin and trimmings from sweetbreads. Cut sweetbreads into thick slices and place in a serving dish. Cover and keep warm. In a skillet, heat butter. Add lamb kidneys, half the truffles, and the mushrooms. Sauté until kidneys are just cooked. Stir in cream, Madeira, and chicken soup. Simmer for 10 minutes. Season to taste with salt. Spoon hot sauce over sweetbread slices; sprinkle with remaining truffles.

Creamed Veal and Mushrooms

Makes 4 servings

1 pound veal leg round steak, thinly sliced
    Salt and pepper
2 tablespoons butter
1 tablespoon olive oil
1 onion, thinly sliced
½ pound mushrooms, sliced
½ cup dry sherry
½ cup half and half
½ teaspoon Worcestershire sauce

Season veal with salt and pepper; melt butter with oil in a large skillet, add veal, and brown on both sides (about 1 minute per side). Remove to a round 2-quart baking dish. In same skillet, sauté onion and mushrooms until tender; spoon over veal. To skillet add sherry, half and half, Worcestershire sauce, and more salt and pepper to taste and heat through. Pour over veal and bake in 325°F. oven 30 minutes, or until veal is tender.

Osso Buco Milanese Style

Makes 4 servings

3 tablespoons salad oil
4 veal shanks, 4 inches long, with meat
3 tablespoons all-purpose flour
1 clove garlic, chopped
½ cup chicken broth
¼ teaspoon Tabasco pepper sauce
6 strips lemon peel
3 anchovy fillets, chopped
    Chopped parsley
    Cooked bow-shaped pasta

Preheat Multi-Cooker Frypan to 360°F. Heat oil in Frypan. Roll veal shanks in flour. Place shanks in Frypan and cook until lightly browned, turning occasionally. Add garlic, broth, 1 cup water and Tabasco sauce. Cover. Reduce heat to Simmer and cook about 1 hour, or until veal is tender. Add more water, if necessary during cooking time. Add lemon strips and anchovy fillets and simmer 5 minutes. Serve, topped with a generous sprinkling of parsley, with cooked pasta.

Carving Veal

Tender—though not always juicy—veal can be carved exactly as lamb is. Remember, always, to slice against the grain. Letting veal stand or "rest" for 20 minutes or so between taking it from the oven and bringing it to the table for serving will make carving easier, true of all meats but most true of veal.

Emincé of Veal

Makes 4 servings

6 tablespoons butter
¾ cup minced onion
1 clove garlic, minced
1 pound very thin Italian-style veal cutlets, cut
    into ½-inch strips
1 can (10½ ounces) Campbell's Condensed
    Cream of Mushroom Soup
1 tablespoon lemon juice
½ teaspoon crumbled tarragon
2 tablespoons Madeira
    Rice pilaf

Melt butter in a skillet; sauté onion and garlic until tender but not brown. Add veal strips and continue cooking until meat is tender. This will take only a few minutes. Stir in remaining ingredients and simmer for 5 minutes. Serve with rice pilaf.

Saltimbocca alla Romana. Campbell Soup Company

Saltimbocca alla Romana

Makes 4 servings

- 8 pieces boneless veal, 3 ounces each, pounded until paper thin
- Salt and pepper
- All-purpose flour
- ⅓ cup butter
- ½ cup dry white wine
- ¼ cup "V-8" juice
- 1 can (10½ ounces) Campbell's Condensed Chicken Broth
- 2 tablespoons lemon juice
- 8 ounces mozzarella cheese, cut into 8 slices
- 8 thin slices prosciutto ham

Sprinkle veal with salt and pepper. Dust veal with flour. In a large skillet heat butter and brown veal slices on both sides. Remove veal and place pieces side by side in a greased shallow baking pan. Sprinkle 3 tablespoons flour into drippings in skillet. Gradually stir in wine, "V-8," chicken broth, and lemon juice. Cook over low heat, stirring constantly, until sauce thickens. Place 1 slice mozzarella and 1 slice prosciutto over each veal cutlet. Bake in a preheated 375°F. oven for 10 minutes, or until cheese melts. Place cutlets on a platter. Spoon hot sauce over meat. Garnish Saltimbocca with watercress sprigs.

Capered Veal Chops

Makes 4 servings

- 2 tablespoons butter or margarine
- 1½ pounds shoulder veal chops or steaks
- ¼ pound mushrooms, sliced
- 1 onion, sliced
- 1 cup chicken broth
- 2 tablespoons all-purpose flour
- 1 teaspoon salt
- ¼ teaspoon freshly ground pepper
- 1 bay leaf
- ½ cup sour cream or heavy cream
- 2 tablespoons capers

Heat butter in skillet. Brown chops lightly on both sides. Arrange in shallow 2½-quart casserole. Sauté mushrooms and onion in drippings in skillet until onion is transparent. Blend chicken broth, flour, salt, and pepper until smooth. Stir into mushroom mixture. Pour over chops. Add bay leaf and cover casserole. Bake at 325°F. 1½ to 1¾ hours, until tender. Check occasionally and add a little more liquid, if needed. Remove chops to warm platter. Discard bay leaf and stir sour cream and capers into drippings in casserole. Spoon over chops and serve immediately.

Veal Burger Steaks

Makes 8 servings

    2 pounds boneless veal, cut in 1-inch cubes
    1 teaspoon salt
    ¼ teaspoon pepper
    ¼ teaspoon basil leaves
    1 large onion, quartered
    1 medium green pepper, quartered and seeded
   10 fresh mushrooms
    8 ounces mozzarella cheese, chilled

Assemble Food Grinder with fine disc. Grind meat into large bowl. Add salt and pepper; mix well. Set aside. Assemble Salad Maker with French fry cutter disc and large bowl. Process onion, green pepper, and mushrooms. Set vegetables aside. Change disc to shredder disc. Process cheese; set aside. Shape meat into 8 patties and arrange on large broiler pan. Broil patties on one side until brown. Turn and broil for 3 minutes. Divide vegetables and cheese equally on patties. Broil until cheese is melted.

Lemon Veal Stew

Makes 6 servings

    2 pounds stewing veal, cubed
    ½ cup sliced onion
    1 bay leaf
    3 peppercorns
    2 teaspoons salt
    4 tablespoons butter
    1 cup sliced mushrooms
    ¼ cup all-purpose flour
    3 tablespoons lemon juice
    2 tablespoons chopped parsley

Place 4 cups of water in Multi-Cooker Fryer and heat to 300°F. Add first 5 ingredients; bring to a boil. Turn dial to first M of Simmer; cook covered skimming off foam as it appears, until meat is tender. Remove bay leaf and peppercorns. In another frypan, melt butter; sauté mushrooms in butter until very lightly browned. Add flour and lemon juice; mix well and add to veal stew. Continue to cook until thickened. Sprinkle with chopped parsley.

Breading

Meat that is breaded should be prepared at least 2 hours before it is cooked. Spread the breaded pieces on a flat platter or tray, not touching; refrigerate uncovered for 2 hours or up to 3 hours. If you follow this method, you'll find that the coating adheres to the meat much better than if the meat is cooked immediately after breading.

Veal in White Wine and Cream

Makes 4 servings

   1½ pounds veal cut from round
    ¼ cup butter
    1 cup dry white wine
    1 can (10½ ounces) Campbell's Condensed
       Cream of Potato Soup
    ⅓ cup light cream
    1 tablespoon lemon juice
    2 tablespoons chopped parsley
       Roesti Potatoes (recipe follows)

Slice veal into strips ¼ inch wide and 2 inches in length. Sauté veal in butter until golden brown. Add white wine and simmer until wine is almost absorbed. Press soup through a sieve and stir soup and cream into veal. Simmer until veal is tender. Stir in lemon juice and parsley. Serve with Roesti Potatoes.

Roesti Potatoes

Makes 4 servings

    4 medium Idaho potatoes
    ½ cup butter

Cover potatoes with water and boil until potatoes are easily pierced but still firm. Peel and grate on a coarse grater. Shape potatoes into 4 large cakes. Sprinkle with salt and pepper on both sides. Fry cakes in butter until richly browned and crusty on both sides.

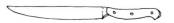

Veal Belle Manière

Makes 4 servings

    8 slices veal, 3 ounces each
    4 thin slices mozzarella cheese
    1 can (2¾ ounces) pâté de foie gras, chilled
       Pepper
       All-purpose flour
    ⅓ cup butter
    1 can (10½ ounces) Campbell's Condensed
       Cream of Mushroom Soup

Pound slices of veal until paper thin. Top 4 of the slices with a slice of cheese and a slice of the chilled pâté. Top with remaining veal slices and press together. Sprinkle both sides of the "sandwich" with pepper and dip into flour. Heat butter in a large skillet and brown veal on one side. Turn carefully and brown on the other side. Pour off excess fat. Spoon soup over veal, cover, and simmer slowly for 10 minutes. Serve at once.

Wiener Schnitzel

Makes 4 servings
  4 veal cutlets (1 pound)
  3 tablespoons lemon juice
     Salt and freshly ground pepper to taste
  1 egg, beaten with 1 tablespoon water
  ¼ cup flour
  ½ cup dry bread crumbs
  2 tablespoons butter or margarine
  1 tablespoon olive oil
     Lemon wedges
     Anchovy fillets

Wipe cutlets with damp cloth and pound thin. Sprinkle with lemon juice and marinate in glass dish about 10 minutes. Pat dry and season with salt and pepper. Dip in egg, then in flour. Shake off excess, then dip in bread crumbs. Shake off excess and refrigerate 30 minutes. Heat butter and olive oil in heavy skillet and brown cutlets over medium heat, about 3 minutes on each side, or until golden brown. Garnish with lemon wedges and anchovy fillets.

Roast Veal Paysanne

Makes 6 servings
  3 pounds boneless veal leg
  3 slices lean bacon, cut into long strips
  ¼ cup diced salt pork
  ¼ cup butter
     All-purpose flour
  2 tablespoons chopped parsley
  1 bay leaf
  ¼ teaspoon crumbled thyme
  1 can (10¾ ounces) Campbell's Condensed Old
     Fashioned Vegetable Soup
  1 cup dry white wine
  1½ cups sour cream
     Salt and pepper
     Rice pilaf

Lard the veal with thin strips of bacon, using a larding needle. Combine salt pork and butter and fry until salt pork is golden brown. Roll veal in flour; brown on all sides. Add parsley, bay leaf, thyme, soup, and white wine. Cover and bake in a preheated 350°F. oven for 1½ to 2 hours, or until meat is tender. Remove meat to a platter; keep warm. Stir sour cream into pan drippings. Strain sauce; reheat only until hot—do not boil. Season to taste with salt and pepper. Spoon sauce over slices of veal. Serve with rice pilaf.

Veal Kidney Stew

Makes 6 servings
  6 veal kidneys
     Salt and pepper
  ¼ cup butter
  1 cup diced carrots
  1 cup diced onions
  1 cup sliced celery
  ¼ cup all-purpose flour
  ¾ cup Burgundy
  1 can (10¾ ounces) Campbell's Condensed Old
     Fashioned Vegetable Soup
  1 can (10½ ounces) Campbell's Condensed Beef
     Broth
     Cooked rice or noodles

Soak kidneys in cold water for 30 minutes. Slice, removing all gristle and tubes. Season and brown slices quickly in butter in a large skillet over high heat. Remove cooked kidneys to a platter and reserve. Add carrots, onions, and celery to pan drippings and sauté until vegetables are wilted. Sprinkle with flour. Stir in wine, vegetable soup, and beef broth. Cook over low heat, stirring occasionally, until vegetables are tender. Add kidneys and simmer until sauce bubbles. Serve with rice or noodles.

Braised Veal Kidneys

Makes 6 servings
  6 whole veal kidneys
  ¼ cup butter
  ¼ cup finely chopped shallots or white onions
  4 crushed juniper berries
  1 tablespoon white wine
  1 tablespoon port wine
  1 can (10½ ounces) Campbell's Condensed
     Chicken Broth
  2 tablespoons cornstarch
  ¼ cup water
  2 tablespoons Dijon-style mustard

Remove skin, fat, and muscle from kidneys and soak in cold water about half an hour. Heat butter and sauté kidneys until brown on all sides. Add shallots and juniper berries. Sauté until shallots are wilted. Add wines and chicken broth. Mix cornstarch with water and stir into sauce. Cook over low heat, stirring constantly, until sauce thickens. Stir in mustard.

Picnic Fare

Whether you fill up a picnic basket for the park or beach, or just want a simple, easy meal, a sandwich is a tempting way to take time out during a busy day.

Chef's Sandwich

Makes 4 sandwiches
- 4 French bread rolls, split, buttered
  Lettuce leaves
- 2 hard-cooked eggs, sliced
- 4 slices Armour Star Cooked Ham
- 4 slices Armour Star Cooked Salami
- 2 slices process American cheese, cut in julienne strips
- 2 slices Swiss cheese, cut in julienne strips
  French salad dressing

For each sandwich, cover bottom half of roll with lettuce, egg slices, one slice ham, one slice salami, cheese strips, 1 tablespoon salad dressing and top of roll.

Uitsmijter

Makes 1 sandwich
- 1 or 2 slices of white bread, buttered '
  Cold roast veal
- 1 or 2 fried eggs
  Salt
  Pepper
  Capers

On 1 or 2 slices of white bread place liberal portion of cold, cooked, thinly sliced veal. Top with 1 or 2 fried eggs. Season. Sprinkle 2 or 3 capers on each egg.
On the run: In Holland, *uitsmijter* is what you order if you have 5 minutes flat in which to eat something substantial. With 1 egg it is called a *halve* ("half") *uitsmijter,* and can be eaten even more quickly.

Chef's Sandwich. Armour Food Company

Poor-Boy Sandwich

Makes 4 sandwiches
- 4 hard rolls, sliced in half
- 1 tablespoon vinegar
- 2 tablespoons salad oil
- 4 1-ounce slices smoked ham
- 12 thin slices cucumber
- 4 1-ounce slices process American cheese
- 8 thin slices tomato

Combine vinegar and salad oil; brush on cut surfaces of buns. On each bottom half, place 1 slice ham, 3 slices cucumber, 1 slice cheese (cut to fit bun), and 2 slices tomato. Replace tops of buns.

Italian Beef

Makes 10 sandwiches
- 1 1-pound loaf Italian or French bread
- 1½ cups beef stock
- 1 cup water
- 3 tablespoons tomato paste
- ½ teaspoon dry red pepper, crushed
- 1 teaspoon salt
- 1 bay leaf
- ¼ teaspoon instant granulated garlic
- 20 slices cooked beef, ⅛-inch thick

Combine beef stock, water, tomato paste, crushed red pepper, salt, bay leaf, and garlic in a 10-inch skillet; cover and simmer for 45 minutes to 1 hour. Add sliced cooked beef to seasoned stock in skillet and heat together an additional 15 minutes. While meat is heating through, cut Italian bread in half lengthwise. Then cut crosswise into 10 sections. To serve, dip each bread piece into stock. Arrange 2 beef slices on the bottom half, completing with top half of bread slice. Serve hot.

Pot Roast of Beef Sandwich

Makes sandwiches as desired

1	4 to 5 pound top-quality beef pot roast
2	carrots, scraped and quartered
2	onions, quartered
2	ribs celery, cut in chunks
2	cloves garlic, minced
½	cup chopped parsley
1	bay leaf
	Salt
	Red Relish Layer (recipe follows)
	White Relish Layer (recipe follows)
	Bread slices, buttered
	Salad greens

Brown pot roast on all sides. Put into a Dutch oven with carrots, onions, celery, garlic, parsley, bay leaf, 2 cups water. Season with salt. Cook at low simmer until fork-tender. Remove meat and cool, then refrigerate. Reserve pan gravy for next steps. Prepare Red Relish Layer and White Relish Layer.

To make sandwiches, place overlapping slices of pot roast on buttered slices of bread. Season with salt and pepper. Cover with ½-inch slice of jellied relish. Surround bread with curly greens (chicory, lettuce, escarole) and serve brightly open-face, so that the jewel-like jellied layer gets a chance to show.

Red Relish Layer

2	envelopes unflavored gelatin
1	cup tomato juice
1	cup pan gravy from pot roast
2	tablespoons tomato paste
1	tablespoon prepared mustard
2	teaspoons onion juice
3	drops Tabasco pepper sauce
1	cup chopped celery
¼	cup chopped sweet pickle

Soften gelatin in ½ cup of the tomato juice. Measure pan gravy from roast; add water to make 2 cups. To 1 cup of this gravy add softened gelatin in tomato juice, remaining ½ cup tomato juice, tomato paste, mustard, onion juice, and Tabasco sauce. Heat until gelatin is dissolved. Cool. Refrigerate until consistency of unbeaten egg white. Add celery, and pickle. Pour into loaf pan. Refrigerate.

White Relish Layer

1	envelope unflaovred gelatin
½	cup dill pickle juice
1	cup pan gravy from pot roast
½	cup mayonnaise
2	tablespoons prepared horseradish, drained
	Salt, white pepper
2	tablespoons chopped chives
1	cup chopped cucumber (seeds and pulp removed
½	cup chopped dill pickle

Soften gelatin in pickle juice. Place remaining cup pan gravy in saucepan, add softened gelatin, and heat until gelatin is dissolved. Cool, stir in mayonnaise, and horseradish; season with salt and white pepper. Refrigerate until consistency of unbeaten egg white. Stir in chives, cucumber, and dill pickle. Pour over stiffened layer of Red Relish and refrigerate overnight.

Hearty Tacos

Makes 8 servings

1	can (16 ounces) refried beans
1	can (7 ounces) Spam, chopped
2	tablespoons taco sauce, mild or hot
8	taco shells
	Shredded Monterey Jack cheese
	Shredded lettuce
	Chopped tomato

In medium bowl, combine refried beans, Spam, and taco sauce, stirring until well mixed. Spoon into taco shells. Place filled shells in baking dish; cover and bake in 400°F. oven about 15 minutes, or until warm. Serve with cheese, lettuce, tomato, and extra taco sauce.

Nice to know: Guacamole or diced avocado also make great toppings for tacos.

Roast Beef for Sandwiches

Makes 16 to 20 big sandwiches

1	8-pound boneless sirloin roast
	Hard rolls, sandwich buns, or rye bread

Wipe meat with a damp cloth. Place on a rack in a shallow pan. Roast uncovered at 325°F. until meat thermometer reaches 140°F. Slice thinly, serve hot—several slices per serving—on hard rolls, sandwich buns, or rye bread.

Point to remember: If you're going to serve the beef cold, take it out of the oven a few minutes before the thermometer reaches the 140°F., or "rare," mark—the meat cooks a bit more out of the oven.

Burritos

Makes 6 servings

    2 large green peppers, seeded and diced
    1 large onion, chopped
    ½ cup vegetable oil, divided
    1 pound lean ground beef
    1 can (8 ounces) whole kernel corn, drained
    2 cloves garlic, minced
    1½ teaspoons salt
    ¼ teaspoon freshly ground pepper
    2 to 3 tablespoons chopped hot peppers (fresh or
        canned) or ½ to 1 teaspoon crushed red
        pepper
    ¾ cup Sun-Maid® Seedless Raisins
    ¾ teaspoon oregano
    ¼ cup cider vinegar
    1 can (16 ounces) refried beans
    12 flour tortillas
    2 cups shredded cheddar cheese
    2 cups sour cream
    ¼ cup sliced pimiento-stuffed green olives

Sauté the green peppers and onion in ¼ cup of the oil until soft but not browned. Add the beef and cook, stirring occasionally, until lightly browned. Skim off excess fat. Add the corn, garlic, salt, pepper, hot peppers, raisins, oregano, vinegar, and ¾ cup water. Heat gently to boil. Reduce heat, cover, and simmer for 20 minutes. Uncover and cook over medium-high heat, stirring frequently, until the meat mixture is fairly dry, but not burned. Remove from the heat and set aside. In a large skillet, heat the remaining ¼ cup oil. Carefully add the refried beans and cook, stirring occasionally, until oil is absorbed and beans are a little crusty. Preheat the oven to 350°F. Grease a 13x9x2-inch baking dish. Spread some of the bean mixture on a tortilla. Spoon about ⅓ cup of the meat down the center of the tortilla, then sprinkle with a little cheese. Fold opposite side of tortilla over the filling and place the burrito in the prepared dish. Repeat until all the tortillas are filled. Stir the sour cream until smooth and spoon over burritos. Sprinkle with any remaining cheddar cheese (or grate a little extra) and bake for 20 minutes. Top with the sliced olives.

Worcestered Wimpys

Makes 6 servings

    1 tablespoon oil
    1½ pounds lean ground beef
    1 can (8 ounces) tomato sauce
    ¼ cup chopped onion
    2 tablespoons Lea & Perrins Worcestershire Sauce
    1½ teaspoons salt
    6 hamburger buns, split

In a large skillet, heat oil. Add beef; cook and stir until brown, about 10 minutes; drain off excess fat. Stir in tomato sauce, onion, Lea & Perrins, and salt. Simmer covered for 5 minutes. Serve over hamburger buns.

Reuben Grill

Makes 4 sandwiches

    ⅓ cup Wish-Bone Thousand Island Dressing
    8 slices rye bread
    ¼ pound sliced Swiss cheese
    ¼ pound sliced corned beef or roast beef
    1 can (8 ounces) sauerkraut, drained
    2 tablespoons butter or margarine

Spread Wish-Bone Thousand Island dressing on bread. On 4 slices, place equal amounts of cheese, beef, and sauerkraut; top with remaining bread. In skillet, melt butter; cook sandwiches in butter until brown on both sides.

Some Homemade Sandwich Sit-besides

Vegetable garnishes in one form or another seem to be perfect partners for meat, fish, or poultry sandwiches—they're pleasant to see on the sandwich plate and a delicious contrast to the sandwich itself.

Artichoke Hearts Vinaigrette: Cook 1 package of frozen artichoke hearts according to package directions and drain. Combine ¼ teaspoon of freshly ground pepper. Marinate the artichoke hearts in the mixture for at least 4 hours.

Asparagus Vinaigrette: Marinate cooked fresh or frozen asparagus as above; if you like, substitute raw or briefly cooked sliced fresh mushrooms in ¼ cup of lemon juice, ¼ cup of olive oil, and ½ teaspoon of salt. if you like, add a little onion juice to the marinade.

Spring Garden Mélange: In a bowl, combine chopped celery, diced cucumber, thinly sliced radishes, chopped green pepper, sliced scallions (include some of the green tops), and chopped parsley in whatever proportions suit you. Add just enough sour cream to hold the mixture together. Season the vegetables liberally with salt and freshly ground pepper. (If you prefer, or if waistlines dictate, add cottage cheese whirled in the blender instead of the sour cream.) Serve the vegetables in a lettuce cup—a refreshing complement to almost any sandwich.

Sloppy José

Makes 3 or 4 servings
- ½ cup chopped celery
- ¼ cup chopped green pepper
  Butter or margarine
- 1 can (15 ounces) Hormel Tamales
- 1 can (15 ounces) Hormel Chili–No Beans (or with Beans)
- 1 loaf (8 ounces) Italian bread
  Shredded cheddar cheese
  Sliced green onions

Sauté celery and green pepper in 2 tablespoons butter until tender. Remove papers from tamales; slice tamales into bite-size pieces. In medium saucepan, combine tamales, chili, celery, and green pepper; cook until hot, stirring occasionally. Halve bread lengthwise, then cut into sections; spread with butter and toast lightly. Place bread, cut side up, on ovenproof serving plates or on a baking sheet. Spoon chili mixture over bread; sprinkle with cheese. Broil until cheese melts. Garnish with green onions.

Ham 'n' Egg Sandwiches

Makes 8 to 10 servings
- 1 pound cooked ham, cut in 1-inch pieces
- 2 hard cooked eggs, halved
- 1 medium onion, quartered
- 1 package (8 ounces) cream cheese, at room temperature
- 1 cup mayonnaise
- 1 teaspoon dry mustard
  Rye bread slices

Assemble Food Grinder with fine disc. Grind ham, eggs, and onion into large mixer bowl. Assemble Mixer. Add cream cheese, mayonnaise, and dry mustard to ham mixture and mix at Low then at Medium-Low until well mixed. Generously spread on slices of rye bread and broil for 5 minutes, or until bread is toasted and ham mixture is hot. Serve immediately.

Cheese-and-Beef Sandwich

Makes 4 sandwiches
- 8 slices whole wheat bread, buttered
- ¾ cup snipped dried beef, firmly packed
- ⅓ cup mayonnaise
- ½ cup grated process American cheese

Rinse dried beef well. Dry. Combine beef, mayonnaise, cheese. Spread on 4 slices of bread and top with remaining slices.
Note: These are make-aheads that can profitably spend some time in the freezer.

Sloppy José. Courtesy of Geo. A. Hormel & Co.

Pablos Tortas
with Bistec Picado
(Pablos Meat Pie)

Makes 6 servings

    ½ cup oil
    1 medium clove garlic, minced
    6 large French Rolls, split
    1 package (8 ounces) Pablos Refried Beans,
        heated
    2 cups Bistec Picado (recipe follows)
    ½ cup Pablos Salsa
    2 cups shredded lettuce
    1 large tomato, chopped
    ½ cup green onion, sliced
    1 avocado, sliced
    ½ cup sour cream

In pie plate, combine oil and garlic. Scoop out soft inside from rolls. Take top half of cut roll and dip into oil mixture. Brown on hot griddle, cut side down. Spread bottom halves of rolls with refried beans. Top with Bistec Picado, salsa, lettuce, tomato, onion, and avocado. Spread top half of roll with sour cream. Place over filling.

Bistec Picado

Makes 6 servings

    1 pound round steak, cut 1-inch thick
    2 tablespoons oil
    ½ cup red pepper, chopped
    1 small onion, chopped
    1 large clove garlic, minced
    1 can (8 ounces) stewed tomatoes
    ⅓ cup Pablos Salsa
    1 teaspoon chili powder
    1 teaspoon Worcestershire sauce
    ½ teaspoon salt
    ¼ teaspoon pepper

Freeze steak 1 hour. Cut into thin strips. In skillet, brown steak in oil. Add red pepper, onion, and garlic. Cook several minutes, until vegetables are limp. Add tomatoes, salsa, chili powder, Worcestershire sauce, salt, and pepper. Cover and simmer 30 minutes, until beef is tender.

Pablos Tortas with Bistec Picado. Hernke Foods

Hamburgers

Makes 8 servings

>   2 pounds boneless beef chuck, shoulder, or
>   round, cut in 1-inch pieces
> 1½ teaspoons salt
> ½ teaspoon pepper

Assemble Food Grinder with fine disc. Grind meat into large bowl. Lightly mix in salt and pepper. Shape into 8 patties. Broil on both sides until brown, or cook in a little butter in a skillet over medium heat. Do not overcook.

Filled Hamburgers
Follow recipe for Hamburgers. Divide each patty in half and pat into thin patties. Put a thin slice of onion or cheese or both on one patty, top with second patty, and press together at edges. Cook as directed.

Onion Hamburgers
Follow recipe for Hamburgers, grinding 1 or 2 medium onions, quartered, with meat. Mix lightly but well before shaping into patties.

Hawaiian Hamburgers
Mix 1 can (8¾ ounces) crushed pineapple, drained, and ½ cup flaked coconut. Set aside. Follow recipe for Hamburgers, mixing 1 tablespoon soy sauce and ½ teaspoon ground ginger with meat. Shape into patties. Cook as directed. Top each patty with 1 tablespoon pineapple-coconut mixture.

Italian Hamburgers
Follow recipe for Hamburgers, grinding 1 small onion with meat. Mix in 1 teaspoon oregano leaves. Shape into patties; broil. Top each patty with slice of mozzarella cheese and broil to melt cheese. Top with hot canned pizza sauce.

Hearty Hero Burgers

Makes 6 to 8 servings

> ¾ cup Wish-Bone Thousand Island Dressing
>   3 pounds ground beef
> 1½ cups shredded cheddar cheese
> ¼ cup finely chopped green pepper
> ¼ cup minced onion
>   1 tablespoon dried parsley flakes
>   2 teaspoons salt
> ¼ teaspoon pepper
>   6 to 8 hero rolls

In large bowl, combine all ingredients except hero rolls. Shape mixture into oblong burgers. Grill or broil until done. Serve in split hero rolls.

Heavenly Hamburger Toppers

Blue Cheese and Sour Cream Topping: Mix ⅓ cup crumbled blue cheese with ⅔ cup sour cream and 2 tablespoons thinly sliced green onion. Place green bell pepper ring on each hamburger and fill center with cheese mixture. Top with additional sliced green onion, if desired.

Olive Topping: Combine ⅓ cup halved stuffed green olives, ⅓ cup halved ripe olives, 3 tablespoons mayonnaise, and 3 tablespoons sour cream. Mix lightly.

Creamy Mustard Topping: Combine ¼ cup prepared mustard, ½ cup mayonnaise, and 1 tablespoon very thinly sliced onion. Mix well.

Cheddar Cheese Topping: Melt slice of cheese on hamburger, add pickle strip, a dash of catsup, and some chopped parsley.

Guacamole Topping: Mash 1 large ripe avocado. Stir in 1½ teaspoons lemon juice, 1½ teaspoons grated onion, ¼ teaspoon salt, and 6 drops hot pepper sauce. Spoon onto meat and top with tomato slices.

Round-the-World Burgers

Makes 6 servings

>   1 envelope Lipton Onion-Mushroom Soup Mix
> 1½ pounds ground beef
> ½ cup water

In large bowl, combine all ingredients. Add any one of the following variations and shape into 6 patties. Grill or broil until done.

Typically British Burgers
Add ½ cup shredded cheddar cheese, 1 tablespoon Worcestershire sauce, and ¼ teaspoon thyme. Serve on English muffins; top with additional cheese and a sprig of parsley.

South of the Border Burgers
Omit water and add ½ cup chopped tomato and 1 can (4 ounces) chopped chilies. Serve on corn toaster cakes or corn bread; top with shredded lettuce, additional chopped tomatoes, sliced ripe olives, or shredded Monterey Jack cheese.

Indian Curry Burgers
Omit water and add ½ cup sour cream, ½ cup raisins, and ½ teaspoon curry powder. Serve on pita bread; add dollop of sour cream blended with curry powder. Top with chopped peanuts.

Greek-Style Pocket Bread

Makes 6 servings

    1 pound boneless sirloin steak, partially frozen
        and cut in paper-thin strips
    1 small onion, halved
  ½ medium green pepper, seeded and halved
    6 large fresh mushrooms
  ¼ cup red wine vinegar
    2 tablespoons sesame seed or olive oil
    1 clove garlic
  ½ teaspoon salt
  ½ teaspoon oregano leaves
  ¼ teaspoon pepper
    6 pita breads
      Toppings (optional): cucumber, coarsely
        chopped; tomato, coarsely chopped; alfalfa
        sprouts; sour cream

Put steak strips into large bowl. Assemble Salad Maker with French fry cutter disc. Process onion, green pepper, and mushrooms into bowl with steak. Put vinegar, oil, and seasonings into "Mini-Blend" container and process at Chop until garlic is finely minced. Pour over steak and vegetables; cover. Refrigerate for 1 hour. Pour steak and vegetables into a large skillet and cook over medium-high heat. Cut or break pita bread in half crosswise. With slotted spoon, fill pocket with filling. If desired, top filling with cucumber, tomato, alfalfa spouts, and/or sour cream.

Sweet and Sour Burgers

Makes 6 servings

    1 envelope (1.35 ounces) onion soup mix
  ½ cup water
    1 egg, beaten
  1½ pounds boneless beef chuck, cut in 1-inch pieces
    1 cup sauerkraut, drained
  ¾ cup whole cranberry sauce
  ¼ cup chili sauce
    3 tablespoons brown sugar
    6 onion rolls

Combine onion soup mix, ¼ cup water, and egg in large bowl. Assemble Food Grinder with fine disc. Grind beef into the bowl; mix thoroughly. Shape into 6 patties. Put sauerkraut, cranberry sauce, chili sauce, brown sugar, and remaining water into small saucepan; mix well. Simmer 20 minutes, stirring occasionally. Slit and toast onion rolls. Broil or grill meat patties to degree of doneness desired. Put patties on buns and top with sauerkraut mixture.

Arabian-Style Pocket Bread

Makes 4 servings

    1 pound boneless lamb shoulder, cut in paper-
        thin slices
  ¼ cup peanut or other vegetable oil
  ¼ cup olive oil
    3 green onions, cut in 1-inch pieces
  ½ teaspoon dried mint
  ½ teaspoon ground cinnamon
    3 sprigs parsley, stems removed
    2 tablespoons butter, at room temperature
    2 tablespoons all-purpose flour
    1 cup milk
    1 clove garlic
  ½ teaspoon dill weed
    4 pita breads

Put lamb into small bowl. Assemble Blender. Put oils, onion, mint, cinnamon, and parsley into "Mini-Blend" container and process at Chop until onion is finely chopped. Pour over meat and cover. Refrigerate for 1 hour. Drain off and discard marinade. Brown meat in medium skillet until meat is cooked. Remove from heat. Assemble Blender. Put remaining vegetables except pita bread into blender container. Cover and process at Chop until garlic is minced. Pour into skillet with meat and heat slowly, stirring constantly until sauce is thickened. Stir to coat meat. Cut or break pita breads in half crosswise and fill with meat mixture.

French-Toasted Hamwiches

Makes 4 servings

    8 slices firm-type bread
      Softened butter or margarine
      Prepared mustard
    4 slices cooked ham
    8 slices cooked chicken
    2 eggs
  ⅔ cup milk
  ¼ teaspoon salt

Spread bread with softened butter, then with a little mustard. Place ham on 4 bread slices, topping each ham slice with 2 chicken slices. Top with remaining bread. Heat Multi-Cooker Frypan to 340°F. Melt 1 tablespoon butter in frypan. Combine eggs, milk, and salt. Beat with Mixmaster Hand Mixer until blended. Dip both sides of sandwiches into egg mixture; sauté in melted butter until well browned on both sides.

Hot Off the Grill

It's almost an American tradition—the backyard barbecue.
What follows are many memorable summer's nights' worth
of great-tasting burgers, kebabs, steaks, and other specialties
for the grill.

Round Steak Sizzler

Makes 8 servings
- ¾ cup catsup
- ½ cup Lea & Perrins Worcestershire Sauce
- ⅓ cup oil
- 1 teaspoon salt
- 1 3-pound boneless beef round steak

In a small bowl, combine catsup, Lea & Perrins, oil, and salt. Place steak in a snug-fitting bowl or doubled plastic bag. Pour catsup mixture over steak. Cover or fasten and refrigerate for 24 hours. Remove steak from marinade. Place on a rack over hot charcoal. Grill until done as desired, about 12 minutes on each side for medium, brushing with marinade occasionally. Or, if desired, place on a rack in a broiler pan. Place under a preheated hot broiler; follow preceding directions for cooking.

Delish-Kebabs

Makes about 6 servings
- 1 envelope Lipton Onion Recipe Soup Mix
- 1 cup dry red wine
- ¼ cup oil
- 1 tablespoon soy sauce
- 1 clove garlic, finely chopped
- 1 2-pound boneless round steak, cut into 2-inch cubes
- 12 mushroom caps
- ½ pint cherry tomatoes
- 2 small green peppers, cut into chunks

In large shallow baking dish, combine Lipton Onion Recipe Soup Mix, wine, oil, soy sauce, and garlic; add beef. Cover and marinate in refrigerator, turning occasionally, 4 hours or overnight. On skewers, alternately thread beef, mushrooms, tomatoes, and green pepper. Grill or broil, turning and basting frequently with remaining marinade, until done.
Idea: Serve side dishes of three-bean salad, coleslaw, potato salad, grated carrots, pickled beets, or cucumbers and onions so that each guest might have his or her choice.

Round Steak Sizzler. Lea & Perrins

Special Stuffed Burgers

Makes 6 servings
- 1 envelope Lipton Onion-Mushroom or Onion Recipe Soup Mix
- ⅓ cup water
- 1½ pounds ground beef
- 6 slices process American cheese, quartered
- 6 slices bacon
- Pickles (optional)

In large bowl, combine Lipton Onion-Mushroom Recipe Soup Mix, water, and ground beef. Shape into 12 patties. Arrange cheese on 6 patties; top with remaining patties and seal edges tightly. Wrap sides with bacon and secure with wooden toothpicks. Grill or broil until done. Top, if desired, with pickles.
Idea: Serve with pork and beans or with a combination of vegetables, such as zucchini and tomatoes.

Barbecued Steak Sandwiches

Makes about 8 servings
- ½ cup Wish-Bone Italian Dressing
- 1 2½- to 3-pound steak (your favorite cut)
- ½ cup catsup
- 4 drops hot pepper sauce
- 1 tablespoon sugar
- 1 teaspoon dry mustard
- 2 tablespoons cornstarch
- 1 cup cold water
- Toasted hamburger rolls

In large shallow baking dish, pour Wish-Bone Italian Dressing over steak. Cover and marinate in refrigerator, turning occasionally, 4 hours or overnight. Remove steak, reserving marinade. In medium saucepan, heat reserved marinade, catsup, hot pepper sauce, sugar, mustard, and cornstarch blended with water. Simmer, stirring occasionally, 5 minutes or until sauce is thickened. Grill or broil steak, turning and basting frequently with sauce, until done. To serve, arrange thinly sliced steak on hamburger rolls and top with remaining sauce.

Barbecue Basics

All grills except the most primitive have a device for regulating the amount of space between the source of heat and the cooking food by raising or lowering the firebox or raising or lowering the grill. This is helpful once cooking is underway, but it's also necessary to have the fire at the proper temperature when the food is put on to cook. Some barbecue chefs determine this through a combination of instinct and prayer, but a grill thermometer is likely to be more accurate. Use it to check the temperature at food level—that is, where the meat is going to be placed, whether on the grill or on the spit. Keep these temperatures in mind:

hot fire	375°F. or over
medium fire	about 325°F.
slow fire	200 to 275°F.

In most cases, meat should be at room temperature before it goes on the grill. If frozen, it should be thawed. Fish fillets are the exception—they need so brief a cooking that starting them from the frozen state results in moist, properly cooked fish, not overdone.

Grilled meats can be cooked by timing (see chart), but the doneness of spit-roasted meats should be determined by checking the internal temperature with a meat thermometer. The "instant" kind is simple to use for outdoor cooking. With it you can check the internal temperature simply by inserting the thermometer briefly in the meat, rather than by leaving it in place throughout the roasting.

In making a grill fire, most people err on the side of too much rather than too little. It takes about 2 pounds of charcoal to cook a 5- to 6-pound steak 1½ inches thick. If the fire is too hot for your purpose, spread it out into a more open pattern (using tongs). Keep tools at hand to lift the meat away from the fire for a brief time if flare-ups occur—and they generally will. If you get an extensive flare-up from dripping fat, don't panic. Get the food off the grill if you can. Douse the fire with baking soda or salt or—as a last resort—water.

Barbecued Kebabs

Makes 4 servings

- ¼ cup minced onion
- 2 tablespoons cooking oil
- 1 can (6 ounces) tomato juice
- 1 tablespoon brown sugar
- 1 tablespoon cider vinegar
  Dash cayenne
- 4 small red potatoes, halved
- 1 large green pepper
- 2 small onions
- 1 can (12 ounces) Spam, cubed
- 8 mushrooms

In small saucepan, sauté onion in oil until transparent. Add tomato juice, brown sugar, vinegar, and cayenne; bring to a boil. Lower heat and simmer barbecue sauce, uncovered, 10 minutes. Wash potatoes but do not peel. Cook in small amount boiling salted water until tender; drain. Seed and cut green pepper into 16 pieces. Cut each onion into 4 wedges. Alternate potato, green pepper, Spam, mushrooms, and onions on long skewers. Place on broiling pan; brush with barbecue sauce. Broil at least 3 inches from heat source 15 minutes, turning and brushing with sauce after 5 and 10 minutes.

Meatball Kebabs

Makes 6 servings

- 1½ pounds ground lean beef
- 1 cup fine dry bread crumbs
- ⅓ cup minced onion
- ¼ cup pickle relish
- ¼ cup water
- 3 tablespoons Lea & Perrins Worcestershire Sauce
- 1 egg, lightly beaten
- 1½ teaspoons salt
  Green pepper cubes
  Cherry tomatoes

In a large bowl, lightly combine beef, bread crumbs, onion, relish, water, Lea & Perrins, egg, and salt. Shape into about 18 meatballs. Arrange on skewers alternately with green pepper and cherry tomatoes. Broil over hot charcoal until done as desired, about 8 to 10 minutes, turning occasionally. Or arrange skewers on a rack in a broiler pan; place under a preheated hot broiler until done as desired, about 8 to 10 minutes, turning occasionally.

Kebabs

A kebab is a small piece of meat. Add "shish," a skewer, and you have shish kebab, a Near Eastern dish that we have made our own, particularly since the cookout became a warm-weather way of life in this country.

Arabians, Armenians, Persians, Syrians, and Turks all cook kebab style, and so do the French, (*en brochette*), but it was probably primitive man who got the idea going, Once he learned that he preferred his meat cooked, it must have been a relatively short step from throwing a chunk of meat into the fire where it was burned on the outside and raw within, to impaling the meat on a stick to cook it over rather than in the flames.

As time went by, refinements were added. Meat was cut into uniform pieces so that it would cook evenly. Presently vegetables (found growing wild, later from cultivated patches) were strung on the skewer to add variety to the meal. When the people were on the move—hunting, fighting, taking their flocks to new pastures—their spears and presently their swords did double duty as weapons and as al fresco cooking equipment.

Before anyone understood that cold would help preserve meat, or had any way to harness the necessary cold, meats were often cooked with spices and herbs and other savory seasonings to disguise the fact that they were—in the genteel term for it of a later day—"turned." From this arose the use of marinating mixtures to tenderize the meat, and sauces and bastes to add succulence as it cooked.

The skewers themselves were refined, too. From swords and spears and fresh-cut green sticks they evolved to kitchen utensils desigend for this particular use: pointed pieces of wood or bamboo or metal, sometimes with handsome handles of elaborately carved or chased wood or metal. Presently the spit was devised, turned by hand- (often a small boy) or sometimes by dog-power. Then came the idea of stewing meat in liquid. Stoves were invented, and their ovens in which meat could be roasted. For a time, except for nomadic peoples, the kebab was out of favor. But now here we are again, kebabing all sorts of food and enjoying these tender, deliciously flavored morsels cooked on a skewer.

String it on a stick: Lamb was the earliest domestic meat to be skewer cooked—the Near Eastern peoples did not raise beef, but they had flocks of sheep. Kid (tender and juicy) and goat (strong and tough) were also used. Beef and pork and fowl joined the list when skewer-cooking spread to other parts of the world. Lamb was—and is—still one of the choice kebab meats; it (and mutton) are liked throughout Europe, and particularly in the British Isles.

Meat for skewer-cooking may be from tender cuts, or can be tenderized by marinating or by the use of a commercial meat tenderizer. For those who like beef rare, cubes should be strung very close together; for those who like their beef well done, cubes are allowed air space all around. Pork, although delicious when cooked in this manner, is the hardest meat to control—it must be served well done, and that is sometimes difficult without drying the meat or burning it. Spareribs, cut in narrow strips, and threaded back and forth on skewer with vegetables between the folds, are probably the best pork choice. Shrimp kebabs are very good, and cook in a brief time. The same is true of oysters and scallops and chunks of lobster tail. Sausages of several sorts and slices of bacon (fold slices accordian-style) add variety. So do lamb or veal kidneys, and chicken livers. Often today, several kinds of meat join on one skewer for a mixed-grill meal.

There's room for more: What goes well on a skewer along with the meat? All sorts of good things. Here are some ideas:

    whole, medium-size mushroom caps
    pitted ripe or stuffed green olives
    squares of seeded green or sweet red peppers
    mild chili peppers
    chunks of zucchini or yellow crookneck squash
    small whole potatoes, or pieces of large ones
      (parboiled)
    small whole white onions (partially cooked)
    fresh or preserved kumquats
    whole cherry tomatoes or halved or quartered
      larger ones
    spiced crab apples
    chunks of yam or sweet potato (partially cooked)
    cubes of tofu (bean curd)
    wedges of lemon, lime, or orange (unpeeled)
    strips of pimiento
    1½-inch cuts of carrot or parsnip (partially
      cooked)
    cubes of eggplant
    cubes of turnip or rutabaga (partially cooked)
    fresh or canned pineapple chunks
    halved fresh peaches or apricots, unpeeled
    small whole or chunks of large dill pickles
    water chestnuts, bamboo shoots
    halved artichoke hearts or whole bottoms
    fresh or dried dates or figs
    chunks of banana (lemon-dipped)
    whole small sweet pickles, watermelon pickle
    2-inch chunks of corn on the cob
    chunks of jerusalem artichoke (partially cooked)

The only thing you need to bear in mind, when you are deciding what goes with what on a skewer, is the length of time the meat will require to cook. That should guide you in choosing appropriate go-alongs that will cook in about the same length of time.

Smoked and Barbecued Loin of Pork

Makes 10 to 12 servings

  1 **3-pound boned center-cut loin of pork**
     Hardwood chunks or chips
  1 **can (16 ounces) Ocean Spray Jellied Cranberry**
     Sauce
  ½ **cup catsup**
  ⅓ **cup firmly packed light brown sugar**
  ¼ **cup soy sauce**
  ¼ **cup bottled meat or steak sauce**
  1 **clove garlic, minced**
  ½ **teaspoon salt**

Prepare a water smoker for grilling as manufacturer directs. With a knife, score the fat side of pork loin in a diamond pattern; let meat stand about 30 minutes, or to room temperature. Soak some wood chunks in water for 15 minutes. Add soaked wood to coals. Place water pan in position and fill with water. Place pork on grill rack. Cover and cook 3 hours, or until pork is almost 170°F. on a meat thermometer. Add more coals and wood halfway through cooking time. While meat is grilling, in a small saucepan, combine cranberry sauce and remaining ingredients. Heat to boiling, stirring, over medium heat. Cover partially and simmer over low heat 10 minutes. Brush some sauce on pork; continue to grill 15 minutes, or until nicely glazed and temperature reaches 170°F. To serve, transfer pork to cutting board; cut into thin slices and serve with additional sauce.
Note: Pork can also be dry-smoked in a covered grill. Pork should be placed on grill over a foil drip pan surrounded with coals and wood. Cook about 1½ hours.

Sweet-and-Sour Kebabs

Makes 4 servings

  ¼ **cup sugar**
  1 **tablespoon cornstarch**
  ¾ **cup Ocean Spray Cranberry Juice Cocktail**
  2 **tablespoons cider vinegar**
  2 **teaspoons soy sauce**
  1 **pound kielbasa (Polish sausage) or knockwurst**
  2 **medium green peppers**
  2 **medium red cooking apples**

Prepare grill for barbecuing. To prepare sweet-and-sour glaze, in a small saucepan, combine sugar and cornstarch. Stir in cranberry juice cocktail, vinegar, and soy sauce. Cook over medium heat, stirring constantly, until mixture thickens; boil 1 minute. Remove from heat. Cut sausages into 1½-inch chunks. Cut each apple into 6 or 8 wedges; core wedges. On long metal skewers, thread sausages, peppers, and apples. Grill skewers 6 inches above low-glowing charcoals until sausages are lightly brown. Brush kebabs with sweet-and-sour glaze, turning occasionally. Serve kebabs with leftover glaze.

Sweet-and-Sour Kebabs. Ocean Spray Cranberries

Q. *Why marinate meat, and when is it appropriate to do so?*
A. Generally, a marinade is used to soak the meat to tenderize it and/or give it added flavor. Quite often, such a marinade can double as sauce with which to baste the kebabs as they cook, or a different basting sauce may be used. (Bear in mind that highly sweet things—syrups, molasses, sugars—tend to burn easily.)

Marinades usually consist of a fat (salad or olive oil), an acid (vinegar, wine, lemon juice), and seasonings such as soy sauce, Worcestershire sauce, prepared mustard, puréed fruit, crushed garlic or garlic juice, grated onion or onion juice, smoke flavoring, and a variety of herbs and spices. Tender meats, such as shellfish, chunks of lamb leg, or sirloin steak, sausages, and so on, need not be marinated to tenderize them but can be to flavor them if you wish. Marinated or not, all kebabs profit from being brushed with a savory sauce as they cook.

Smoked and Barbecued Loin of Pork. Ocean Spray Cranberries

Barbecued Pork Chops

Makes 6 servings

    1 medium onion, quartered
    1 clove garlic, halved
    1 stalk celery with leaves, cut into chunks
    1 small green pepper, seeded, cut into chunks
    1 cup catsup
    2 tablespoons wine vinegar
    1 tablespoon Worcestershire sauce
    1 teaspoon salt
    ¼ teaspoon pepper
    6 lean pork chops, 1 inch thick

Place all ingredients except chops in Oster Blender. Cover and process at Chop until vegetables are very finely chopped. Set aside. Preheat Multi-Cooker Frypan to 360°F. Rub a small amount of the fat from the chops over bottom of Frypan. Add chops and brown well on both sides. Pour mixture from Blender over top of pork chops. Cover, reduce heat to Simmer, and cook 45 minutes, or until chops are tender. Turn occasionally during cooking.

Spicy Barbecue Sauce for Spareribs

Makes 6 servings

    1 can (10½ ounces) Campbell's Condensed Consommé
    1 can (10¾ ounces) Campbell's Condensed Tomato Soup
    2 tablespoons molasses
    ¼ cup firmly packed dark brown sugar
    ¼ cup lemon juice
    1 teaspoon chili powder
    1 teaspoon dry mustard
    1 teaspoon crumbled oregano
    2 cloves garlic, mashed
    2 racks spareribs, about 6 pounds

In a saucepan, combine all ingredients except spareribs and simmer for 10 minutes. Roast rib racks in a shallow pan in a preheated 350°F. oven for 1 hour. Drain excess fat. Brush sauce over partially cooked ribs. Continue roasting ribs for 30 to 40 minutes, brushing with sauce every 10 minutes. If barbecuing, partially cook ribs as directed above; place ribs 6 inches above gray coals, brush with sauce, and grill for 20 minutes on each side. Brush with sauce every 10 minutes. Makes enough sauce for 2 racks of spareribs.

TIME/TEMPERATURE CHART FOR MEAT COOKED ON THE GRILL

meat cut	thickness, weight, or size	fire temp.	cooking time each side (in minutes)				
			very rare	rare	med. rare	medium	well done
beef							
beef steak	1 inch	hot	4	5 to 6	7	7½ to 8	10 or more
beef steak	1½ inches	hot	5	6 to 7	8 to 9	10	12 to 15
beef steak	2 inches	med. to hot	7 to 8	8 to 10	10 to 15	16 to 18	20 or more
beef steak	2½ inches	med. to hot	10 to 12	12 to 15	15 to 17	18 to 23	25 or more
flank steak	whole	hot	3 to 4	4 to 5	5 to 6	(must be rare to be tender)	
hamburger	1 inch	med. to hot	3	4	5	6	7 or more
tenderloin	whole	medium	10 to 12	12 to 15	15 to 17	18 to 23	(don't ruin!)
ham			(fully cooked ham: reduce time by 5 minutes)				
slice	1 inch	low to med.	—	—	—	—	15
slice	1½ inches	low to med.	—	—	—	—	20
lamb							
chops, steaks	1 inch	medium	—	4 to 5	6	6 to 7	8 to 9
chops, steaks	1½ inches	medium	—	5 to 6	7	8 to 9	10 to 11
chops, steaks	2 inches	medium	—	6 to 7	8	9 to 10	12 to 14
butterflied leg	whole	low to med.	—	—	—	30, total	40, total (turn several times)
pork							
chops, steaks	1 inch	low to med.	—	—	—	—	14 to 18
chops, steaks	1½ inches	low to med.	—	—	—	—	16 to 24
spareribs	whole rack	low	—	—	—	—	60 to 90, total (turn often)

Luau Lamb Grill

- ½ cup Sue Bee Honey
- 1 cup pineapple juice
- ¼ cup lemon juice
- 3 tablespoons butter or margarine
- 1 teaspoon Worcestershire Sauce
- 1 teaspoon prepared mustard
- 1 teaspoon garlic salt
- ¼ teaspoon ginger
- 2 tablespoons chopped mint leaves (optional)

Cut 2 pounds boneless lamb shoulder into 1½-inch cubes. Arrange meat, pineapple chunks, green pepper slices, and mushrooms on skewers.
Combine all ingredients and simmer in a sauce pan for 10 minutes. Brush marinade generously over kabobs. Grill for 15-20 minutes, or until tender, turning often and basting with marinade. Serve over fluffy seasoned rice. Makes 6-8 servings.

Taco Burgers

Makes 12 servings
- 1 envelope Lipton Onion, Beefy Onion, or Beef Flavor Mushroom Soup Mix
- 2 pounds ground beef
- ½ cup finely chopped green pepper
- 1 medium tomato, chopped
- 2 teaspoons chili powder

In large bowl, combine all ingredients. Shape into 12 oblong burgers. Grill or broil until done. Serve, if desired, in taco shells or frankfurter rolls and top with shredded lettuce, grated cheddar cheese, and chopped tomatoes.

Orange Barbecued Pork

Makes 4 servings★
- 1 teaspoon cornstarch
- 1 packet Butter Buds, made into liquid
- ⅓ cup frozen orange juice concentrate, undiluted
- ⅛ teaspoon ground cinnamon
- ⅛ teaspoon ground cloves
- 1 pound lean, boneless pork tenderloin

Dissolve cornstarch in Butter Buds. Add orange juice, cinnamon, and cloves. Mix well. Pour over pork and refrigerate covered 1 to 2 hours. Remove meat from marinade and reserve. Place pork on preheated barbecue grill. Cook about 15 minutes each side, basting occasionally with reserved marinade, or until meat thermometer registers 180°F. to 185°F.
★By using Butter Buds instead of vegetable oil in this recipe, you have saved 228 calories per serving.

Smoke-Cooking—An Aromatic World of Barbecuing

In smoke-cooking, or smoking, heat from charcoal or wood coals cooks the food while chunks or chips of smoldering hardwood impart a distinctive aroma and smoky flavor. Hickory (available where barbecue equipment is sold) is the most popular wood, but oak, mesquite, walnut, pecan, cherry, apple, alder, and aspen also qualify. Softwoods (pine, spruce, cedar, and fir) are not recommended, for they create a bitter taste and coat the inside of the smoker. Before adding wood chunks or chips to the hot coals, they must be soaked in water 15 to 30 minutes so that they will smoke, not burst into flame.

Three types of equipment for smoking are available at gourmet cookware or hardware stores—water smokers, large covered grills, and shallow grills. The water smoker, which resembles a dome-covered metal drum, has a water pan in which water, fruit juice, wine, beer, marinade, basting sauce, or a combination of these liquids is added. The pan is placed between the hot coals and food to create a moist atmosphere. There's no need to baste or turn the food, for the slow, even cooking makes for wonderfully tender and juicy meat.

Both the water smoker and large covered grill are used primarily for whole cuts of meat and poultry. A shallow grill—such as a hibachi—is best used for barbecuing thin or flat cuts of meat and poultry, seafood, and kebabs. Most grills burn charcoal for fuel, but gas and electric models are also available. For a more pronounced smoky flavor, the water smoker is superior to the covered grill, for foods cook more slowly in it. To further enhance the smokiness, a few drops of natural liquid hickory smoke can be added to the liquid or to the marinade or basting sauce.

Apple 'n' Sauerkraut Sausage. Armour Food Company

Kielbasa Skillet Casserole. Sun-Maid Growers of California

Something Extra Quick and Easy

Feeling rushed but don't want to give up the pleasures of a home-cooked meal? May we suggest one of the following meat dishes designed especially with you in mind?

Kielbasa Skillet Casserole

Makes 6 servings

   1½ pounds kielbasa (Polish sausage) or knackwurst
   3 tablespoons butter or margarine
   1 large onion, sliced
   ½ cup Sun-Maid® Seedless Raisins
   ⅓ cup cider vinegar or lemon juice
   1 tablespoon prepared mustard (optional)
   1 bay leaf, crumbled
   ¼ teaspoon ground cinnamon
   1 small red cabbage, (about 1½ pounds), coarsely shredded
   6 small new potatoes, scrubbed
   2 apples, cored and sliced
     Rye bread
     German mustard

Slash the sausage at 2-inch intervals to prevent the skin from bursting. Heat the butter in a large skillet and brown the sausage lightly; remove from the pan. Add the onion, and sauté until soft but not browned. Add the raisins, vinegar, mustard, bay leaf, cinnamon, and ½ cup water, stirring until smooth. Mix in the cabbage, top with the sausage and potatoes, and bring to a boil. Reduce heat, cover and simmer for 15 minutes; add the apple slices, cover and simmer 15 minutes longer, or until potatoes are fork tender. Place the sausage on a warmed platter, surrounded with the cabbage, apple slices, and potatoes. Serve with plenty of rye bread and German mustard.

Apple 'n' Sauerkraut Sausage

Makes 6 servings

   1 pound Armour Star Kielbasa, cut in 1-inch pieces
   1 can (27 ounces) sauerkraut, drained
   1 cup chopped apple
   ¼ cup firmly packed brown sugar
   ¼ cup water
   ½ teaspoon caraway seed

Combine all ingredients in fry pan; cover. Simmer 30 minutes, or until heated through.

Hash-Stuffed Peppers

Makes 6 servings

   6 medium-size green peppers
   1 cup water
   ½ teaspoon salt
   2 tablespoons butter or margarine
   ½ cup minced onion
   2 cups diced cooked corned beef
   1 cup diced cooked potatoes
   ½ cup soft bread crumbs
   1 can (8 ounces) tomato sauce
   1 tablespoon Lea & Perrins Worcestershire Sauce

Cut a thin slice from the stem of each green pepper scoop out seeds. In a large saucepan, bring water and salt to boiling point. Add peppers. Simmer covered for 5 minutes; remove peppers and drain. In a medium saucepan, melt butter. Add onion; sauté for 2 minutes. Stir in remaining ingredients. Spoon into pepper shells. Place in a greased 10x6x1½-inch baking pan. Bake uncovered in a preheated moderate oven (350°F.) until hot, about 30 minutes.

Sausage Fried Rice

Makes 6 servings

    2 cans (5 ounces each) Armour Star Vienna
        Sausage in Beef Stock, sliced diagonally in
        thirds
    1 jar (2½ ounces) sliced mushrooms, drained
    ½ cup sliced green onions and tops
    ¼ cup vegetable oil
    3 cups cooked rice
    2 tablespoons soy sauce
    ½ teaspoon salt
    2 eggs, beaten

In a wok or large fry pan, cook sausages, mushrooms, and green onions in oil over medium heat 5 minutes; stir in rice, soy sauce, and salt. Heat, stirring occasionally, 8 to 10 minutes. Reduce heat; stir in eggs. Cook, stirring constantly, until eggs are cooked. Serve immediately.

Franks 'n' Hot Potato Salad

Makes 4 servings

    2 cans (15½ ounces each) German potato salad
    4 Armour Star Dinner Franks

Spoon potato salad into fry pan; top with franks. Cook covered on medium heat 20 minutes.

Zucchini-Beef Bake

Makes 6 servings

    4 zucchini, cut in ¼-inch slices
    1 cup chopped onion
    ½ cup chopped celery
    2 tablespoons vegetable oil
    1 pound Naturally Tender Ground Beef
    1 cup sliced mushrooms
    1 can (6 ounces) tomato paste
    ¼ cup red wine
    1 teaspoon salt
    ½ teaspoon oregano
    ¼ teaspoon pepper
    2 cups (8 ounces) shredded mozzarella cheese

Heat oven to 350°F. Arrange zucchini in 13x9-inch baking dish. In fry pan, cook onion and celery in oil 5 minutes. Add ground beef; cook until beef loses pink color. Stir in mushrooms, tomato paste, wine, and seasonings; simmer 5 minutes. Spoon cooked mixture over zucchini; sprinkle with cheese. Bake at 350°F. for 25 minutes, or until cheese is light brown.

Skillet Sausage Sweets

Makes 4 servings

    ¼ cup finely chopped onion
    ¼ cup butter or margarine
    2 tablespoons all-purpose flour
    1 can (15¼ ounces) pineapple chunks, drained
        (reserve syrup)
    ⅓ cup water
    ⅓ cup firmly packed brown sugar
    1 pound Armour Star Polish Sausage, cut in 1-
        inch pieces
    3 cups sliced cooked sweet potato

Cook onion in butter, 2 to 3 minutes; stir in flour. Add reserved syrup and water; cook, stirring constantly, until thickened. Stir in pineapple, brown sugar, and sausage. Top with sweet potatoes. Cook covered 15 to 20 minutes, or until heated.

Baked Ham and Egg Loaf

Makes 6 servings

    ¼ cup butter or margarine, softened
    8 slices white toast
    2 cups diced cooked ham
    4 eggs, lightly beaten
    3 cups milk
    1 cup (4 ounces) shredded sharp cheddar cheese
    1 tablespoon Lea & Perrins Worcestershire Sauce
    ¼ teaspoon salt

Spread butter on toast. Cut each slice into fourths. Arrange half of the toast in the bottom of a greased 10x6x1½-inch baking pan. Top with half the ham. Repeat layering. In a medium bowl, combine eggs, milk, cheese, Lea & Perrins, and salt; mix well. Pour over toast and ham. Place in a larger pan. Pour hot water into the larger pan to a depth of 1 inch. Bake in a preheated slow oven (325°F.) until a knife inserted in the center comes out clean, about 1 hour and 40 minutes.

Sloppy Joes Potatoes

Makes 4 servings

    4 large baking potatoes
    1 can (15¼ ounces) Armour Star Sloppy Joes,
        heated
    1 cup (4 ounces) shredded cheddar cheese

Heat oven to 400°F. Scrub potatoes; prick with fork. Bake at 400°F. for 1 hour. Remove potatoes from oven. Cut crisscross gash in potato tops; squeeze gently until potato pops up through opening. Pour ⅓ cup Sloppy Joes on each potato; top each with ¼ cup cheese. Return to oven; bake until cheese melts.

Wilted Lettuce Salad with Bacon

Makes 8 servings
- 1 quart torn iceberg lettuce
- 1 quart torn bibb lettuce
- ½ cup sliced radishes
- ⅓ cup sliced green onions
- 8 slices Armour Star Bacon
- ¼ cup sugar
- ¼ cup vinegar
- ½ teaspoon salt
- Dash pepper

Combine lettuce, radishes, and onions in a large salad bowl; toss lightly. Cook bacon until crisp; drain, reserving drippings. Crumble bacon; sprinkle over salad. Add remaining ingredients to drippings; bring to a boil over medium heat, stirring constantly. Pour over salad; toss lightly and quickly until lettuce wilts.

Cold Cuts

Also called luncheon meats and sandwich meats, these are available in wide and tempting variety in supermarket refrigerated cases in packages—cooked, sliced, and ready to serve. They can be had at meat markets, too, and at delicatessens or delicatessen departments, sometimes packaged in the same manner, sometimes sliced to order.

Considering that we are gobblers of sandwiches in huge numbers, it's no wonder that tasty and convenient cold cuts are so popular. But their usefulness and goodness doesn't end there. A platter of cold cuts makes a welcome change as a main dish, particularly on a warm summer night, accompanaied by potato salad (hot or cold) or macaroni salad, with a platter of raw vegetables and a savory dressing to dip them in, or a bowl of zippy coleslaw. Or if you have a family turned off by liver, try them on lightly sautéed slices of liver sausage accompanined by creamed new potatoes and peas and a salad of pickled beets.

One of the easiest and most welcome meals for a large crowd is a spread of build-your-own sandwich makings, with several kinds of cold cuts, several cheeses, and several breads, plus mustard, pickles, and relishes, and a bowl of crisp lettuce leaves for the finishing touch. If you want to be a bit more elaborate, add a dish of three-bean or white-bean salad, or a salad made of several cooked vegetables mixed with minced celery and onion, dressed with garlicky mayonnaise. This is the blame-it-on-someone else mixture called French Salad by the English, Italian Salad by the French, and Russian Salad by the Italians—heaven only knows what the Russians call it—probably because in its early versions it was a sort of sweep-the-kitchen mélange. Made on purpose, rather than to use up leftovers, it's truly delicious, and a nice change from potato salad. With all this, beer is the beverage of choice, coffee is always acceptable, and big glasses of (don't turn up your nose) icy cold milk taste just right. On a hot day, iced tea and/or cold fruit punch.

We've strayed somewhat from cold cuts—thinking up party refreshments, even the simplest, can do that to you.

Cold-cut fanciers probably have a list of availabilities at their fingertips. But for those of you who haven't ventured far into the field, tending to think of cold cuts as bounded on the north by bologna and on the south by liver sausage, with no man's land between, there's a wide world a-waiting. Here's a sampling to get your thinking aimed in the right direction. All of these are ready to eat straight from the package, but some may be warmed if you prefer. Heat them, foil-wrapped, in regular or microwave oven, or frizzle briefly in fat in a skillet, or steam gently in the top of a double boiler.

Sliced meats: corned beef, smoked beef, tongue, pastrami, baked or cooked ham, pork loin, breast of chicken or turkey, smoked turkey.

Sausages: bologna in various sizes, several kinds of cervelat, summer sausage, mortadella, hard or genoa salami, pepperoni, thuringer, Lebanon bologna, New England-style sausage.

Liver luncheon meats: braunschweiger (sometimes with flecks of green pistachio nuts), liver sausage (often flavored, as with bacon), and white-rimmed liver cheese loaf.

Luncheon loaves: peppered loaf, pickle and pimiento, chopped ham, honey loaf, headcheese (and souse, its close kin), olive loaf, jellied tongue, blood-and-tongue pudding, jellied corned beef, jellied veal loaf, ham-and-cheese loaf, dutch loaf.

A recent development is turkey cold cuts. In plentiful supply and low in fat and in calories, turkey is being used as a subtitute for the more usual meats (beef or pork or a beef-pork combination) in many kinds of luncheon meats. Look for turkey bologna, salami, pastrami, ham, summer sausage, and old-fashioned meat loaf, as well as sliced cooked turkey breast, smoked turkey, and smoked turkey breast. Your favorite flavor a new way—isn't modern technology wonderful?

Panned Beef and Beans

Makes 4 servings
   2 tablespoons oil
   ⅓ cup chopped onion
   ½ clove garlic, minced
   1 pound lean ground beef
   1 can (10¾ ounces) Campbell's Condensed
      Vegetarian Vegetable Soup
   ½ soup can water
   1 can (1 pound) baked beans in tomato sauce
   1 cup chopped celery
   2 tablespoons Lea & Perrins Worcestershire Sauce
      Cooked macaroni or spaghetti

In a large skillet, heat oil. Add onion and garlic; sauté until tender, about 5 minutes. Add beef; cook and stir until browned, about 5 minutes; drain off excess fat. Stir in remaining ingredients. Bring to boiling point. Reduce heat and simmer covered until mixture is slightly thickened, about 15 minutes. Serve over macaroni or spaghetti.

Crown Roast of Franks

Makes 8 to 10 servings
   2 pounds frankfurters
   ⅔ cup Wish-Bone Italian Dressing
   1 cup sliced celery
   ½ cup chopped onion
   4½ cups diced cooked potatoes (about 8 medium)
      or 3 cans (16 ounces each) whole potatoes,
      drained and diced
   ½ teaspoon caraway seed

Make 2 1-inch cross cuts through tops of one end of frankfurters. Thread frankfurters together through center with cotton twine. Tie twine together to form a circle of frankfurters. In large skillet, heat ⅓ cup Wish-Bone Italian Dressing and cook celery and onion until tender. Add potatoes, caraway seed, and remaining dressing; cook 10 minutes, stirring occasionally, or until heated through. Preheat oven to 375°F. In 8-inch round baking pan or foil-lined cookie sheet, stand frankfurters on uncut ends to form "crown"; spoon potato mixture into center. Completely cover frankfurters with foil; bake 20 minutes. Remove foil and bake an additional 10 minutes, or until heated through.

Nutrition Note
Luncheon meats are high in protein. Store them, unopened, in the refrigerator—be guided by the "last day of sale" date stamped on them. After the package is opened, keep the meats refrigerated and closely covered; store up to 1 week.

Stew 'n' Biscuit Bake

Makes 2 to 3 servings
   1 can (24 ounces) Dinty Moore Beef Stew
   ¼ cup sour cream
   1 cup biscuit mix
   ¼ cup water

In 1½-quart casserole, combine stew and sour cream. Bake in 425°F. oven. Meanwhile, in small bowl, stir biscuit mix and water to make a soft dough. Drop by spoonfuls into hot stew. Bake about 20 minutes, until biscuits are lightly browned.

Franks 'n' Kraut Goulash

Makes 6 servings
   ½ cup chopped onion
   3 tablespoons butter or margarine
   6 Armour Star Dinner Franks, cut in half lengthwise
   1 can (27 ounces) sauerkraut, drained
   1 cup sour cream
   1 teaspoon sugar
   ½ teaspoon caraway seed
   ½ teaspoon paprika
   ¼ teaspoon salt

Cook onion in butter 5 minutes. Add franks and sauerkraut; heat covered 15 minutes. Stir in remaining ingredients; continue heating uncovered 5 minutes.

Speedy Chinese Stir-Fry

Makes 2 servings
   1 package (10 ounces) frozen Chinese-style stir-fry vegetables
   1 cup shredded cabbage
   2 tablespoons chopped green onion
   2 tablespoons cooking oil
   1 can (7 ounces) Spam, diced
   ¼ cup water

Heat 10- or 11-inch skillet until very hot. Remove seasoning packet from vegetables. Spread vegetables, cabbage, and onions over bottom of skillet. Pour oil evenly over vegetables; stir to coat pieces. Cover and cook 2 minutes, stirring once. Add Spam; sprinkle seasonings over mixture and add water. Cook and stir about 2 minutes until serving temperature.

Index